Language Learning and Teacher Education

BILINGUAL EDUCATION AND BILINGUALISM

Series Editors: Professor Colin Baker, *University of Wales, Bangor, Wales, Great Britain* and Professor Nancy H. Hornberger, *University of Pennsylvania, Philadelphia, USA*

Recent Books in the Series

Language Use in Interlingual Families: A Japanese-English Sociolinguistic Study
Masayo Yamamoto
Cross-linguistic Influence in Third Language Acquisition
J. Cenoz, B. Hufeisen and U. Jessner (eds)
Learners' Experiences of Immersion Education: Case Studies of French and Chinese
Michèle de Courcy
Language Minority Students in the Mainstream Classroom (2nd edn)
Angela L. Carrasquillo and Vivian Rodríguez
World English: A Study of its Development
Janina Brutt-Griffler
Power, Prestige and Bilingualism: International Perspectives on Elite Bilingual Education
Anne-Marie de Mejía
Identity and the English Language Learner
Elaine Mellen Day
Language and Literacy Teaching for Indigenous Education: A Bilingual Approach
Norbert Francis and Jon Reyhner
The Native Speaker: Myth and Reality
Alan Davies
Language Socialization in Bilingual and Multilingual Societies
Robert Bayley and Sandra R. Schecter (eds)
Language Rights and the Law in the United States: Finding our Voices
Sandra Del Valle
Continua of Biliteracy: An Ecological Framework for Educational Policy, Research, and Practice in Multilingual Settings
Nancy H. Hornberger (ed.)
Languages in America: A Pluralist View (2nd Edition)
Susan J. Dicker
Trilingualism in Family, School and Community
Charlotte Hoffmann and Jehannes Ytsma (eds)
Multilingual Classroom Ecologies
Angela Creese and Peter Martin (eds)
Negotiation of Identities in Multilingual Contexts
Aneta Pavlenko and Adrian Blackledge (eds)
Beyond the Beginnings: Literacy Interventions for Upper Elementary English Language Learners
Angela Carrasquillo, Stephen B. Kucer and Ruth Abrams
Bilingualism and Language Pedagogy
Janina Brutt-Griffler and Manka Varghese (eds)
The English Vernacular Divide: Postcolonial Language Politics and Practice
Vaidehi Ramanathan

For more details of these or any other of our publications, please contact:
Multilingual Matters, Frankfurt Lodge, Clevedon Hall,
Victoria Road, Clevedon, BS21 7HH, England
http://www.multilingual-matters.com

BILINGUAL EDUCATION AND BILINGUALISM 48
Series Editors: Colin Baker and Nancy H. Hornberger

Language Learning and Teacher Education
A Sociocultural Approach

Edited by
Margaret R. Hawkins

MULTILINGUAL MATTERS LTD
Clevedon • Buffalo • Toronto

Library of Congress Cataloging in Publication Data
Language Learning and Teacher Education: A Sociocultural Approach
Edited by Margaret R. Hawkins.
Bilingual Education and Bilingualism: 48
Includes bibliographical references and index.
1. Language and languages–Study and teaching–Social aspects.
2. Language teachers–Training of. I. Hawkins, Margaret R. II. Series.
P53.8.L3625 2004
418'.0071–dc22   2004002823

British Library Cataloguing in Publication Data
A catalogue entry for this book is available from the British Library.

ISBN 1-85359-764-3 (hbk)
ISBN 1-85359-763-5 (pbk)

Multilingual Matters Ltd
UK: Frankfurt Lodge, Clevedon Hall, Victoria Road, Clevedon BS21 7HH.
USA: UTP, 2250 Military Road, Tonawanda, NY 14150, USA.
Canada: UTP, 5201 Dufferin Street, North York, Ontario M3H 5T8, Canada.

Typeset by Wordworks Ltd.
Printed and bound in Great Britain by the Cromwell Press Ltd.

Contents

Acknowledgements

My deep gratitude goes to all the authors included in this volume, for their enormous patience through a lengthy process, and for their willingness to stick with this project. Thanks, too, to Bonny Norton for her early contributions and participation. I owe more than I can say to Ken Zeichner, who I consistently rely on for sound professional advice, on this as on everything else. A special thanks to the folks at Multilingual Matters, especially Mike and Tommi Grover, for believing in the book and my ability to pull it off, and for all the help along the way. A special mention, too, for Marjukka Grover and Ken Hall at Multilingual Matters, for shepherding it (and me) through the process, and answering the endless questions. Anne Gray did a masterful editing job, and Chung-Pei Tsai's help in proofing and indexing was invaluable.

I dedicate this book to my children – Becky, Annie and Sam – who put up (as always) with endlessly hearing, 'Not now, I'm working.'

Margaret R. Hawkins

Author Biographies 2004

Alison Beynon is a language teacher who is developing the 'multiliteracies approach' at a range of sites in Johannesburg. She coordinates the EFL program at Wits Language School, trains EFL teachers working in a refugee program and directs a remedial literacy program for teenagers in the township of Alexandra. She believes the modality most neglected, yet most promising in remedial and EFL teaching, is 'bodywork', and this forms the core of her integrated cultural program.

Donald Freeman is Dean of Graduate and Professional Studies in Language Teacher Education at the graduate School for International Training in Vermont, where he directs the Center for Teacher Education, Training, and Research. He is author of books and articles on teacher education and teacher-research, and works regularly with educators in various settings in different parts of the world. His current work focuses on documenting development and change in practitioner knowledge in relation to student learning.

James Paul Gee is the Tashia Morgridge Professor of Reading in the Departments of Curriculum and Instruction and Educational Psychology at the University of Wisconsin-Madison. He works in the areas of sociolinguistics, discourse studies, literacy learning, and situated cognition. Among other books, he is the author of *Social Linguistics and Literacies* (1990), *The Social Mind* (1992), *An Introduction to Discourse Analysis* (1999), and *What Video Games Have to Teach Us About Learning and Literacy* (2003).

Margaret R. Hawkins is an Assistant Professor in the Department of Curriculum and Instruction at the University of Wisconsin at Madison, where she directs the ESL and Bilingual certification and graduate programs. Her professional career includes teaching and scholarship in the areas of literacies, sociolinguistics and language teacher education. Current projects include collaborative research on the language and literacy development of young English language learners in schools, and supporting/researching school-based initiatives on home–school relations.

Jennifer Miller is a Senior Lecturer in the Faculty of Education at Monash University in Melbourne where she teaches postgraduate courses in TESOL and teacher education. Her work explores language acquisition and identity, cultural diversity, qualitative methodology in applied linguistics and teachers' work. Her book, *Audible Difference: ESL and Social Identity* (2003) explores the politics of speaking and representation for immigrant students in high schools. She continues to research in this field.

Sarah Miller is a former graduate student in the Bilingual, ESL and Multicultural Master's program in the School of Education, University of Massachusetts at Amherst. Her teaching experience includes TESOL with children, teenagers and adult immigrant populations, as well as private students, German and music.

Pippa Stein is an English teacher educator at the University of the Witwatersrand, Johannesburg. Her research interests are in social semiotics, multimodality and literacy pedagogies within contexts of poverty. She has published in the Harvard Educational Review, TESOL Quarterly and has chapters forthcoming in G. Kress and C. Jewitt (eds) *Multimodal Literacy,* published by Peter Lang (New York) and B. Norton and K. Toohey (eds) *Critical Pedagogies and Language Learning*, published by Cambridge University Press.

Jerri Willett is a Professor at the University of Massachusetts in the Language, Literacy and Culture Doctoral Concentration. She directs the ACCELA Alliance, an inquiry-based professional development program for teachers and administrators focused on supporting English Language Learners (ELL). Her current research examines the social and political processes shaping the co-construction of language practices in classrooms and communities and how these practices are related to the academic and language growth of ELLs.

Part 1

Introduction

Introduction

MARGARET R. HAWKINS

This book took shape from discussions among language teacher educators in the process of reconceptualizing and redefining their practices within the emergent shift of perspective (in the fields of second language acquisition and applied linguistics) from viewing language learning as an isolated individual phenomenon to viewing it as one inherently embedded in and shaped by situated social interactions. What might this changing theoretical landscape mean for language teaching, and what implications might there be for teacher educators' practices across diverse contexts? Those of us involved in these conversations, as well as others, continue to explore the theories that drive our work, and how they impact our teacher education practices. In this volume we share some of our thinking and work, with hopes that all language teacher educators and language teachers will find it a useful catalyst for reflections and discussions that lead to continuous transformations in practice.

Shifting Perspectives

From a sociocultural perspective, no language – e.g. English – exists as a general thing. Rather, each language is composed of many different 'social languages,' that is, different styles of language that communicate different socially-situated identities (who is acting) and socially-situated activities (what is being done). Every social language communicates in use, as it creates and reflects specific social contexts, socially-situated identities that are integrally connected to social groups, cultures, and historical formations. These identities and activities (whether that be a rap artist performing on a street corner, a laboratory physicist using instrumental data to prove a theory, or an ESL teacher trying to convince other school staff that 'these kids' aren't deficient) are each deeply embedded in a network of ways of feeling, being, thinking, valuing, acting, and interacting – ways that themselves co-relate to the 'grammar' of the social language and which, with that language, carry a bevy of ideological and culturally-specific information about what is 'right', 'normal' and 'appropriate' (Gee, 1996). Since a social language is so integrally tied to socially-situated identities, language teaching and learning is always about acquiring new identities, and transforming identities in a context where learners' previous identities are respected and leveraged in the service of acquiring new ones.

The fields of English as a Second Language, English as a Foreign Language, and Foreign Language (hereinafter referred to as ESL/EFL/FL) are historically rooted in a very different conception of language and grammar. ESL/EFL/FL have tended to see a language as the sum of all its grammatical parts (hence the role of 'grammar teaching,' where a language like English is treated as some general all-purpose set of forms). Even as the fields have evolved into current notions of communicative approaches to language, and the focus has turned to form-in-service-of-function, views of language remain predicated on notions of universality, uniformity, and consistency of usage. The prevalent view is still that of grammatical forms, and their relationship to meaning, not that of contextually customized patterns (co-relations) across all levels of grammar that define genres and social languages, as these are integrally connected to socially-situated activities and identities in the modern world.

Sociocultural theory, then, takes up issues of the co-relationships between language, culture, context, and identity. I would like to focus, for a moment, on context. One major divide between traditional and social/cultural views of language is that a social/cultural perspective acknowledges that language is never decontextualized, never used outside of a particular 'discourse'. And the discourses of our modern world are rapidly changing, as are the identities of our language learners. In the light of 'New Times' (Hall, 1993), and the fast-moving shifts in technological, cultural, communicative, and economic environments, those of us involved in language education have an ever-more-pressing need to reflect on who our language learners are, and what our goals are. What lifeworlds are we preparing learners to participate in? What roles will they take on? What languages/identities/cultural knowledge/literacies/etc. will they need to do this? And how is this learning best supported?

Teacher Education

The field of teacher education is also experiencing a paradigm shift. It originally focused on a view of teaching as a technical endeavor – teachers needing to acquire and be able to employ specific skills and practices – then moved to viewing teaching as a cognitive process, with a focus on uncovering, analyzing and shaping teachers' thinking. Most recently the focus is shifting to critical teacher education, a view of teachers as transformative agents, whose responsibilities include ensuring equal educational access for all students. Ken Zeichner (1998: 31) refers to this as ' ... a movement toward a more critical and reflective pedagogy that (is) sensitive to the social and political dimensions of teaching.' The assumptions, respectively, were that teachers could learn 'best practices' that could then be applied across all teaching contexts; that teachers could develop appropriate attitudes and ways of thinking that would enable them to make conscious and informed decisions; and that teachers with sensitivity to and under-standings of the ways in which power (predicated on factors such as culture, class, gender, and language) works in our society to position our learners could work to ensure equity to all learners. All of these, together, are laudable goals. While perhaps the notion of universal 'best practices' is misguided, certainly teachers need a tool kit of teaching ideas, methods and materials from which they can draw and on which they can build. And the notion of conscious and informed decision-making is crucial, as is a view of the role of teacher as a catalyst to ensure equal educational access and promote social change.

In and of themselves, however, these notions don't impart an under-standing of what learning/acquisition is, nor how it happens. Thus, while they may offer teachers some practical skills, opportunities to reflect on taken-for-granted assumptions and practices, and an awareness of the social worlds in which they teach (and in which they and their students live), they don't provide a foundation on which to coordinate decisions about what to teach, how to deliver instruction, and how to structure learning environments. Sociocultural perspectives on learning begin to fill that gap.

Many theorists, researchers, and practitioners who recruit sociocultural theories to inform their work draw heavily on the work of Lev Vygotsky – in particular, on the notion of the Zone of Proximal Development (ZPD) (Vygotsky, 1987). Vygotsky's ZPD introduced the concept of learning as occurring through social interaction with adults or more capable peers. More recently, notions of communities of learners (Brown, 1994; Rogoff, 1994), and communities of practice (Lave & Wenger, 1991), have been developed, where learning is seen as a social apprenticeship to the practices (including language practices, activities, values and belief systems) of specific situated communities. Thus the work of teachers is framed as establishing and supporting classroom communities in which learners collaboratively engage in situated (socially sanctioned) activities (with guidance and facilitation) to come to new understandings and take on new practices (learning). This diverges from traditional and well-documented practices of teaching as rote learning and memorization, and traditional participation patterns such as initiation-response-evaluation (Cazden, 1988; Mehan, 1979).

For teachers, then, this is a huge shift. It suggests embracing a foundation for their work where 'to teach' means creating an environment where learners can interact and collaboratively negotiate new language, concepts, and understandings. And the impact is not just on 'what they know' (i.e. internalized in-the-head knowledge), but on 'who they are.' The impact of teaching and schooling shapes the identities of learners both within and outside the classroom, and the identities that learners acquire impact their engagement with 'learning.' And this, ultimately, determines what forms of languages/literacies/practices they acquire, and which communities and lifeworlds they will ultimately have access to. Thus teachers not only influence the lives of their individual learners, but also contribute to the social transformation of the larger social world. And this makes it crucial that teachers engage in thoughtful, informed, and reflective critical practices. It is a huge responsibility, and challenge.

For teacher educators, the responsibility is twofold. Certainly such views indicate the need (and responsibility) to foster critical and reflective practices in the teachers they prepare. But they call for a change not only in the *content* of what teachers learn through teacher education, but also in the *process.* For teacher educators, it becomes crucial to engage in critical, reflective practices as well, and to envision their work as creating learning communities within which they also participate as teachers and collaboratively negotiate new understandings of their profession and practices. Teacher educators, too, must establish new practices and take on new roles. And what this might look like, and what it might mean, especially for the field of language teacher education, is an area that has received little attention in the professional literature, and is at the heart of this book.

The Book

This focus of this book is an exploration of what such shifts in beliefs and practices might entail. An important component, however, is that it does not just delve into these issues in a theoretical manner. While we do present theoretical perspectives, the book explores pedagogical issues, and 'uptake' in our fields. It begins with a framing of sociocultural theory specifically applied to language and learning. We then present accounts from teacher educators discussing classroom and programmatic practices that are informed and shaped by these perspectives. We gain a view of what, if teacher educators take these perspectives and views seriously, their teacher education practices might look like (here we mean not to be prescriptive but to present examples of some of the sorts of reflection and practices currently being engaged in).

In order to explore what these socioculturally-oriented teacher preparation practices might mean to ESL/EFL/FL teaching, we then present accounts from teachers 'trained by' (socialized into) these sorts of discourses – these accounts describe and analyze their pedagogical approaches and practices. In conclusion, the book discusses implications for the field. Because these issues are critical to language learners, teachers, and teacher educators internationally, the accounts range across diverse global and contextual boundaries.

The format is as follows: we begin with theoretical perspectives in a 'framing' chapter by James Paul Gee (Chapter 1) that identifies key elements of sociocultural perspectives on language and literacy, and provides a framework for what is required for teaching and learning language in a sociocultural sense.

The next section, Sociocultural Approaches to Language Teacher Education, consists of three chapters by language teacher educators. Pippa Stein, Jerri Willett and Sarah Miller, and Margaret Hawkins each discuss a component of a language teacher education course or program that they designed and implemented to align with, and embody, these sociocultural perspectives. Stein (Chapter 2) explores two pedagogical projects with English language teachers in South Africa who come from both historically advantaged and disadvantaged communities. She illustrates some of the delicate social negotiation that took place in these teacher education classrooms around the equitable distribution of what she calls 'students' representational resources' (following Kress, 1997a and 1997b). Stein argues that one of the ways to work with the different values that are attached to students' representational resources is to develop pedagogies that work with what students bring (their existing resources for representation) and acknowledge what students have lost. Willett and Miller (Chapter 3) present a collaborative text, in which they dialogically reflect on their experiences of implementing a course in a University in the Northeast US that explored the possibility of transformational curriculum deliberation and design. Through describing the course and modeling their collaborative reflections, the authors represent their learners' struggles, as well as their own. Hawkins' chapter (Chapter 4), drawing on data from a teacher education class in the Midwest section of the US, analyzes student interaction on a listserve that the class utilized on an extended basis. Hawkins explores how the listserve mediated students' perceptions and understandings (Wertsch, 1991), how these were constructed and debated among participants in this particular learning community (the uptake of issues and theory), and how these learners applied their understandings to and through their particular sociocultural contexts, practices, and identities.

The following section, entitled The Uptake of Sociocultural Approaches in Language Education, comprises papers by Jennifer Miller and Alison Beynon. They discuss their teaching practices and pedagogies in working with language learners, one as director of a 'newcomer center', the other as a language/literacy teacher. Both are 'products' of graduate programs that promote deep engagement with social/cultural theories. Miller (Chapter 5) explores how sociocultural perspectives on language can be incorporated into ESL pedagogy, curriculum and institutional practices in schools. Through the example of an intensive English language reception center for migrants and refugees of high school age in Queensland Australia, Miller identifies a number of convergences and tensions between second language acquisition theory and practice on the one hand, and the transformational directions offered by social discourse theorists on the other. Beynon (Chapter 6) examines the ways in which literacy practices both exclude the social and cultural discourses that children bring with them, and also silence the modalities that support children in their learning. She shows how a situated practice (her South African classroom) uses the linguistic, cultural, social, and personal resources of each child as a central and creative part of the pedagogy. She also shows how multiliteracies (New London Group, 1996) can extend these resources to help children access language and literacy skills in alternative and powerful ways.

In the final section, Implications of Sociocultural Perspectives for Language Teacher Education, Donald Freeman (Chapter 7) highlights substantive themes and issues across chapters, and extends the conversations to examine in depth how viewing language as a social resource transforms traditional views of language teaching and language teacher education. He builds an argument for re-viewing the content and form of language teaching, and explores implications for language teacher educators and professional preparation programs and practices.

References

Brown, A.L. (1994) The advancement of learning. *Educational Researcher* 23 (8), 4–12.
Cazden, C.B. (1988) *Classroom Discourse: The Language of Teaching and Learning.* Portsmouth, NH: Heinemann.
Gee, J.P. (1996) *Social Linguistics and Literacies: Ideologies in Discourses.* London: Taylor & Francis.
Hall, S. (1993) Culture, community, nation. *Cultural Studies* 7, 345–363.
Kress, G. (1997a) *Before Writing: Rethinking the Paths to Literacy.* London: Routledge.

Kress, G. (1997b) Multimodal texts and critical discourse analysis. Unpublished paper, Institute of Education, University of London.

Lave, J. and Wenger, E. (1991) *Situated Learning: Legitimate Peripheral Participation.* Cambridge: Cambridge University Press.

Mehan, H. (1979) *Learning Lessons.* Cambridge, MA: Harvard University Press.

New London Group (1996) A pedagogy of multiliteracies: Designing social futures. *Harvard Educational Review* 66, 60–92.

Rogoff, B. (1994) Developing understanding of the idea of communities of learners. *Mind, Culture, and Activity: An International Journal* 1 (4), 209–229.

Vygotsky, L.S. (1987) *The Collected Works of L.S. Vygotsky* (Vol. 1): *Problems of General Psychology.* Including the volume *'Thinking and Speech'.* R.W. Reiber and A.S. Carton (eds). New York: Plenum.

Wertsch, J.V. (1991) *Voices of the Mind: A Sociocultural Approach to Mediated Interaction.* Cambridge, MA: Harvard University Press.

Zeichner, K. (1998) The new scholarship in teacher education. Division K Presidential address delivered at the American Educational Research Association Annual Meeting, San Diego, CA.

Part 2

Sociocultural Perspectives on Language and Learning

Chapter 1

Learning Language as a Matter of Learning Social Languages within Discourses

JAMES PAUL GEE

Introduction

In this chapter, I argue for a sociocultural perspective on what is involved in literacy and language learning at any level, whether for children or adults. This perspective makes two key claims. First: people do not primarily learn language at the level of things like 'English' or 'Russian'. Rather, they learn one or another of a great many different varieties of English that I will call 'social languages' (Gee, 1996, 1999a). Each social language offers speakers or writers distinctive grammatical resources with which they can 'design' their oral or written 'utterances' to accomplish two inter-related things:

(1) to get recognized by others (and themselves) as enacting a specific socially-situated *identity* (that is, to 'come off' as a particular 'kind of person') and

(2) to get recognized by others (and themselves) as engaged in a specific socially-situated *activity.*

Thus, each distinctive social language allows a speaker or writer to be recognized as a socially-situated 'who doing *what'* (Wieder & Pratt, 1990).

The second claim is that, in anything like the traditional ways in which philosophers, linguists, and psychologists have talked about meaning for things like words, phrases, and sentences (e.g. in terms of definitions, concepts, stored representations), at the level of social languages, *there is no such thing as meaning.* In social languages, meaning is not something that is 'stored' in the head and then looked up or accessed. It is actually 'customized', built, or assembled (however we want to phrase the matter) here and now, on the fly, on the spot, 'on line' when and as we speak/write or listen/read (Barsalou, 1999; Clancey, 1997).

Below, I will first lay out the key elements of a sociocultural perspective

13

on language and literacy. I will then show these elements at work in concrete examples. The most extended example involves a Korean graduate student trying to use, not 'English' per se, but a social language that will allow her to enact successfully the identity of an advanced doctoral student accomplishing the very consequential activity of getting a faculty member to take her on as a thesis student.

In the final section of this chapter, I will briefly discuss what is required for teaching and learning language in the sociocultural sense developed here, with particular reference to learners I will refer to as 'authentic beginners'. Let me take a moment here and say what I mean by the term 'authentic beginners'. In other work, I have used the term 'latecomers' for such learners, since they are people who arrive at learning sites after some other learners have already engaged in a good bit of consequential learning practice in terms of which they come to look smart or gifted and the latecomers come to look 'slow'. But, as Pippa Stein (personal communication) has pointed out to me, the term 'latecomer' has the unfortunate (and untrue) implication that it is the latecomers' fault that they have arrived 'late in the game'. So, I will switch to the term 'authentic beginner'.

I will use the term 'authentic beginners' for people, whether children or adults, who have come to learning sites of any sort *without* the sorts of early preparation, pre-alignment in terms of cultural values, and sociocultural resources that more advantaged learners at those sites have. For example, it has long been argued in the educational literature (e.g. Heath, 1983; Gee, 1996) that schools resonate (in many cases, for historical and arbitrary reasons) with the values and practices of certain types of (usually middle class) homes. Children from these homes are 'false beginners' when they enter school to begin their formal introduction into literacy and school-based learning. They come to look like 'quick studies' when they pick up early school-based literacy so quickly. On the other hand, children from some minority and lower-socioeconomic homes are 'authentic beginners', having come from homes with other sorts of (often equally complex) values and practices with regard to literacy and language, ones that do not resonate with early schooling. They are treated as if they are 'slow' even when they are, in fact, making substantive progress. Worse yet, their induction often skips things that teachers assume they 'should' already know because, in fact, 'false beginners' already take these things for granted.

The Korean doctoral student I will discuss below, like many foreign students in the United States, came to her US graduate school as an 'authentic beginner', as, indeed, do many native English speaking minority and lower-socioeconomic students. She was, of course, well educated, and no beginner in that sense. But she was an authentic beginner in her attempts to master the sociocultural identity (and concomitant practices) of being a graduate student in a US research-based university. When she entered graduate school, she was treated as if she were a co-equal beginning graduate student, while, in fact, many of her fellow students were false beginners who came to graduate school 'pre-aligned' for success, based on their earlier experiences – in this case experiences that may have taken place anywhere between (or throughout the course of) their early home-based socialization and their college careers.

As the Korean student failed to make rapid progress, she was progressively treated as a 'failure' in relation to her fellow students. And, of course, no one ever felt the need to teach her what they assumed any graduate student in a US research university already knew, even when, perhaps, it was obvious she did not know such things. In fact, some of what she needed to know was so taken for granted and unconscious to her fellow graduate students and her professors that they could not in any case have articulated the knowledge she needed.

What I want to concentrate on here is not just the injustice of pretending that people are all equivalent beginners when some are authentic beginners and some are false ones. I want to concentrate, as well, on just what it is that authentic beginners often don't know but do need to know if they are to ever 'catch up' with false beginners, but which 'insiders' often can't or won't tell them. However, I must also admit that our whole idea of 'catching up' is itself in serious need of interrogation (Varenne & McDermott, 1998). In many sites, especially in schools, we set the 'norm' in terms of the performance of the most advanced false beginners and then pretend that learners making quite 'normal' and adequate progress, by any rational standards, are not 'really learning'.

Teaching Social Languages, Not 'Language'

So, my first claim is this: Teaching and learning language and literacy is not about teaching and learning 'English', but about teaching and learning specific social languages. The best way to see what I mean by a 'social language' is to consider some examples (Gee, 1996). First, consider the two excerpts below from the talk of a young woman (we'll call her 'Jane') who recorded herself speaking to her parents and to her boyfriend. In both cases, she was discussing a story she had already discussed with her classmates in a college class earlier in the day. In the story, a character named Abigail wants to get across a river to see her true love, Gregory. A river boat captain (Roger) says he will take her only if she consents to sleep with him. In desperation to see Gregory, Abigail agrees to do so. But when she arrives and tells Gregory what she has done, he disowns her and sends her away. There is more to the story, but this is enough for our purposes here. Students in the class had been asked to rank order the characters in the story from the most offensive to the least.

In explaining to her parents why she thought Gregory was the worst (least moral) character in the story, the young woman said the following:

To parents at dinner:
Well, when I thought about it, I don't know, it seemed to me that Gregory should be the most offensive. He showed no understanding for Abigail, when she told him what she was forced to do. He was callous. He was hypocritical, in the sense that he professed to love her, then acted like that.

Later that night, in an informal setting, she also explained to her boyfriend why she thought Gregory was the worst character. In this context she said:

To boyfriend late at night:
What an ass that guy was, you know, her boyfriend. I should hope, if I ever did that to see you, you would shoot the guy. He uses her and he says he loves her. Roger never lies, you know what I mean?

Note that Jane designs or crafts her language in the two cases quite differently. She is using two different grammars; she is speaking two different social languages. To her parents, she carefully hedges her claims ('I don't know', 'it seemed to me'); to her boyfriend, she makes her claims straight out. To her parents, she uses formal terms such as 'offensive', 'understanding', 'callous', 'hypocritical' and 'professed'; to her boyfriend, she uses informal terms like 'ass' and 'guy'. She also uses more formal sentence structure to her parents ('it seemed to me that ...', 'He showed no understanding for Abigail, when ...', 'He was hypocritical in the sense that ...') than she does to her boyfriend ('... that guy, you know, her boyfriend', 'Roger never lies, you know what I mean?').

Jane repeatedly addresses her boyfriend as 'you', thereby noting his social involvement as a listener, but she does not directly address her parents in this way. In talking to her boyfriend, she leaves several points to be inferred, points that she spells out more explicitly to her parents (e.g. her boyfriend must infer that Gregory is being accused of being a hypocrite from the information that, though Roger is bad, at least he does not lie, which Gregory did in claiming to love Abigail).

Now, what is the point or purpose of using two different social languages with different grammars here? Why can't Jane just use one of these social languages both to her parents at dinner and to her boyfriend at night?

Different social languages allow Jane to make visible and recognizable two different versions of *who* she is, two different socially-situated identities. In one case, to her parents at dinner, she is 'a dutiful, intelligent, and respectful daughter' in the terms of a certain sort of (upper-)middle-class culture. In the other case, to her boyfriend at night, she is 'an intimate, but cautioning, girlfriend to and for her boyfriend.' These socially-situated identities are inherently social and relational. Jane fashions for herself a position in social space that, in turn, creates positions (relative to hers) for others to occupy. In one case she creates a position or identity for her parents as people who have done 'right' by her education; in the other case, she creates a position or identity for her boyfriend as an intimate who had, nonetheless, better realize what her expectations for romance and relationships are.

Different social languages allow Jane to make visible and recognizable two different *doings*, two different socially-situated activities. It is a common activity, in certain sorts of middle-class homes in the US, that children from a very early age display their knowledge in school-based forms of language at dinnertime. Though she is a college student, Jane still carries out this activity with her parents at dinner in the context of school topics. While people like Jane may sometimes talk to their parents at dinner in this way, not all people do. This is a distinctive activity that research has long connected with both success in school and the formation of school-based identities and identifications. To her boyfriend, Jane is using language to carry out a quite different activity. She is both bonding to him and fashioning for him the sort of value system and identity she wants any boyfriend of hers to have.

Let me give one more example of two different social languages used by the same person to enact different identities and activities. This example will make clear that social languages, enacting distinctive identities and activities, are highly relevant in professional and academic settings. To see this, consider the two extracts below, the first from a professional journal, the second from a popular science magazine, both written by the same biologist on the same topic (examples are from Greg Myers's excellent and important book, *Writing Biology* (Myers, 1990: 150):

(1) Experiments show that *Heliconius* butterflies are less likely to oviposit on host plants that possess eggs or egg-like structures. These egg-mimics are an unambiguous example of a plant trait evolved in response to a host-restricted group of insect herbivores. (Professional journal)

(2) *Heliconius* butterflies lay their eggs on *Passiflora* vines. In defense the vines seem to have evolved fake eggs that make it look to the butterflies as if eggs have already been laid on them. (Popular science magazine)

The first extract, from a professional scientific journal, is about the *conceptual structure* of a specific *theory* within the scientific discipline of biology. The subject of the initial sentence is 'experiments', a *methodological tool* in natural science. The subject of the next sentence is 'these egg mimics'; note how plant parts are named, not in terms of the plant itself, but in terms of the role they play in a particular *theory* of natural selection and evolution, namely 'co-evolution' of predator and prey (that is, the theory that predator and prey evolve together by shaping each other). Note also, in this regard, the earlier 'host plants' in the preceding sentence, rather than the 'vines' of the popular passage.

In the second sentence, the butterflies are referred to as 'a host-restricted group of insect herbivores', which points simultaneously to an aspect of scientific methodology (as 'experiments' did) and to the logic of a theory (as 'egg mimics' did). Any scientist arguing for the theory of co-evolution faces the difficulty of demonstrating a causal connection between a particular plant characteristic and a particular predator when most plants have so many different sorts of animals attacking them. A central methodological technique to overcome this problem is to study plant groups (like *Passiflora* vines) that are preyed on by only one or a few predators (in this case, *Heliconius* butterflies). 'Host restricted group of insect herbivores', then, refers to both the relationship between plant and insect that is at the heart of the theory of co-evolution and also to the methodological technique of picking plants and insects that are restricted to each other so as to 'control' for other sorts of interactions.

The first passage, then, is concerned with scientific methodology and a particular theoretical perspective on evolution. By contrast, the second extract, from a popular science magazine, is not about methodology and theory, but about *animals* in *nature*. The butterflies are the subject of the first sentence, and the vine is the subject of the second. Further, the butterflies and the vine are labeled as such, not in terms of their role in a particular theory. The second passage is a story about the struggles of insects and plants that are transparently open to the trained gaze of the scientist. Further, the plant and insect become 'intentional' actors in the drama: the plants act in their own 'defense' and things 'look' a certain way to the insects, who are 'deceived' by appearances just as humans sometimes are.

So the scientist has designed his language differently in the two cases. In turn, he has accomplished different *activities* (in the professional case, a report of experimental results; in the popular case, an illuminating description of nature) and enacted different *identities* (in the professional case, experimental scientist; in the popular case, expert observer of nature).

Situated Meanings and Cultural Models

I now want to turn to the second key claim I made at the beginning of the chapter: in anything like the traditional ways in which we have talked about meaning for words, phrases, and sentences, at the level of social languages, *there is no such thing as meaning*. Traditional work in linguistics and psychology has argued that words are associated with general meanings, concepts, or representations that are 'stored' in the mental lexicon and 'looked up' (accessed) when they are required for speaking/writing or listening/reading (see Clancey, 1997 for an overview). And, this is certainly the view that has informed most traditional language and literacy pedagogy.

More contemporary work, however, especially that stemming from recent 'connectionist' (or related) approaches to the mind, suggests that this traditional viewpoint is not, in fact, true (Barsalou, 1999; Clancey, 1997; Clark, 1997; see Gee, 1999a for an overview and more citations to the literature). Words do not have general meanings. In fact, in an important sense, they don't have any stable meanings at all. Rather, they are associated with different 'situated' or 'customized' meanings in different contexts. A *situated meaning* is an image or pattern of elements from our embodied experience of the world, including our experience of texts and conversations, that we *assemble* 'on the spot', in context, as we communicate, based both on the way we construe that context and on our past experiences.

For example, consider the following two utterances: 'the coffee spilled, get a mop'; 'the coffee spilled, get a broom'. In the first case, triggered by the word 'mop' in the context, for 'coffee' you assemble a situated meaning something like 'dark liquid we drink'. In the second case, triggered by the word 'broom' and your experience of such matters, you assemble either a situated meaning like 'grains that we make our coffee from' or like 'beans from which we grind coffee'. Of course, in a real context, there are many more signals as to how to go about assembling situated meanings for words and phrases.

Situated meanings don't simply reside in individual minds. Very often they are negotiated between people in and through communicative social interaction (Hutchins, 1995; Shore, 1996). For example, suppose a partner in a relationship says something like 'I think good relationships shouldn't take work'. A good part of the ensuing conversation might very well involve mutually negotiating (directly or indirectly through inferencing) what 'work' is going to mean for the people concerned, in this specific context, as well as in the larger context of their ongoing relationship. Furthermore, as conversations, and, indeed, relationships, develop, participants often continually revise their situated meanings.

Words such as 'work' and 'coffee' *seem*, of course, to have much more general meanings than are apparent in the sorts of situated meanings we have discussed so far. But words have no such general meanings. Whatever generality we sense them to have is due to the fact that words, with their situated meanings, are always associated with or trigger the application of what I will call 'cultural models' (D'Andrade & Strauss, 1992; Gee, 1999a; Holland & Quinn, 1987; Shore, 1996; Strauss & Quinn, 1997). Cultural models are 'storylines', families of connected images (like a mental movie), or (informal) 'theories' shared by people belonging to specific social or cultural groups. Cultural models 'explain', relative to the standards of the group (though often at a fairly taken-for-granted and unconscious level), the sorts of situated meanings that people tend to assemble for their words and phrases. Cultural models are usually not completely stored in any one person's head. Instead, they are distributed across the different sorts of 'expertise' and viewpoints found in the group, much like a plot to a story (or pieces of a puzzle) that different people have different bits and pieces of and which they can potentially share in order to mutually develop the 'big picture'.

The cultural model connected with 'coffee', for example, is, for some of us, something like this: berries are picked (somewhere? from some sort of plant?) and then prepared (how?) as beans or grain to be made later into a drink, as well as into flavorings (how?) for other foods. Different types of coffee, drunk in different ways, have different social and cultural implications, for example, in terms of status. This is about all I know of the model; the rest of it (I trust) is distributed elsewhere in the society should I need it.

Cultural models are nearly always ideologically laden – for example, the cultural model of coffee held by many groups of people involves correlations among various coffee practices and diverse social and class identities. It is also important to note that to 'know' a situated meaning is not merely being able to say certain words (e.g. 'a cup of coffee') but to be able to *recognize* a pattern (such as a cup of coffee or 'yuppie coffee') in a number of settings and variations.

To look at this point in a more consequential domain than coffee, consider the notion of 'light' in physics. First of all, our everyday cultural model for 'light' is not the same as the model (theory) of 'light' in physics – that model is the specialized theory of electromagnetic radiation. It is more overt and articulated than most cultural models. In physics, 'light' is associated with a variety of situated meanings: as a bundle of waves of different wave lengths, as particles (photons) with various special (e.g. quantum-like) properties, as a beam that can be directed in various ways and for various purposes (e.g. lasers), as colors that can mix in various fashions, and so on.

If one wants to start 'practicing' with light so as to learn physics, then one must acquire experiences that lead to the acquisition of a few situated ('in situ') meanings. Otherwise, one really cannot understand what the theory of light has to explain, at least not in any way that could efficaciously guide pattern recognition and action and reflection. And what does it mean to 'recognize' situated meanings? Situated meanings are patterns of associated features from embodied experience, such as 'light as a particle that behaves in term of various sorts of contrived (experimental) observations in certain characteristic quantum like ways' or 'grains of a certain color and texture associated with certain sorts of containers'. To recognize such things is to be able to re-cognize (reconstruct in terms of one's pattern-recognizing capabilities) and to act-on-and-with these various features and their associations in a range of contexts. One's body and mind have to be able to be situated with – coordinated by and with – these correlated features in the world.

A Final Example Relevant to Teaching Language and Literacy

To get at the workings of social languages, situated meanings, and cultural models, I want now to develop an extended example. After a number of years of graduate work, a doctoral student from Korea had been 'dropped' by her advisor. She went to see a different faculty member to ask if he would take her on as a doctoral student, even though it was clear to both of them that her prior work had not been evaluated all that highly by her previous advisor. However, that work had been carried out in an area that was both notoriously difficult and not really all that relevant to what the student wanted to do for her thesis. It was clear, however, that she would need a good deal of further training in the new faculty member's area before she could start her thesis work in earnest. In the course of a discussion about her past work and her future prospects, when the faculty member was showing some reluctance to take her on as a student, the student said the following:

It is your job to help me, I need to learn.

This utterance is, of course, in impeccable English. But it is, nonetheless, all 'wrong' (a strong term, I know, but I use it on purpose: real consequences happen to people when they get things wrong in this way). In this context, it had the wrong 'design'. In a profound sense, in a sense crucial to teaching language and literacy, it was 'ungrammatical'. It used a wrong social language, one that communicated a wrong identity, a wrong activity, wrong situated meanings, and operated within a wrong cultural model *in the context of this (sort of) department and university.*

Here's what went wrong. Considering the whole conversation between this student and faculty member, it appears that one of the cultural models the student was operating with was a distinctive model of faculty–student relationships, a model that made situated sense of many of her words and of her utterance as a whole. Her cultural model worked something like this:

Cultural model:
A faculty member (who is in a 'helping' profession) is morally obligated, by virtue of the definition of the position and job he or she holds, to give aid to a student (who in a sense is in the role of a 'client' or 'patient') who is having problems and who needs help learning – just so long as the student wants to work hard. It does not matter how much time or how much effort this will require from the faculty member. In return, the student will give the faculty member deference, respect, loyalty, thanks, and certain forms of assistance.

I have no idea whether this cultural model is connected in any way to Korean culture, nor does it matter in the least for my purposes here. And, indeed, in some settings (e.g. in many elementary schools), lots of US teachers do, in fact, operate by something much like this model. Unfortunately, this model is not one with (or within) which many doctoral advisors at research universities operate. Many of them operate with a cultural model something like the following:

Cultural model:
A faculty member is willing to give a good deal of time and effort to doctoral students who are near their thesis work (especially students he or she has not trained from the beginning) only when they have shown they can 'make it', produce good work, and become a 'credit' to the faculty member, thereby justifying the effort that the faculty member puts into the student (and takes away from his or her own research).

The Korean student, having the wrong cultural model, also enacted the wrong socially-situated identity. She enacted the identity of a needy, problem-plagued, suppliant. In fact, her cultural model implied that the needier students were, the more the faculty member was obligated to help them (provided they were willing to keep working hard). This is just the identity that is guaranteed, in many doctoral programs in US research universities, to get you no advisor or, indeed, to lose one you already have. The identity this student needed to enact was that of a self-motivated, advanced graduate student with goals that no longer fit her previous advisor, but with growing interests and potential strengths and skills in the other faculty member's area.

In addition to her wrong cultural model and situated identity, this student enacted the wrong socially-situated activity. In fact, she enacted several different wrong activities simultaneously. In the overall context, her utterance enacted simultaneously the activities of an exhortation (for the faculty member to do his 'duty'), supplication (for the faculty member to help a needy person), persuasion, and a request for the faculty member to be her new doctoral advisor. Exhortation and supplication are wrong activities for this setting. Thanks to this fact, and all the other aspects of this student's performance, her persuasion and request were not likely to work either.

Exhortation for the faculty member to do his moral duty can be heard as insulting (implying he doesn't know his duties) and inappropriate in a professional context in which the morality to which the student is appealing comes across as 'extra-professional'. Indeed, this student also brought up her Christian faith in the midst of the conversation. She told the faculty member (though in a low-key way) that she was confident that God had brought her to him and meant him as the 'right' advisor for her. This, too, created an 'extra-professional' reference that keyed the faculty member to see her exhortation as, in some sense, 'spiritual', and not just 'professional'.

The student's other activity – supplication – served to suggest weakness, when a potential doctoral advisor is, in fact, looking for strengths that will merit his or her efforts. Of course, all these features (her wrong socially-situated identity, cultural model, and activities) undermined her further activities of request and persuasion, rendering both ineffective (eventually not only with this faculty member, but with every other relevant doctoral advisor in the department).

Finally, the student's wrong identity, activities, and cultural model communicated the wrong situated meanings for her words, while, in turn, these situated meanings helped create the wrong identity, activities, and cultural model. These things – identity, activity, cultural models, and situated meanings – are all reflexively related. Each both creates and reflects – at one and the same time – all the others. They are a 'package deal' and that's why one has to get the whole package right.

For example, in the student's utterance, within its overall context, the word 'help' took on the situated meaning, here and now, of something like 'charitable assistance'. For success here, it needed to have a situated meaning something like 'professional guidance' (as it might have had if she said something like: 'With your help, I believe I can write a really good thesis'). Or, to take another example, the student's word 'need', in this context, took on the situated meaning of 'neediness' in the sense of: 'my ability to learn is inadequate without a good deal of effort on your part'. Instead, it ought to have taken on the situated meaning of 'good, but still able to be supplemented' in the sense of something like: 'my high-level ability to learn will be supplemented by your advanced professional expertise' (as it might have had if she said something like 'though I have a pretty good beginning background in your area, I need your help to deepen my knowledge of the area').

Of course, much more went into this Korean student's situation than I have covered here, and my analysis is, in reality, based on my knowledge of a much wider context. But I want to stress, nonetheless, that there were no 'objective' and 'neutral' judgments independent of discursive interactions to be made about the student, for example about the answer to the question, 'Was she a "good student"?' Her grades, papers, and the comments of other faculty members were, of course, themselves the products of discursive interactions in which social languages, socially-situated identities and activities, situated meanings and cultural models were at play.

Discourses

The Korean student did not need to learn more 'English' (in fact, she was well aware that her English was better than, or certainly no worse than, other Asian students who fared better than she did with the faculty). She needed to learn how to design utterances within a specific form of language (a specific social language) so as to trigger a specific identity, as well as specific activities and specific situated meanings, with their associated cultural models. So more – much more – is at stake than 'just' language.

Let me say, then, that what this student needed to get right was not English, but what I will call a 'Discourse' (with a capital D; see Gee, 1996, 1999a). Just using the 'right' social language will not, in and of itself, ensure that you are successfully recognized as enacting the 'right' socially-situated identity and activity. You have to get more than just the language right. You have to get 'other stuff' right, as well. The notion of 'big D Discourse' is meant to capture this fact. By a Discourse I mean ways of combining a specific social language with specific ways of acting-interacting-thinking-believing-valuing-feeling, as well as ways of coordinating, and getting coordinated by, other people, various tools, technologies, objects, and artifacts, and various 'appropriate' times and places in order to be recognized as enacting a socially-situated identity and an appropriately-related activity. Examples include being-and-doing an advanced graduate student recruiting a thesis advisor (Figure 1.1); being-and-doing an urban Latino gang member warning another gang member off one's turf; being-and-doing a cutting-edge nuclear physicist arguing the unique virtues of one's teams detector, etc.

The Korean student knew English (whatever that really means). She did not, however, even after years in graduate school, know the Discourse of being-and-doing a graduate student in a research university in the United States. She did not have the social language(s) that go with this identity. She could not enact the activities that this identity requires. She could not situate her meanings in actual contexts in ways that communicated the right 'on the spot' meanings and triggered the right cultural models.

Now someone is bound, at this point, to ask, perhaps in exasperation, 'But what's this got to do with literacy? How well did this student write?' Of course, I want to suggest that these are the wrong questions. For students like this one, teaching and learning language and literacy ought, I believe, to be about learning social languages within Discourses, not about oral or written 'English' per se. And Discourses always involve multiple ways of acting-interacting-speaking-writing-listening-reading-thinking-believing-valuing-feeling with others at the 'right' times and in the 'right' places so as to be recognized as enacting an 'appropriate' socially-situated identity. It's a 'package deal' – it does you no good to get bits and pieces of the Discourse 'right', you have to get the whole thing 'right'.

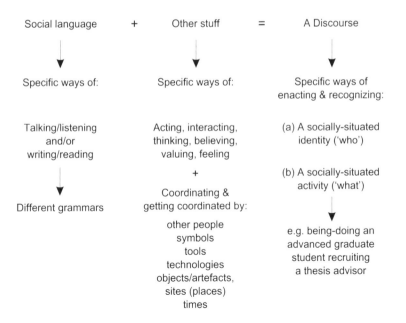

Figure 1.1 Discourse

The fact that the Korean student did not understand the social language, situated meanings, and cultural models required for her to be-and-do an advanced graduate student seeking a thesis advisor certainly led the faculty member to suspect that the student did not understand the sorts of related social languages, situated meanings, and cultural models required for diverse writing tasks in the Discourse in which she was seeking his mentorship. Reading her work (as well as reading new work she wrote at the faculty member's request) simply bore that out. The grammatical errors in her writing were a minor matter. Her failure to situate (customize) meaning in terms of the sorts of experiences, conversations, texts, and cultural models that instantiate the Discourses that she was attempting to write within was the problem. In fact, ironically, perhaps, her words, phrases, and sentences had only the sorts of general and 'canned' meanings that have traditionally been thought, incorrectly, to be what meaning is all about. Yes, someone had taught her 'English' – and it did her little good.

Political complications

Discourses are inherently and irredeemably 'political' and so is the process of acquiring them. They are political in three ways:

(1)   Internal to a Discourse there are almost always hierarchical positions (e.g. doctoral advisor–thesis advisee).
(2)   Discourses are partly defined in relationships of alignment and conflict with other Discourses (e.g. the Discourse of being-and-doing a certain sort of middle-class child is more compatible with the forms of language, practices, and values of early school-based Discourses than is the Discourse of being-and-doing a child in some non-middle-class homes and in the homes of some non-Anglo ethnic groups).
(3)   Discourses are harder to acquire and often tension-filled for many of those whom I called 'authentic beginners' above – people who are often marginalized by the Discourse they are attempting to acquire 'late'. Authentic beginners (whether children or adults) are people who come to the acquisition of a Discourse without the sorts of early preparation, pre-alignment, or sociocultural resources that have given more advantaged learners a 'head start'.

When I first developed this example in an address at the annual US TESOL conference in New York in 1999 (Gee, 1999b), it was clear that many in my audience were growing progressively more uncomfortable, as, indeed, they should have been (and were intended to). In fact, I purposely did not say what had happened to the Korean student, so as not to obscure the fact that what was going on in this meeting most certainly involved the workings of power. And, of course, status, age, gender, and ethnicity were all part of the workings of power here – though, I must also add that the student had already been turned down by several other potential advisors, including several female professors.

In the questions after my talk, one member of the audience suggested that the remedy here was more 'cultural understanding' on the part of faculty. This remark drew approval from the audience, mostly people who were ESL teachers or teacher educators (the session was sponsored by the Teacher Education Interest Section of TESOL). Though, of course, I am all for more cultural understanding, there was also a part of me that wished to respond to this remark by saying: 'I certainly wouldn't want YOU training foreign graduate students at my university' – at least if the person's remark was meant to suggest that faculty advisors should (or would) simply and charitably accept any sorts of cultural understandings in lieu of those demanded by their academic Discourses and often also by the 'economics' of graduate education as it actually exists. After all, doctoral degrees are training people to participate in (and even excel at) a new 'culture', namely the one constituted by their discipline.

Of course, this is not to imply that academic Discourses and academic institutions do not badly stand in need of political and cultural revitalization. Nonetheless, it may be the case that ESL teachers and teacher educators, who often think of their profession in terms of 'service', in fact, often accept and act in terms of the cultural model that I have attributed to the Korean student (the 'moral response to neediness' model). If this is true, it might indicate a rather deep irony. The people responsible for helping students like the Korean student I have discussed here may unwittingly, as part and parcel of their own social and political positioning within the Discourses of the university, pass on or, at least, reinforce cultural models that will help those students to fail.

So, while I certainly advocate much greater cultural understanding on the part of everyone in the university, at the same time, I do not want students like the one I have discussed here to pay the price while she waits for us to bring off a revolution in the political, economic, and cultural relationships within powerful institutions in our society. While we go about fighting for that revolution, I would suggest that we make both ourselves and our students more aware of how language works in terms of social languages, Discourses, situated meanings, cultural models, situated identities, and situated activities. But, then, perhaps, this is what my questioner meant by 'cultural understanding'.

Thus, I think it a first task (hard and long enough in its own right) that we make ourselves and other faculty across disciplines aware that students who are struggling may be 'authentic beginners', operating with distinctive situated meanings and cultural models, who do not realize that the faculty member is, however unconsciously, looking for different ones. In turn, we need, then, to make 'authentic beginners' meta-aware of the sorts of social languages, situated meanings, and cultural models in terms of which 'false beginners' are operating and succeeding.

The Korean student I have discussed here, even within the confines of our current institutional structures, *did not need to fail*. If a call for more 'cultural understanding' is a way to avoid acknowledging that, then it is, itself, an evasion of responsibility. Since I have now made the points I have wanted to make with this example, I can tell the 'end of the story'. The faculty member worked for many months with this student, conducting normal and consequential interactions with her (e.g. office hours, courses, directed research) while often rising to the meta-level, within the interactions themselves, in order to ask questions about and to discuss the forms of language and the sorts of situated meanings and cultural models that seemed to be at play both in her speech and writing and in mine. Of course, she made progress. Unfortunately, she was nearly a decade into her graduate work and eventually both her visa and her University eligibility lapsed. It was 'too late' – she needed to have been recognized and treated as an 'authentic beginner' years before.

Finally, let me say, too, that the points I have made about this example are not meant to be about foreign graduate students only and per se. They are meant to apply to all types of 'authentic beginners', whether they be first graders learning to read or college students seeking access to academic Discourses.

Teaching and Learning Social Languages

A key question, then, is this: What is required for the acquisition of a social language within a Discourse, and not just bits and pieces of a 'big' language like English, especially for authentic beginners? This should, to my mind, be the leading issue in research on language and literacy learning of all sorts. As a start, I would hypothesize that it requires at least the following (see New London Group, 1996; Gee, 2000):

(1) *Situated meanings:* Learners must learn, in production and reception, how to situate/customize meaning in the midst of practice, that is, how to assemble, here and now, the detailed, nuanced meanings that both construct and reflect specific identities, activities, and cultural models. They must gain feedback, inside and outside actual practice,

as to whether they are producing and recognizing the right situated meanings – see (5) below for a related point.

(2) *Cultural models:* Learners must gain meta-awareness about what cultural models are relevant to specific identities and activities within specific Discourses. They must come to see how these cultural models are triggered in actual contexts of practice by specific situated meanings.

(3) *Identities:* Learners must come to know (eventually at an unconscious and automatic level) what it feels like, in mind and body, to enact a specific identity. Authentic beginners, in particular, must also gain conscious meta-awareness about how specific identities within specific Discourses align themselves with or conflict with their other identities in other Discourses.

(4) *Activities:* Learners must be able to 'pull off' not just language, but 'moves' in the 'game'. They must know where in the game (activity) they are, what game (activity) they are in and how it is placed within larger activity systems.

(5) *Social languages:* Learners must come to see how the form (design features) of a specific social language – as they craft and comprehend utterances within it – fit with or fail to fit with specific identities, activities, situated meanings, and cultural models. They must get feedback about this matter both inside and outside actual practice.

(6) *Critical framing:* Discourses do not often encourage critique of their own values and practices – they usually ensure that their core members are 'true believers'. For authentic beginners to a Discourse, though, such critique is often important, both to allow them to work on any conflicts that may exist between their old Discourses and their new ones, and to acknowledge the fact that 'mainstream' Discourses have often denigrated immigrants, minorities, and lower socioeconomic people. Critical framing involves juxtaposing the ways and values of different Discourses, and framing one Discourse within the ways and values of another. This process allows learners to compare and contrast different Discourses (and their values and their practices) as part and parcel of the learning process. For example, the Discourse of academic psychology treats intelligence in ways that almost completely ignore what some people in their 'lifeworld' Discourses (i.e. when they are being-and-doing 'everyday', non-specialized people) call 'street smarts'. Comparing and contrasting 'school smarts' and 'street smarts' is a good way both to learn and to critique approaches to intelligence in academic psychology.

(7) *Transformed practice:* It is often the case that authentic beginners to a Discourse are allowed to master the Discourse only enough for them to become 'colonized' members of it, and never really experience the power of transforming their own practices and changing the values and practices of others in the Discourse. They never become real producers and innovators in the Discourse, but only ritualized producers and consumers of it. Giving authentic beginners and marginalized learners the power to transform practice is an important aspect of social justice. One way to do this is to allow learners to 'inflect' practices in the new Discourse they are acquiring with features of their old Discourses, but never as a substitute (always as a supplement) to mastery. For example, some African-American academics can, to quite effective purposes, inflect some of their academic practices, some of the time, with features of talk and interaction from their African-American family or community-based Discourses, while still getting recognized as having successfully pulled off the academic Discourse. For authentic beginners, I believe it is a sine qua non, in most cases, that they become, in the acquisition of any one 'mainstream' Discourse, sociologists and critical theorists of Discourses in general. It is necessary that they come to understand how Discourses work to help and harm people, to include and exclude, to support and oppose other Discourses. It is necessary that authentic beginners develop strategies to deflect the gate-keepers of Discourses when their newly-won and hard-fought-for mastery may be challenged or begin to fail them. It is necessary that they develop the power to critique and resist the impositions of Discourses when these Discourses are used to construct people like themselves as 'inferior' (often because they are authentic beginners). Authentic beginners must learn to 'play the game', but they must also learn to 'talk strategy' and, at extreme points, to 'call the game'. Their teachers must not only be masters of the Discourse or Discourses to which they are apprenticing their learners, they must be masters, as well, of what we might call the 'political geography of Discourses'.

References

Barsalou, L.W. (1999) Language comprehension: Archival memory or preparation for situated action. *Discourse Processes* 28, 61–80.

Clancey, W.J. (1997) *Situated Cognition: On Human Knowledge and Computer Representations.* Cambridge: Cambridge University Press.

Clark, A. (1997) *Being There: Putting Brain, Body, and World Together Again.* Cambridge, MA: MIT Press.

D'Andrade, R. and Strauss, C. (eds) (1992) *Human Motives and Cultural Models.* Cambridge: Cambridge University Press.

Gee, J.P. (1996) *Social Linguistics and Literacies: Ideology in Discourses* (2nd edn). London: Taylor & Francis.

Gee, J.P. (1999a) *An Introduction to Discourse Analysis: Theory and Method*. London: Routledge.

Gee, J.P. (1999b) Learning language as a matter of learning social languages within Discourses. Paper delivered at TESOL '99, New York, March 9–13.

Gee, J.P. (2000) New people in new worlds: Networks, the new capitalism, and schools. In B. Cope and M. Kalantzis (eds) *Multiliteracies: Literacy Learning and the Design of Social Futures* (pp. 43–68). London: Routledge.

Heath, S.B. (1983) *Ways with Words: Language, Life, and Work in Communities and Classrooms*. Cambridge: Cambridge University Press.

Holland, D. and Quinn, N. (eds) (1987) *Cultural Models in Language and Thought*. Cambridge: Cambridge University Press.

Hutchins, E. (1995) *Cognition in the Wild*. Cambridge, MA: MIT Press.

Myers, G. (1990) *Writing Biology: Texts in the Social Construction of Scientific Knowledge*. Madison: University of Wisconsin Press.

New London Group (1996) A pedagogy of multiliteracies: Designing social futures. *Harvard Educational Review* 66, 60–92.

Shore, B. (1996) *Culture in Mind: Cognition, Culture, and the Problem of Meaning*. New York: Oxford University Press.

Strauss, C. and Quinn, N. (1997) *A Cognitive Theory of Cultural Meaning*. Cambridge: Cambridge University Press.

Varenne, H. and McDermott, R. (1998) *Successful Failure: The School America Builds*. Boulder, CO: Westview.

Wieder, D.L. and Pratt, S. (1990) On being a recognizable Indian among Indians. In D. Carbaugh (ed.) *Cultural Communication and Intercultural Contact* (pp. 45–64). Hillsdale, NJ: Erlbaum.

Part 3

Sociocultural Approaches to Language Teacher Education

Chapter 2

Re-sourcing Resources: Pedagogy, History and Loss in a Johannesburg Classroom

PIPPA STEIN

Introduction

In this chapter I engage with some of Gee's ideas around learning to 'play the game' in relation to students whom he calls 'authentic beginners' (Gee, 1999). I will refer to such students in my own context, South Africa, as 'historically disadvantaged' and 'historically advantaged' to emphasize the historical basis on which students come to acquire certain kinds of education, epistemologies, values, identities and resources. I argue that in the case of historically-disadvantaged students, the process involved in what Gee calls learning to 'play the game', 'talk strategy' and 'call the game' (Gee, 1999) is a challenging and emotionally-laden project for both learners and their teachers and requires imaginative and culturally-sensitive peda-gogical interventions. Such interventions can be built on establishing a classroom community that works creatively, productively and critically with participants' diverse socially-situated identities and histories.

Learning to 'play the game' involves multiple levels of learner and teacher commitment. Not only do learners have to gain control of the target language in all its dazzling complexity, but they have to develop critical awareness and resistance to the possible ways in which they are being constructed as 'inferior' by different discourses. For teachers, not only do they have to teach the target language and critical literacy, but they have to deal with what happens in classrooms when students come face to face with their own *loss*: the loss of decent education, resources and networks of association, all of which culminate in a loss of power: power that they see shining in their fellow white students who had access to better schools and resources simply because they were white. I am referring, of course, to the legacy of the apartheid education system or 'Bantu Education' during the period from 1953 to 1994, which was premised on racial segregation and discrimination, poor funding and low standards of education.

Representational Resources

What I offer is a window into two classrooms with in-service and pre-service English teachers where both historically-advantaged (mostly white) students and historically-disadvantaged (mostly black) students make up the classroom community. My focus is on the delicate social negotiation that took place in these classrooms around the distribution of what I shall call the students' *representational resources*. This term comes from the work of Kress (1997a, 1997b) and Kress and Van Leeuwen (1996, 2001), and describes the range of available resources across semiotic modes that human beings draw on when they make meaning – including the linguistic in its written and spoken forms, the visual, the gestural, the sound, and the multimodal performance. Each text produced can be viewed as a complex sign. In the act of meaning-making in classrooms, students produce multiple signs, (in textual forms) across semiotic modes, in different genres, drawing on multi-semiotic resources within particular communicative practices which they need in order to succeed in this domain. In developing an adequate theory of semiosis in relation to the new communicational land-scape, Kress has stated:

> An adequate theory of semiosis will be founded on the recognition of the 'interested action' of socially located, culturally and historically formed individuals, as the remakers, the transformers, and the re-shapers of the representational resources available to them. (Kress, 1997b: 19)

Central to this theory of semiosis is the idea of change, 'transformative action', in which the human being is constantly engaged in a process of re-designing his or her available resources for representation. Kress (1997b: 19) has called this process 'the remaking of resources in the process of their use, in action and in interaction.' Meaning-making as a process of transformative action or 'work' produces change both in the object being transformed and in the individual who is the agent of the transformation.

In post-apartheid South Africa, the new Constitution promotes funda-mental principles of equity, redress and democracy. In the wider educational community, these principles are inseparable from the promotion of redress and equity in pedagogical and assessment practices. However, the promo-tion of equity poses the complex and fraught question of what resources are available and to whom, and what resources are needed for the range of pedagogical tasks in the classroom. Resources have different values attached to them according to the social occasion in which the resources are being deployed. I call these values *exchange values*. Certain kinds of literacy resources have high exchange values in school settings. Often historically-disadvantaged students come to class without sufficient access to these highly-valued resources, but with other resources that are deemed to have, in the school setting, low exchange value. Such multi-semiotic resources often go unrecognized or are marginalized in school settings. What I am proposing are pedagogies in which the existing values attached to representational resources are reconfigured to take into account a broader notion of semiotic resources. One of the ways to do this is to integrate ideas of *affect, history* and *community* into the meanings attached to resources that have high exchange values. I shall return to these issues later.

Both projects I mention deal with the subject of multiliteracies (New London Group, 1996; Cope & Kalantzis, 2000) and multimodality (Kress & Van Leeuwen, 1996, 2001), which is the use of multiple semiotic modes in the making of meaning. In the first project, which I call the 'Performing the Literacy Archive Project', students explore their literacy histories in performance. Fundamental to the construction of this performance is each student's individual literacy history, in other words, the value ascribed to each student's semiotic resources is equal. In the second project, the 'Photographing Literacy Practices Project', students work with photographs, visual design and writing to produce a photographic exhibition for the public on the subject of literacy practices in diverse sites. In this project, the majority of the historically-disadvantaged students came to the class without any prior experience of taking photographs or making a visual poster or display. In the Bantu Education system, there was no art education for secondary school students, and students rarely, if ever, did visual display or design projects at school. The white students in this class – all female – had all had some experience both of photography, and of designing and writing up a display chart.

The Focus on Literacy

Issues of literacy and access to it are at the heart of educational success in South African schools. Writing in English is the dominant literacy practice in schools where the majority of children speak English as a second, third or fourth language. At the end of schooling, students have to write an exit examination, the results of which determine their access to tertiary education and the job market. What literacy is, how people acquire it (or don't), what it does and its relationship to language, power and access, is critical to language teacher education. Literacy has a history (Barton, 1994). Teachers carry with them sets of beliefs, practices and contexts in relation to literacy which they have accumulated since early childhood – what Freeman and Johnson (1998) call teachers' *experiential knowledge-base* of literacy. This knowledge base is located in each individual's history of literacy in his or her social world – family literacy, community literacy, school literacy – in other words, all the different domains in which each one of us has encountered forms of literacy throughout our lives. This knowledge of literacy resides in our memories and our senses, in flashes of images that come to us when we remember those first words we read on the page (*Janet and John. Look. See the aeroplane.*), in our language/s, and in words and phrases that make up our networks of association in the mind (Gee, 1992) in relation to what we know, remember and feel about literacy. I call this kind of work on literacy history exploring the literacy archive: working with teachers' archives of knowledge and experience about literacy and the ways in which this archive constructs their present beliefs, knowledge and affect in relation to literacy.

The Limits of Language

My interest as a language teacher educator is in *productive* diversity: exploring pedagogies that work with students' diverse representational resources in productive ways. A central feature of such pedagogies is recognizing the limits of language as a communicative channel in expressing the arc of human experience. When giving expression to the richness of memory, words are not enough. Much of memory is located in images and in our senses. In the act of making meaning, we have an array of multi-semiotic resources at our disposal which extend beyond language into gesture and particular uses of the body, into visual images, music and silence. From a pedagogical point of view, I devise a lot of classroom tasks that consciously work with multimodality, across modes and communicative practices, to incorporate the multiple ways of representation evident in different contexts and communities.

The Classroom as Community

Central to the way I work with productive diversity is conceptualizing the classroom as a social and community space in which diverse groups of people come together to produce meaning. In South Africa, we are engaged in a difficult and painful process of social and political transformation. This involves coming to terms with the past in order to 'invent' a different South African identity that takes into account the cultural and linguistic diversity of the country's people. This identity quest impacts on many aspects of the way we live, including our social relations in classrooms. Through constructing the classroom as a community whose goal is to produce textual objects in response to specific tasks, for real audiences, certain kinds of synergies are produced that incorporate and juxtapose individual identities within larger social groupings. These kinds of juxtapositions in the collaborative process work to reconfigure – in varying degrees of intensity – students' existing sets of relations to the object of investigation. This process of reconfiguration produces some form of *change*, both in the object being transformed, and in the individual who is the agent of his or her own meaning-making.

Re-sourcing Resources: Working with Affectivity and History

I argue that any account of pedagogical practice that works with the varying degrees of access or representational capital that students bring to the classroom setting needs to take seriously issues of *affectivity* and *history*. In the contexts I describe, where students who have benefited from a particular ideological system work side by side with students who have been disadvantaged by this same system, it is the saying of the unsayable, that which has been silenced through loss, anger or dread, which enables students to re-articulate their relationships to their pasts. Through this process of articulation, a new energy is produced that takes people forward. I call this process of articulation and recovery *re-sourcing resources*: taking the resources we have which are taken for granted and invisible to a new context of situation and community to produce new meanings. Through this re-articulation in a new site, we come to see what we have in a different way: the source is re-sourced. In this sense, then, re-sourcing resources is a transformative activity that helps us come to new understandings about who we are, what we feel and what we know: it is a cognitive, affective and social activity that helps us to discover our humanity. But critical to this transformation is how the classroom functions *as a community* and how, *as a community*, it is able to contain the deep feelings that arise when students come face to face with loss.

Performing the Literacy Archive Project

The classroom context and practice

Performing the Literacy Archive Project is part of an INSET language teacher education course I run on sociocultural perspectives on literacy, including work by the New Literacy Studies (Heath, 1983; Street, 1984, 1993; Gee, 1996; Prinsloo & Breier, 1996) and the International Multiliteracies Project of the New London Group (1996; Cope & Kalantzis, 2000). The New Literacy Studies and the International Multiliteracies Project reject a view of literacy as an autonomous, neutral skill that can be applied universally to all contexts and domains. The project situates literacy very much within the social world: literacy is a social practice that is embedded in specific contexts, is used for particular purposes and produces different effects according to its domain of use. Thus what literacy is (how people view it) and what it does is 'situated' (to return to Gee's framework) within specific discourses, histories, identities, activities, and cultural models that produce certain sets of beliefs and practices around it. The International Multiliteracies Project expands this view to include multiple communicative practices (what has been called 'The New Communicative Order' across semiotic modes) to account for the ever-increasing range of communicative systems being produced by the new technologies. This project links these multimodal communicative practices to the New Work Order in the global workplace and explores the implications of these articulations for language and literacy in schools.

All the students in the group speak English as a primary or additional language. Many students are multilingual, speaking at least three of the eleven official languages of the country. The students come from a range of cultural, linguistic, and geographical contexts from South Africa and from Sub-Saharan Africa. There is usually a mix of historically advantaged and disadvantaged South African students in this group. The course is designed to work at a number of levels in order to integrate the students' representational resources – their cross-cultural perspectives and diverse multiliteracies – into the course content and practices. Students have seven weeks in which to prepare a multimodal, multilingual performance piece that works with their individual literacy histories. This performance is assessed on a group basis only, and forms part of a larger assessment that includes written research reports of literacy practices in specific contexts. In terms of the management of the actual task, I usually select the small working groups, mixing students across languages, cultures, histories, gender, race, and educational backgrounds. Students then spend time in these groups sharing their literacy histories and preparing for their transformation into a performance piece with all its features of visual design, music, dance, gesture, costumes and spectacle. I stress to students that what they are doing is a literacy history and that literacy is the pivotal point around which the history is constructed. And I encourage them to weave together these diverse histories and languages, like a braid, into a coherent narrative that takes into account their convergences and divergences.

Literacy archives performances

Each time students present their performances, I am struck by the powerful effects the project has on the participants both as individuals and as members of the classroom community (Stein, 1998). I have chosen two extracts of performance texts by students that vividly convey some of the complex issues around what counts as literacy, and the consequences of having or not having access to it. Obviously this written text cannot convey in any full sense the power of the performance, but I ask you to imagine a small seminar room in Johannesburg full of excited, nervous adults laughing at themselves and at each other, as they display their costumes and props for the play. The cast of characters includes students dressed up as their mothers, fathers, nannies and teachers. The performance begins. A young black woman dressed as a 10- year-old girl shyly takes the stage to begin her monologue:

In 1968, I was ten years old and in Standard One when I came to Petanenge ('Put Leg') village in the Northern Province, so named because of the river one has to cross to reach the place. The community in Petanenge was illiterate, if I may use the word in its traditional sense. Without a single school, teacher or doctor. Our house, just like many houses surrounding us, was mud built. We often had to go for days without proper meals. Many families lived in degradation. The fathers worked on the mines in Johannesburg and Pietersburg – many never came back to their families and they left them destitute. There was little or no motivation for learning. My two sisters and I were amongst the few who stuck to school. Since the place did not have any electricity or tele- phones, communication was limited to letter writing. Many people would come to us every week to ask us to read or write letters for them. The majority would be women who wanted to communicate with their husbands, children or boyfriends. These were the most humbling moments I could remember from my youth, humbling because many of the old people would entrust me with the most private and intimate news of their lives. Old men would squat and old women would kneel when asking for my services. This was a gesture only accorded elderly people or important members of the community. Old people would ask me to write letters to their sons who were enticed to the city and were no longer prepared to come home. The sufferings of these people would be shamelessly shed. What I dreaded most was to read letters, telegrams and messages informing the relatives about deaths in the family. This was not uncommon for a community where people worked on the mines. I would watch helplessly while my aunt tried to comfort the poor father, mother, wife.

Let me draw you to the fact that when I started reading these letters I was a young girl of ten. I began to think that, by right, women were inferior to men as the women around me were subjected to shame and humiliation. Men could decide on how many children they wanted, while they stayed for years in Johannesburg, entertaining themselves with other women, expecting their wives to wait for them. Some women tried to go against this but were met with great criticism from both genders. Fathers were not prepared to fund their daughters' education while they were prepared to do it for their sons.

At the tender age of ten, I was a letter reader and a letter writer for my village. Through my access to literacy, I came to know the ways of men and women. I feel now that I was exposed too early to adult life and in a way, I feel robbed of my childhood.

What you now witness is a poignant scene between this young girl and a woman from the village who brings in a letter she has just received from her husband. The letter is written in Tsonga, the local language. The young girl slowly reads the letter aloud in Tsonga and in English. The woman begins to weep. Her husband is demanding that she procure a second wife for him – her own sister.

A different group of students, a different year. This time, the cast of characters includes a group of four men dressed in traditional African cloths, blankets, skins and assegais, carrying their faded school certificates from apartheid Bantu Education days, a Voortrekker lady from the Great Trek, and a visiting Japanese student clutching large posters full of beautiful Japanese and Chinese calligraphy. She carefully pins up her calligraphy on the walls of the classroom, creating a vivid backdrop to her performance. She then begins speaking in Japanese while a member of her group provides a running translation in English.

Rumiko (speaking in Japanese): From the time I was seven years old, my parents forced me to go to lots of schools every day after normal school, like electric piano, calligraphy and the abacus. When I was ten years old, my parents forced me to go to juku where we learn the same subjects but with better teachers. Even on Sunday I went to swimming school because my mother didn't want to play with me – she needed a rest. So my parents never taught me to read books. If they had I would have become a child who loves reading. I didn't like my private high school because my teacher insulted my mom and me when I told him the fact that my mother was illiterate. Teachers often asked for the parents' responses in writing. In the morning before the teacher collected the forms from the pupils, the pupils showed them to one another to compare the calligraphy skills. I hated it because I had to hide my mom's illiteracy every time. I always filled in the forms myself. In Japan you are regarded as an illiterate person if you can't read and write difficult Chinese characters even if you can write in two kinds of Japanese characters.

Jenny (in English): So even though your mother could write two different Japanese characters she was regarded as illiterate because she couldn't write Chinese characters? Seems like Japan has a very narrow definition of literacy …

Rumiko (in English): If my mother could hear you now she would be very happy!

The literacy performance brings together a complex interweaving of identity, cultural memory and history through autobiographical narrative that students find compelling in its own right. The act of remembering or reconstructing the truth about one's literacy history is not just an act of repetition. It has the potential to become both a validation and a recovery of that history. The concept of multiliteracies is liberatory for many students because it places value on multiple forms of representation, not only writing in standard English. Many students have come to see that, for example, the multilingual songs and dances of their communities form part of the multiliteracies of that community. In addition, the task is structured on the assumption that all students have a story to tell and *each story has equivalent value* at the outset. In terms of an equitable distribution of representational resources in this task, all things are assumed equal, and everyone has to have a voice in the final project. Ensuring that each history is represented in some way forms part of the evaluation criteria for the assessment of the task.

For many of the students, watching the performances evokes a wide range of feelings: empathy, nostalgia, curiosity, pleasure, humor as well as anger, regret, envy and pain. Watching the literacy histories of historically-advantaged students can reveal in stark ways the cultural and symbolic capital that needs to be accumulated in order to 'play the game'. The experience of watching can unleash bitterness and regret for what has been lost, and anger at those who produced this loss. However, because of the nature of the project, this sense of loss and anger is examined, in varying degrees of depth, through the long whole-group discussions we have together directly after the performance, in the same room, in which everyone talks about what they felt during the show, the images they were moved by, what the histories tell us about ourselves, our education systems, our country, and our identities. Drawing on Freire's work (1970), these discussions form part of a critical pedagogy and dialogue in relation to the group's collective histories: they acknowledge what people have lost and attempt to explain the sociological and historical conditions that have produced, and continue to produce, these inequities. They also move into discussions of what it means to take action in relation to these inequities. For example, it is hoped that, through such dialogues, students can act to change the conditions of literacy acquisition for their own children.

These discussions are not primarily intended as forms of therapy in coming to terms with South Africa's long and painful history. Rather, they aim to provide a platform for historical and social analysis that may enable people to channel their anger into different forms of social action. These discussions are for me the most important part of the project because it is in these moments that the most poignant and powerful moments can occur: when as a group, we come face to face with our past, and with each other, black and white. One black woman student said, 'What these stories show is the kind of access to books, films, education I didn't have … even now I sit in this room as an Honours student, in this elite university, with everyone else, I still feel there are deep problems with access …' A long discussion then ensued on this point. Another historically- disadvantaged student wrote a reflective paper on the literacy project that articulates her cognitive and affective engagement with the task:

> When we were first asked to write out our literacy histories, I could not remember any of my early experiences with literacy. By conversations with my parents, the memories came flooding into my head. I could recall my first experience with paper, the written word and language. I enjoyed thinking about my childhood memories. Some of these memories were painful to think about, like the fact that I did not have many books when I was little, since my parents were financially disadvantaged. But I recall my father bringing home pamphlets, greeting cards, and almost everything he had printed (this puts a smile on my face, my literacy history was not as sad as I had originally thought). What I found difficult to do thereafter, was to put my literacy history onto paper. At that stage they were still in the form of pictures (I feel that I think in pictures) and converting the pictures into words was a difficult task. Eventually I opted to tell my group my literacy history. In telling I wasn't limited to using words, I used gestures, my tone of voice changed when I recalled something exciting like when I folded paper into boats

and raced them in a puddle of water when it rained. I also recall shedding a tear when I retold the story of how my father was robbed of an education. For me, in telling the stories and doing the literacy performances, my literacy experiences were brought to life. When I wrote my literacy history the words were lifeless and the experiences were lost in the past. When I performed the literacy history, I could once again be the five-year-old child who enjoyed folding paper.

This process of recovery is encapsulated in the line, 'I could once again be the five-year-old child who enjoyed folding paper.' The recovery of loss in some form can take place through the emphasis on community, identity and affectivity in the small groups. These issues are later taken to larger groups for more analytical discussions and critical reflection. This *re-sourcing of resources*, in which that which is taken for granted and invisible is re-evaluated, is perfectly captured in her words ' ... this puts a smile on my face, my literacy history was not as sad as I had originally thought.'

To return to Gee's metaphor about the game, I would claim that the Performing the Literacy Archive Project attempts to level the playing field of the game in that the game can belong to everyone: everyone has a history to tell and resources to draw on to do this. In this kind of game playing, students with disadvantaged educational backgrounds can 'call the game' and transform what counts as the game – although the extent to which this occurs will depend on the interpersonal power relations in the small group. In the following project, I explore what happens when the game belongs only to some, and the majority of students do not have the necessary resources to draw on in order to play it.

Photographing Literacy Practices Project

The classroom context and practice

This project was carried out with a class of third year ESL and English home language undergraduate students at the University of Witwatersrand, who were completing language-in-education courses. The class consisted of a mix of historically-advantaged women (mostly white) and historically-disadvantaged men and women (mostly black). The course, based on the social uses of literacy in different contexts and sites (Heath, 1983; Street, 1984, 1993; Barton, 1994; Prinsloo & Breier, 1996), had a research component in which students were required to select a site in which literacy was a communicative practice. They had to research the various ways in which literacy was being used in this site, in particular modes and for specific purposes. Once they had selected the site, they were each given a disposable camera with exactly fourteen shots in which they had to capture the literacy practices in this site to use in a photographic display and exhibition that would open to the public on a specific day. Each student was required to design his or her own display chart with the following components:

- an arrangement of photos with captions;
- an explanatory text for viewers contextualizing the project;
- standard, accurate, written English.

After this photographic exhibition, students were required to write:

- a research report using the photographs as a reference point;
- a reflective account of what they encountered and felt about the project and process.

Thus the total assessment package required students to produce multi-modal textual forms across a range of modes and genres:

- a collection of photographs *in the visual mode* as examples of a certain photographic genre of 'display' and 'report';
- a *visually designed multimodal* display poster in the genre of 'exhibit' which would be posted on a wall;
- a series of explanatory captions *in writing* for the photographs;
- an explanatory page *in writing* which explains the whole project for the viewer;
- an academic essay *in writing* and *in the visual mode* (using the photographs) which describes and analyzes the uses of literacy in the chosen site.

At least 60% of the students in this class had no previous experience of designing posters or charts, taking photographs or writing explanatory texts as required on the poster. The remaining 40% had a good deal of experience in visual design at school. All the students had three years of academic literacy with varying degrees of competence.

The use of photography

I use visual communication as the entry point into the research process because I am interested in how we engage in different semiotic modes and the ways in which these modes impact on how we see and think and feel. Many historically-disadvantaged students experience difficulties with academic writing in English, as English is their additional language. I thought that if the students used their eyes first – their powers of observation – this way of seeing would be a form of situated activity that would connect them in a concrete way to the context and the subject. By going into a place – an office, a school, a factory, a church – and looking carefully at what people were doing and saying in relation to literacy in order to make decisions about what to 'capture' in photographs, this procedure would give them some control over the object of study. The idea was that this control would help them to generate *cognitive* concepts about literacy in this site in more focused ways, which they could then describe and analyze in very grounded ways. Thus the starting point for *thinking* was *seeing (or observing)*. The activity of selecting what was to be represented in the fourteen photographs would produce an amplification of their own seeing- the idea of focused seeing as an activity of knowledge making. A student from this group who had never used a camera before explains how he engaged with this process of focused seeing:

> Before I took photographs I realized that I have to go to the site I have chosen and look at what I should capture on film. It was very difficult to select what I should capture as it was not easy to decide what counts as literacy. To understand what literacy practices are, I had to consult some books which deal with the subject. When I took the photos I ensured that I place myself at a position that would make me to take good and clear pictures, which reflect my point of view. In some cases I had to organize the children in a particular way so that the photo could reveal what I want the viewers to see. This project has revealed that photos can speak for themselves ... they do not only complement what is written.

Another student wrote, 'I had to learn to see how others would see.' According to Sontag (1977), to photograph is *to appropriate* the thing photographed. It means putting oneself into a certain relation to the world *that feels like knowledge*, has the semblance of knowledge, and therefore, like power. A photograph furnishes evidence. It passes for incontrovertible proof that something exists or has happened. Referring to the practice of taking travel snaps, Sontag explains:

> As photographs give people an imaginary possession of a past that is unreal, they also help people to take possession of space in which they are insecure...The very activity of taking pictures is soothing, and assuages general feelings of disorientation that are likely to be exacerbated with travel. (Sontag, 1977: 9–10)

This research project does require of students that they 'travel' into unfamiliar zones and 'take possession of a space' in which they are insecure. The taking of photographs as the first stage in this research project was surprisingly enabling for all students, but most of all for the students who had never used a camera before. Through the use of fail-proof Fuji and Kodak technology, all the photos worked. No one produced bad photos. Students were coming into a new object of study through the visual – through their eyes – and they had to communicate their evidence through the visual medium first. They then had to develop explanations of their practices both visually and in writing for a specific audience. Thus the *aesthetic* became a factor at the level of academic textual practice.

In this project, there were different exchange values in the group from the outset in terms of the representational resources needed for the task. Some students' resources were 'worth' more than others. The question for me, as the teacher, was what to do about the differences in exchange values. One way might be to use the teacher or textbook to mediate access to what is needed through sufficient scaffolding for each student who is outside the zone of access. This can be done on an individual basis. The route I chose was to work with the classroom as a community in which some form of redistribution of the necessary resources would take place. But the social negotiation around this redistribution can be very tricky and depends for some degree on the goodwill of those who have the resources. Sensing that the situation might be difficult, I decided that the way to handle the imbalance in resources was to openly acknowledge them, to provide an historical explanation of how and why such differences had come about, and to recruit the class as a community in which, *together*, students might set about re-organizing the redistribution of 'symbolic' capital. I then consciously left the class to enable students to take agency in relation to this redistribution. When I returned to class one hour later, the students were absorbed in their projects, helping each other, using the resources they had available productively and generously. This negotiation had taken place because those who had the cultural capital were prepared to share it and those who needed it felt entitled to ask for it: a reason for working together, which made sense, had been created. This particular social negotiation depended on goodwill: if there is goodwill lacking, resentment and animosity follow.

To return to Gee: what is often necessary is for someone to facilitate the process of learning how to play the game, in very real and concrete ways. In this classroom, those who knew the game were side by side with those who wanted access to the game. Through setting up the classroom as a generative community of practice in which skills sharing was critical to the public success of the project, where the stakes were raised to include an outside, public audience, work was produced that went way beyond what I had expected. Students worked together creatively and productively, drawing on one another's skills, which the 'advantaged' students were happy to share. We opened the exhibition and 90 teachers came and saw the students' work. Afterwards a student, who calls herself a 'first-time doer' wrote:

> First of all, it was the first time for me to be able to use a camera. In our township schools around the country we were not involved in such projects. For many black students it was the experience of a life-time (meaning, *a first time experience*). I learnt how to organize a poster creatively ... During the beginning of the year the AELS 300 students were full of individualization. We were grouped according to friends ... With the introduction of this project we changed and became a team, a family who helped each other. We learnt to tolerate each other regardless of race, gender, ethnicity and status. This is a very important project. In future I think it should be given more time for the first-time doers to acquire enough skills. We were all committed to making this project a success. The more united we stood the stronger we became. I think we even surprised ourselves. We grew and acquired new skills for the workplace. Teamwork and creative work created a wonderful working environment full of new challenges.

Another student, whose exchange value was the highest in the class because she was a very skilled design student, wrote afterwards:

> The greatest achievement of this assignment in my opinion was the end. Not because the assignment was over, but because the collaboration and comradeship had begun. This was the first time that I collaborated with my fellow students. Helping them consolidate their efforts and my involvement in that process was astounding and truly awakening.

Conclusion

A question I have been asked several times in relation to the projects described above is: isn't this kind of pedagogy an abdication of responsibility in relation to developing academic literacy? Some teachers think that the time devoted to developing multiliteracies (in this instance, the visual, oral and performance modes) is time wasted, time that should be spent on developing and sustaining students' skills in written academic English. My response is that literacy learning requires a social context in which learners' identities and histories are central to the formation of that context. Identities emerge in diverse forms of representation: language is only one mode in which this can occur. In both the projects described above, a relationship is established between identity, history, community and creativity that unleashes productive energies at affective and cognitive levels. New intellectual and social connections are produced in these formations that break through previously-established boundaries, feeding unconsciously and consciously into learners' understandings of their social world. In classrooms into which students bring diverse representational resources that are differently valued in the school setting, one of the ways to work with this situation is to develop pedagogies that work with what students bring (their existing resources for representation) and acknowledge what students have lost. This is possible through pedagogies that consciously work with re-sourcing resources: providing students with the opportunity to re-articulate what they have, know and feel within the supportive context of a classroom community which is critically conscious of the powerful effects of culture, ideology and history.

Acknowledgements

I thank Lynne Slonimsky for her contribution to this paper.

References

Barton, D. (1994) *Literacy: An Introduction to the Ecology of Written Language.* Oxford: Blackwell.

Cope, B. and Kalantzis, M. (eds) (2000) *Multiliteracies: Literacy Learning and the Design of Social Futures.* London: Routledge.

Freeman, D. and Johnson, K. (1998) Reconceptualising the knowledge-base of language teacher education. *TESOL Quarterly* 32 (3), Autumn, 397–417.

Freire, P. (1970) *Pedagogy of the Oppressed.* New York: Seabury Press.

Gee, J.P. (1992) *The Social Mind.* New York: Bergin and Garvey.

Gee, J.P. (1996) *Social Linguistics and Literacies: Ideology in Discourses* (2nd edn). London: Taylor & Francis.

Gee, J.P. (1999) Learning language as a matter of learning social languages within Discourses. Paper delivered at TESOL '99, New York, March 9–13.

Heath, S.B. (1983) *Ways with Words: Language, Life, and Work in Communities and Classrooms.* Cambridge: Cambridge University Press.

Kress, G. and Van Leeuwen, T. (1996) *Reading Images: The Grammar of Visual Design.* London: Routledge.

Kress, G. and Van Leeuwen, T. (2001) *Multimodal Discourse: The Modes and Media of Contemporary Communication,* London: Edward Arnold.

Kress, G. (1997a) *Before Writing: Rethinking the Paths to Literacy.* London: Routledge.

Kress, G. (1997b) Multimodal texts and critical discourse analysis. Unpublished paper, Institute of Education, University of London.

New London Group (1996) A pedagogy of multiliteracies: Designing social futures. *Harvard Educational Review* 66, 60–92.

Prinsloo, M. and Breier, M. (1996) *The Social Uses of Literacy.* Cape Town: Maskew Miller Longman.

Sontag, S. (1977) *On Photography.* Harmondsworth: Penguin Books.

Stein, P. (1998) Reconfiguring the past and the present: Performing literacy histories in a Johannesburg classroom. *TESOL Quarterly* 32 (3), Autumn, 517–528.

Street, B. (1984) *Literacy in Theory and Practice.* Cambridge: Cambridge University Press.

Street, B. (ed.) (1993) *Cross-Cultural Approaches to Literacy.* Cambridge: Cambridge University Press.

Chapter 3

Transforming the Discourses of Teaching and Learning: Rippling Waters and Shifting Sands

JERRI WILLETT AND SARAH MILLER

Introduction

Just as authentic beginners and colonized members of a Discourse rarely become innovators (see Gee in Chapter 1), their teachers rarely become innovators in the dominant and official Discourses of teaching and learning, so they are not able to create spaces for their own students to talk back to the dominant Discourses that colonize them. Teachers, of course, may resist and innovate behind the closed doors of their own classrooms, but great efforts are made to ensure that they conform to the official Discourses, and most find there is little time left for innovation or resistance. The State of Massachusetts, for example, has spent millions of dollars on developing curriculum frameworks for both public schools and teacher preparation programs and a testing program to ensure that learning and teaching are aligned with these dominant Discourses. The questions consistently asked by accreditation teams, government funding agencies, employers, and supervisors are 'How does your curriculum and teaching practice align with the frameworks?' and 'Can your learners pass the tests that have been aligned with the frameworks?'

As a result of these mandates, schools are changing dramatically. In one elementary school, copies of the curriculum frameworks replace the display of children's drawings and writing in the halls. In another school district, the teachers are no longer able to create their own professional development plans, as they once did. Instead, they must now attend workshops that teach them how to use the frameworks to develop their curriculum and how to prepare their learners for the MCAS (Massachusetts Comprehensive Assessment System). Principals are being threatened with dismissal if their school fails to do well on these tests, and the State has threatened to close down any School of Education whose student body does not achieve an

80% pass rate on the MECT (Massachusetts Educators Certification Tests). We are all colonized by this Discourse of Accountability: some submit, some resist and others enthusiastically take up its subject positions, believing its ideologies to be the natural order of things. However, the schools with high proportions of English language learners or special needs students and the Schools of Education who value and admit high numbers of students who speak standard English as second language or dialect are the ones most negatively affected by the accountability movement.

It is in this climate of accountability that the faculty and students (in-service or pre-service teachers in public and private schools and agencies) in the Bilingual/ESL/Multicultural Practitioner Area (BEM) at the University of Massachusetts-Amherst renewed our resolve to become critical innovators in the Discourse of teaching and learning. The program has always attempted to support students and faculty as they learn to both participate in and resist the dominant Discourse of teaching and learning, as called for by Gee (see Chapter 1, this volume). But now we needed to find *new ways* to provide them with opportunities to explore identities as 'transformative intellectuals,' a term coined by Henry Giroux (1989: 139). In other words, we wanted to help them become educators who contribute deliberately and critically to the Discourses and practices that constitute schools and society, rather than educators who take on identities as 'ritualized producers and consumers' (Gee, Chapter 1) of dominant Discourses and practices. Challenging the status quo in the current climate, however, has become much riskier, but if we do not fully explore alternative Discourses and practices, we may merely reproduce the inequitable social relations we are attempting to transform through our classroom practices.

This chapter provides an example of how faculty and students are working together to open up spaces outside the boxes into which we have been placed. Our example comes from a course collaboratively designed by BEM faculty to explore the possibilities of transformative curriculum deliberation in the current climate of narrow accountability. In the process of reflecting publicly on our teaching and learning and exposing the ebb and flow of tensions within our work, we argue that contradictions, tensions, misalignments and unpredictable results provide productive possibilities for transformative practice, despite the frustrations they may cause. In practice, such tensions are frequently experienced by participants as failures and perhaps abandoned prematurely, particularly by those working within Discourses that promote hyper-achievement, alignment, and accountability. As we will demonstrate, such work is always unpredictable, so no guarantees are offered. Nevertheless, we construct a hopeful narrative in order to support others' understandings as they encounter tensions in their own transformative practices.

The heart of the chapter is a dialogic commentary that grew out of conversations between the authors as we critically reflected on the contradictions and tensions around which we struggled during the course, and afterwards as we worked on writing this chapter. We each had different roles in the course – Sarah, a student in the course, was a group-process facilitator in one of the teams engaged in curriculum deliberation, and Jerri was one of the instructors who designed the course and who typically teaches it.

In the pages that follow, we first frame the chapter with a discussion of the concept 'performing dialogue and critical reflection across difference,' which was a principle strategy used in this course to enable pre-service and in-service teachers to explore the possibilities of transformative practice. We also present a metaphor that we collaboratively constructed to capture insights from our reflective dialogue. Next, we describe the course and Sarah's curriculum team. Following this, we provide dialogic commentary around the student-produced texts that were the products of curriculum deliberation in Sarah's team. The commentary grew out of our ongoing dialogue about these texts and should not be read as an authoritative interpretation of what 'really happened.' No doubt, had the dialogue occurred between any of the other students and faculty who were involved, the commentary would have looked very different. Indeed, our own interpretations continue to evolve and change as we bring new experiences and conversations to our reflections.

Performing Dialogue and Critical Reflection across Difference: A Theoretical Framing

Many language teacher-educators and teachers are acutely aware of being caught between two contradictory forces. That is, they must prepare teachers and learners to become socialized members of the dominant Discourses, while also protecting them from these Discourses. On the one hand, by taking up their role as agents of socialization, language teachers and teacher educators perpetuate the dominant Discourses that continue to marginalize English language learners and themselves. On the other hand, taking up the role of critical pedagogue frequently produces resistant learners, who may, in fact, desire the colonizer's privileges. Further, this role can also unintentionally position teachers and their learners as ineffective troublemakers who need further surveillance, rather than as transformative intellectuals. This conundrum has led many postcolonial and feminist theorists who have studied the power dynamics operating within transformative projects to ask such questions as, 'Can the subaltern[1] speak?' (Spivak, 1988) and 'Why doesn't this feel empowering?' (Ellsworth, 1989). These questions suggest that 'speaking for' or 'giving agency to' those who are marginalized can be patronizing, reproductive, and ultimately impossible to achieve. Recognizing these challenges, transformative teacher/theorists responded with the questions, 'What kinds of practices are possible once vulnerability, ambiguity, and doubt are admitted?' and simultaneously, 'What kinds of power and authority are taken up in practices we choose?' (Britzman, 1991).

One practice explored by many transformative teacher/theorists is 'performing dialogue and critical reflection across difference' (Burbules & Rice, 1991; Bhabha, 1996; Escobar, 1995; Freire, 1993; Luke & Gore, 1992; McNamee & Gergen, 1999; Rosenberger, 2003; Sidorkin, 1999; Willett *et al.*, 1999). Although differently realized across these teacher/theorists, the idea is that performing sustained dialogue brings into being the possibility, not the guarantee, of new understandings, ways of talking and ways of being. Typically, two conditions are proposed for enabling the productivity of dialogue: (1) co-existing multiple voices speaking from different horizons, and (2) mutual listening to these voices (Cheyne & Tarulli, 1999; Sidorkin, 1999).

Bakhtin's (1981) notion of dialogicality and otherness serves as a platform for much of the theorizing around dialogic practices used by transformative teachers. For Bakhtin, human beings participate in dialogue throughout their lives, using words that others have used in the past for different purposes. They shape their utterances in ways that simultaneously address their interlocutors' previous statements, communicate their own intentions, and anticipate how their interlocutors will respond to what they are planning to say. In the process of their engagement in lifelong dialogue, individuals contribute to the discourses of different and often conflicting voices handed down through generations and across situations. A key insight for a transformative agenda is Bakhtin's assertion that the struggle to understand differences between oneself and others is not only essential to being human, it results in highly productive hybridity, despite forces working against change:

> The collision between differing points of view on the world ... fighting it out in the territory of the utterance ... unconscious hybrids have been ... profoundly productive historically; they are pregnant with potential for new world views, with new 'internal forms' for perceiving the world in words. (Bakhtin, 1981: 360)

In order to achieve legitimacy in these battles of understanding, interlocutors typically reference an implied third person in dialogue. That is, an authority whose 'ideally true responsive understanding assumes ideological expressions (God, absolute truth, the court of dispassionate human conscience, the people, the court of history, science and so forth' (Bakhtin, 1986: 126).

Critical theorists, however, argue that 'third person authorities' are often used to justify powerful but unjust social hierarchies, rather than 'true responsive understanding.' Habermas (1970), for example, posited that systematically-distorted communication (e.g. pre-existing and biased patterns of language and thought) leads to failure to achieve equitable dialogue, and therefore genuine consensus. In response, he developed a theory of communicative competence that could mediate dialogue to ensure 'mutual listening.' Communicatively-competent individuals can make decisions based on mutual concerns rather than ideological domination, if they are willing to explore motivations, unmask false assumptions about the other (e.g. poor people are lazy), and assess true needs and capacities (Wuthnow *et al.*, 1986). Since validity claims are built into the structure of discourse itself and have material existence at the level of speech acts, claims and counter claims become available for the critical analysis and reflection needed to engage in 'genuine dialogue.'

Postmodern theorists, however, countered that it is impossible to set up universal procedures or rules to ensure undistorted dialogue, much less genuine consensus, about what constitutes just practices and structures (Butler, 1990; Ellsworth, 1989; Foucault, 1972; Fendler, 1999; Lather, 1992; Luke, 1996; Spivak, 1988; Weedon, 1987). In order to (re)position critical dialogue and reflection within postmodern discourses, critical theorist/ teachers have developed strategies that open up the possibility for constructing new social relations within the practice of critical dialogue and reflection (some examples include Bhabha, 1996; Escobar, 1995; Fendler, 1999; Sidorkin, 1999; Rosenberger, 2003; Willett *et al.*, 1999). While recognizing the challenges, these teacher/theorists believe that constructing equitable relations is possible, albeit in unpredictable and impermanent ways.

The social conditions under which equitable relations are more likely to come into being include plurality, tolerance, and respect, together with the willingness to engage in such conversations, as suggested by modern critical theorists. Added to this list, however, are a number of strategies suggested by postmodern critical theorists, such as those proposed by Fendler (1999: 186):

(1) problematizing the assumption of autonomous subjectivity (e.g. Juan's ignorance is responsible for failures in communication);

(2)   deconstructing texts constructed during the performance of dialogue (e.g. analyzing how unequal relations are created in dialogue, even though it aims to create parity);

(3)   historicizing the systems of reasoning that have become naturalized (e.g. examining the history of colonial relations involved in the development of the reasoning being used to engage in critical dialogue);

(4)   shifting the analysis to understand the dichotomous relation between the textual subject and the subject-as-reader (e.g. an identity, such as 'Asian-American' is a performance, not a description, and as such can be interpreted in multiple and contradictory ways by both those performing and those interpreting the performance);

(5)   faith rests on unforeseen and uncontrolled possibilities for the future rather than on the ability to solve social problems (e.g. the leverage of an historical analysis of dialogue is critical only in that it challenges common sense at the moment; if it becomes a methodology, it too needs to be interrupted).

We invite readers to perform a deconstructive reading of the text that follows, but we hope that it will, despite its contradictions and tensions, support them in performing their own dialogic encounters. This text (re)presents a critical dialogue between Sarah and Jerri in which we (re)interpret a historical text (a transcript) of a four-month dialogic deliberation among Sarah and her group mates, the parameters of which were structured by Jerri, who was not physically present during most of the performances but whose authority was frequently invoked.

We begin our (re)presentation with a metaphor that emerged for us as we reflected on the dynamic nature of our insights.

Rippling Waters and Shifting Sands: A Metaphor under Construction

The photographs in Figure 3.1 show the dynamic patterns formed by the sand and water in dialogue with one another across time. This dialogue became a metaphor for the way we experienced the effects of the course on our beliefs and values about teaching and learning, and the reactions of others who were touched by the course. Our experiences are the ripples of water undulating over the shoreline. We are the sand, rippled by the water and in turn shaping the ripples of waves yet to come. Just as the photographs capture a dynamic meeting of water and sand, the transcripts of classroom conversations, journals and other products of curriculum deliberation capture moments of dynamic learning and allow us to reflect on and take joy in their intricate complexities, protected momentarily from the

Figure 3.1 Rippling waters and shifting sands

sometimes terrifying and sometimes exhilarating experience of the shifting sands of our understandings.

Jerri: It took a long time for Sarah and I to write this chapter because each time we met we came to see our experiences of the course differently. The chapter was originally a conference paper I had written to illustrate how sociocultural perspectives might look in a teacher education program (Willett, 1999). I drew heavily on a course that my colleague Theresa Austin and I had developed, focusing on the work produced by a group of students from the course in which Sarah participated. Her final paper, in particular, captured the tensions that arose in the process of creating these documents, a reflection of her role as the group-process facilitator. As I crafted my paper, I felt uncomfortable writing about a dialogic practice in such a monologic fashion. Moreover, I was intrigued that, while most of our facts were similar, our interpretations of those facts were very different. So I scrapped my original paper and asked Sarah if she would collaborate with me on writing this chapter. I originally thought that we could quickly put the chapter to rest, since we had both already written the core of it. We just needed to explore some of the interesting differences. Each time we met, however, new interpretations and insights would emerge. The waves that rippled across our writing have been gentle and soothing, helping us to better understand the dramatic and thundering waves that crashed across our experiences of the course. The sand beneath us shifted in both cases.

Sarah: I also began the project believing that my original reflection paper together with a few additional insights would form the core of my contributions to this chapter. Our dialogic reflections on the experience of the course – (re)reflecting and (re)writing – have rippled across me, deepening the learning that began with the course, and revealing two things. First, how invaluable the process of continual (and collegial) reflection is to enriching and broadening the insights and lessons experienced during and after the course, indeed, **any** course. Second, how remarkable the impact of those lessons have been, as they continued to ripple through the subsequent courses, papers, projects, and explorations in my graduate work over the next two years. The initial thoughts I expressed in my original paper, as I reflect on them now, foreshadowed the development of my identity and philosophy as an ESL/multicultural educator.

The Micro-Political Context and Description of the Course

Jerri: Theresa (also a faculty member in the BEM Program) and I were inspired by Henderson & Hawthorne's (1995) *Transformative Curriculum Leadership* and Leo van Lier's (1996) *Interaction in the Language Curriculum.*

Together these two books outlined an emancipatory, interdisciplinary, learner-centered, and language-based approach to curriculum development. On the other hand, we were concerned about the increasing pressure being exerted by the State to prepare our students to develop curriculum around the State Curriculum Frameworks and the MCAS examination, which seemed to be the antithesis of the principles that undergirded our beliefs about learning. In response to these inspirations and concerns, we designed a course to help us to work with the tensions between the two competing ideologies. The following description outlines the course that Theresa and I created.

The course

The course was entitled 'Curriculum Development & Adaptation for Learners Becoming Bilingual through Content.'

Platform

A platform consists of the basic values and beliefs about learning that undergird the design of a curriculum unit. This was our platform:

(1) Education should aim to help learners take action on the world in order to make it more equitable and to reflect critically on their own actions and cultural productions (Freire, 1993). By working on real-life problems together, diverse learners will learn to use the 'genres of power' (Kress, 1999) and their own 'funds of knowledge' (Moll *et al.*, 1992) as resources in making their own visions and voices heard.

(2) Curriculum development is not a technical activity based on knowledge for which there is wide consensus. Rather, curriculum needs to develop through dialogue with stakeholders so that provisional ideas and conclusions emerge from dialogue across differences (Henderson & Hawthorne, 1995).

(3) Power relations between students and teachers, dominant and non-dominant language users, men and women, old hands and newcomers are problematic in the kinds of negotiations we are advocating. These relations should be ameliorated when possible, and held up for critical analysis.

(4) Assessment should not be coercive, nor require students to reproduce our beliefs and values, but the productions of faculty and students (e.g. curriculum, assessment practices, methods, etc.) should receive extensive constructive feedback in terms of how these productions affect others.

Goals

The course aims to support students and faculty, as they engage in critical dialogue and praxis, to explore new ways to design and adapt a curriculum for actual learners in local schools and agencies who are becoming bilingual through content.[2] Structures are designed to enable teams of students to engage in collaborative curriculum deliberation and to critically reflect on what they produce through the deliberative process, and receive multiple forms of feedback from classmates, faculty, and learners in the local schools. Students are asked to draw on a variety of different resources to guide their designs, including:

- the Massachusetts State Curriculum Frameworks;
- principles of transformative leadership, emancipatory and constructivist learning, and interactive language learning (outlined in the textbooks);
- the funds of knowledge, values and interests of their learners and communities;
- the values, experiences and knowledge of all their team members.

Assessment on both the product and process of deliberation consists of feedback from a variety of different sources, including from team mates, classmates, instructors, cooperating teachers, learners in local schools and agencies, and self-reflection.

Instructional design

The major activity in the course is the *deliberation and design of curriculum projects for local classrooms that include learners who are in the process of becoming bilingual*. The class is divided into five Curriculum Teams, each consisting of a Cooperating Teacher (the project is designed for the Cooperating Teacher's classroom), a Group Process Facilitator (who helps the team critically reflect on their interaction within the teams), and two or three members (who bring a variety of different resources and experiences to the team).

Each team is given a resource pack of readings relevant to their project, assembled by the instructors and supplemented by the Team. Teams record their discussions so they can reflect on their group processes and decide for themselves how to run their meetings and develop their projects. Team meetings take up half of the class time and most teams also meet outside of class time and/or visit the classrooms of their Cooperating Teacher.

The teams present their works-in-process three times during the semester so that they can get feedback from their classmates and instructors. Written comments from the instructors are duplicated and distributed to everyone in the class. The first presentation focuses on their platforms (statement of values, beliefs and purposes) and contextual information about the classroom and students for whom they are designing their projects. The second presentation gives an overview of their design and describes one activity that illustrates how their goals could be enacted. The completed project is displayed at a Curriculum Faire at the end of the semester to which all students and faculty in the BEM Program and local teachers and parents are invited.[3]

For the remainder of the time, the full class meets together to engage in dialogue about the principles of curriculum development and adaptation for learners who are becoming bilingual. Full-class meetings follow the professors' agendas and the students' emergent issues. The full class meetings include three kinds of activities: (1) discussions about the assigned readings or film; (2) activities or demonstrations designed to highlight particular issues, principles or skills; (3) feedback on team presentations.

The second major activity in the course is *critical reflection* on the teams' own productions. Teacher-learners engage in three kinds of reflective activities: (1) team dialogue and analysis about their group-process; (2) full-class reflection on the curriculum projects; and (3) a final written reflection on their experiences in the course.

The role of the group-process facilitator is to help the team analyze and reflect on their group processes and products. Each facilitator is responsible for taping and reviewing team deliberations; transcribing a critical incident or an interaction sequence that captures a persistent and salient pattern; and moderating a discussion in which the team analyzes and reflects on the incident or sequence selected by the facilitator. Facilitators are told explicitly that they are not 'team leaders' and that they are not to control 'turn-taking' during curriculum deliberation. Facilitators who agree to take on the role meet with other facilitators several times during the semester to explore creative ways to handle their difficult and sensitive role and they are given papers written by previous facilitators in other courses, but they are not given 'authoritative' methods on facilitation.

The teams moderate the critical feedback discussions on their own presentations to the full class. Although the class is encouraged to give feedback sensitively, the purpose of the discussion is not to give technical feedback, but rather to help the team examine their assumptions about learning and teaching and the consequences of these assumptions on learners who are becoming bilingual. The instructors' commentary focuses on how a particular team presentation contributes to the ongoing classroom dialogue about principles, issues, and concerns relevant to curriculum deliberation and design. This commentary is distributed to everyone in the class.

Finally, in addition to group reflection, each participant is asked to reflect on his or her personal experiences and learning in the course. Typically, course participants reflect on their team's process and final product; the course structure, assignments, methods, and readings; specific concepts or issues that arise in the class, in their meetings or in the reading; and the implications of their experiences on teaching and learning in their own classrooms.

Projects and outcomes from the 1998 implementation

Table 3.1 summarizes the projects that were designed when Sarah was in the course. It illustrates the range of projects that the students produced for a wide variety of educational contexts. We also attempted to find out what happened to these particular projects after the course was completed.

Situating the Social Studies Curriculum Team

Sarah: The Social Studies Curriculum Team consisted of Jan, a monolingual cooperating teacher who taught mainstream Social Studies and had no previous course work that dealt with language minority students; Roland, a multilingual ESL teacher from a country in Africa who had little experience in US classrooms (although he had visited several classrooms); Josh, a second-year ESL teacher in a local high school, who had majored in philosophy, politics and economics as an undergraduate; Bill, a US-born student without formal TESOL training who had three years of experience with adults and teachers in the Czech Republic, and Sarah, a US-born student (who became bilingual as an adult), interested in non-formal and holistic education with two years of TESOL experience at a private boarding high school, and limited overseas experience teaching English.

Our curriculum project (See Figure 3.2) focused on a course in the Social Studies Department in a local high school entitled 'Contemporary Issues.' The course was intended for students who were not performing well academically and were considered 'not college-bound,' some of whom were expected to drop out. Based on discussions in the curriculum course, political events that were occurring in the town, and initial discussions with the students, our team decided to focus on helping students to propose revisions for the school's *Student Handbook* that reflected their issues and concerns (the current handbook outlined an imposed disciplinary code with little input from students). The idea was to engage

Table 3.1 Summary of class projects

Group Name	Group make-up	Classroom	Product	What happened to the Projects?
Hmong-English Literacy	4 Anglo-American females (all ESL teachers). In addition to this adult ESL class, 2 of the teachers also taught ESL in public schools.	Adult bi-literacy program with 1 Hmong teacher and 2 ESL teachers. Grant-funded project.	Developed and implemented a project in which Hmong women wrote a community ethnography for bilingual publication. Collected folk stories, information and photographs about community events, family practices, women's stories, and descriptions of the practice and design of traditional embroidery.	The Hmong women continue to work on their ethnography. They contacted other Hmong communities for advice and ideas through Internet and conferences. Children were brought into the project to interview elders and write about their homeland. Two ESL teachers wrote grants to fund the publishing of the class-produced book. Another member began working in a center for new Americans, using a participatory approach. We lost contact with the fourth member.
Math	3 Anglo-American females, 2 Anglo-American males, 1 Asian male (3 math, 1 EFL, 1 middle school English, 1 doctoral student)	Middle School in heterogeneous & interdisciplinary teams. Focused on math.	Designed a unit for a Middle School organized into teams. The plan was for students to write proposals to the town counsel for the design of a youth hangout. Math class focused on statistical analyses of surveys, budget for the project, and measurements for the design of the project.	The cooperating teacher stated that this project was not implemented after the course finished because the focus of the school turned to exams and there was no time. The next year she was reassigned and was no longer participating in a team. We have no information on the other members.
Social Studies	2 Anglo American females, 2 Anglo American males, 1 African male (4 ESL teachers, 1 history teacher).	High School current events class. Course was typically taken by 'lower-tracked' students, assumed non-college bound.	Designed a project around revisions of the Student Handbook, which emerged out of discussions with the high school students on high absenteeism, drop out rates and the school's punitive response. Students discussed changes to make handbook more respectful and relevant.	Despite responsiveness of students to the project, the handbook changes never materialized during that school year [see Scene VI below for details]. Inspired by the project, however, the students continued the effort to participate in school policy-making. A new principal has been receptive to student participation.

Table 3.1 Summary of class projects (*continued*)

2-Way Bilingual	1 male Latino, 1 female Latino, 4 Anglo-American females (1 ESL, 2 bilingual N-3, 2 reading specialists, 1 teacher educator)	Kindergarten classroom in a new 2-way bilingual program of ½ Spanish and ½ English speakers.	Designed and implemented a curriculum unit aimed to increase status of Spanish in an English dominated school and community. The unit was entitled 'Asi Soy Yo.'	The teacher, also inspired by the bilingual team (*below*), instituted home/school journals with families to help them understand bi-literacy in their homes and conducted a teacher-research project on the changes she made. The ESL teacher (in another school) has become 'critical friends' with the 2-way bilingual teacher. The teacher educator is currently engaged in a critical ethnography of a school–university partnership in a low-income neighborhood.
Transitional Bilingual	4 Latina women (1 counselor, 1 vice principal, 1 bilingual aide, 1 bilingual teacher)	Transitional primary bilingual; multigrade class.	Developed practices that positioned families as curriculum partners. Team made family visits, invited parents into the classroom, and engaged in home/school journals.	All the women are working to improve relations & participation with families. The bilingual teacher is now a staff developer helping 2-way bilingual teachers work with families. She finds that involving Anglo American families is harder work for her than involving Latino families.
Foreign Language	1 Anglo male, 1 Latina female, 2 Asian females, 1 Asian male (all FL teachers in English, Spanish, Chinese, Japanese.)	Intermediate level Chinese classroom at the University level.	Created practices within traditionally structured FL programs that developed cross-cultural learners rather than flawed native-speakers, using interactive methods & incorporating culture as communication.	The institutional structures of their programs & their positions in the hierarchy (instructors) make it difficult to make major changes, but they all reported making small changes in their classes. The Spanish teacher is now in a doctoral program exploring issues of intercultural communication. The Japanese teacher is conducting a teacher-research project in her institution on collaborative group work.

Democracy, Change, and You: Looking at the Student–School Relationship Student Handbook Project

1. Absenteeism survey

[see Scene III, below]

2. Reflection

Students discuss their responses to the Absenteeism Survey.

They reflect on how they could be instrumental in affecting real change in terms of the issues they raised in their survey responses.

3. Scavenger Hunt

Students seek answers in the *Student Handbook* to questions concerning school policies.

4. You're On Camera!

Students write informal survey questions for their peers, teachers, school staff and administrators. They videotape the interviews, and analyze the content.

5. Writing Activities

(a) Free write: Students brainstorm a written response to the following prompt: 'School sucks!'

(b) In-class writing: Students respond in a more structured written format to the questions below: What aspect of school bothers you most? Why does it bother you? Do you think it's possible to change this aspect of school? If no, why not? If yes, how?

(c) Homework: Students describe the 'perfect school,' including, for example, subjects, teachers, scheduling, facilities, rules, extracurricular activities, food, etc.

6. Class Discussion of Writing Activities

Class engages in a guided discussion of the topics they addressed in their writing assignments. They negotiate especially relevant or 'hot' topics/issues they want to tackle in subsequent unit activities.

7. First letter to stakeholders

Class composes and sends a letter to parents, peers, faculty, the school committee and administration, in which they present the Student Handbook Revision Project and their areas of focus. They invite feedback from the community. Letters are translated for families and students when appropriate.

8. Formal surveys

Students collate the responses to their first videotaped interviews with the topics they have chosen to focus on. They develop and carry out the surveys with peers, faculty, administration, and parents. Interviews are recorded with multimedia.

9. Analyze data and reflect on findings

(a) Data analysis: Students analyze the survey results and any responses to their letter. In small groups, they present and discuss the results with their classmates and instructor. They can present their findings via posters, handouts, other visual aids, drama, etc.

(b) Reflection: Students form groups around individual issues/topics in the data, discussing possible solutions and proposed amendments to the *Student Handbook* based on their action research.

10. Final Projects

(a) Small groups: Students create presentations in a variety of media about their research findings and proposed solutions/amendments. They present to other classes, the faculty, parents, the school staff and administration.

(b) Whole class: Students collaboratively compose a second letter to the stakeholders to follow up on the first letter. They present their findings and solutions.

Figure 3.2 Summary of the Social Studies team's project

From my perspective, two primary tensions characterized our deliberative process: Individual vs. Communal and Process vs. Product. The first of these reared its head early in October in our platform discussion of 'values,' when there was disagreement on what values to list for 'the group.' This tension as I understood it then arose between individual differences and the need to negotiate a common list for our presentation; hence we arrived at 'Values Under Construction.' In the final weeks of the semester preceding the Curriculum Faire, certain dynamics around these tensions intensified, causing what I considered a 'collaborative breakdown.'

A second major dynamic of this team was finding a balance between deliberating (Process) and moving forward with the task (Product). One of our strengths as a team was our ability to be creative, generate ideas, and brainstorm activities. Generally speaking, each one of us was committed to this project; that commitment fueled our discussions of authentic, thoughtful, and emancipatory activities on a theme we found to be highly relevant to the students we had in mind. Each team member believed that we had developed a content focus with immense potential for transforming the socio-political context of the students for whom we designed it. We genuinely explored the connections between the activities we designed and the central topics read and discussed in the course. However, when it came time to make a presentation to the class, requiring us to come to consensus and negotiate shared choices/decisions, the 'Collaborative Breakdown' occurred.

The Collaborative Breakdown dynamic comprised the two major tensions mentioned above: Process vs. Product, and Individual vs. Communal. Our 'inability' to (a) successfully negotiate compromise in order to communally represent a group of shared pedagogical values, and to (b) make decisions about curriculum unit activities, or divide tasks to prepare for our major presentations directly resulted from not 'playing by the rules' for collaboration. The Collaborative Breakdown occurred at two points. The first involved the team acknowledging when it was time to 'agree to disagree' when presentation deadlines loomed. The tensions of Process vs. Product and Individual vs. Communal are correlated.

Figure 3.3   Excerpt from Sarah's final reflection paper

students who had disengaged from school while simultaneously helping them improve their academic skills.

As the group-process facilitator, my final reflection paper identified the key issues and questions that arose for me: first, concerning the team's process – the how of collaborative deliberation; second, my role as facilitator and what I learned from the facilitation experience. Figure 3.3 is in an edited excerpt from the paper I wrote at the end of the course.

The Dialogue

In the following pages, we will discuss textual 'scenes' that come from the Social Studies Curriculum Deliberation. Sarah sets the stage for each scene in the prologue; our dialogue with the scene and with each other follows the text. For the scenes, we chose texts capturing the drama that unfolded as the team developed their project: *Scene I* is a transcript excerpt from a team deliberation session; *Scene II* is the curriculum platform deliberated and presented by the team; *Scene III* is a summary of the high school students' responses to a survey developed by the team in response to feedback given to them by the class; *Scene IV* consists of Sarah's notes from a meeting in which the idea for the handbook project emerged from the high-school students' responses to the survey; *Scene V* is a graphic presentation of the team's deliberative process presented at the Curriculum Faire; *Scene VI* is the cooperating teacher's reflection on the impact of the project on the students and on her teaching.

Scene I: Excerpt from a Transcribed Interaction Sequence from the Curriculum Team

Prologue: The following dialogue[4] comes from the third in-class meeting of the social studies curriculum team. The urgent task at hand is preparing a presentation for the next class meeting on a 'curriculum platform,' i.e. the curriculum goals and beliefs about those goals, organizing principles for the curriculum unit, and finally a set of principles and values (as educators) deliberated by the team. In the excerpt, we are negotiating 'team values' for the platform. Significantly, we were operating under a time constraint at a late hour in the evening.

1	**Sarah:**	Do we agree on [the list of values we've generated for our platform]?
2	**Bill:**	One thing I would like is … is to have students be able to critically look at something, critical analysis on their own part.
3	**Sarah:**	Could we say 'reflection'?
4	**Bill:**	Critical reflection …
5	**Jan:**	Mmmm
6	**Roland:**	It's good.
7	**Josh:**	I don't know if we all agree, or if we're just putting these ideas out, 'cause I see some of the things we've already put down as contradicting … or at least I disagree with them
8	**Jan:**	/what do you disagree with?
9	**Bill:**	/well what do you think conflicts? … I see it all as gelling.
10	**Jan:**	Hmmm … I see this flow.
11	**Josh:**	… like one big happy consensus. I want to put in a plug for not necessarily coming to a fast consensus /and, you know … umm …objectivity [one of the words on the list]

	what does that mean? Um ... like whenever I hear that word I get suspicious, especially in the social sciences, and especially in education
12 **Sarah:**	/well, I think as human beings it's ... it's an almost impossible endeavor...
13 **Josh:**	/well then why do we /even have it as a value.
14 **Bill:**	I think you could tie objectivity to open-mindedness
15 **Roland:**	we said ... objectivity ... in the case where the...teacher presents facts ... in US History ... in this year ... America and the Britain had a war ... in this place ... and so forth ... presented objectively ... so ...
16 **Bill:**	/we're confusing ... we're confusing ...
17 **Sarah:**	/so non-biased presentation ...
18 **Roland:**	yes, non-biased presentation ...
19 **Sarah:**	/that's what we meant ...
20 **Josh:**	Is there such a thing, though?
21 **Roland:**	Hmmm? Yes ...! [Emphatic.]
22 **Josh**:	Really? ... the point, what I'm wondering about personally when I hear this word 'objective,' ... that language [suggests] you're trying to associate your value with science, reason, logic ... what did you say, the war between who?
23 **Roland:**	American and Britain ... the war of liberation.
24 **Sarah:**	American Revolution.
25 **Josh:**	OK. Ah, well ah, well, how you talk about that, we could think that we're talking about it in a factual way, and we'd like to believe that, and that teachers do that all the time, and they talk about /'just the facts.' I would wonder whose facts, and what view, and what biases, and when you look at one set of facts, what other facts do you forget, I mean ...
26 **Sarah:**	well ...
27 **Bill:**	/well ... but
28 **Josh:**	/ ... this history of imperialism has been ... has been shuffled to the side, because for so long we've had a whole perspective that [we're] supposedly looking at the facts of history ... the important facts. So I'm just saying, /what is factual ... what is objective ...
29 **Sarah:**	/the facts are not always unbiased ... that's what you're saying.
30 **Josh:**	Yeah, and so I'm highly suspicious ... when I start talking

about a platform and I'm talking about objectivity ... it almost seems like a sham, or farcical, or not honest, on my part. When anyone starts to say, 'let's look at this objectively,' right away I want to say, now why is his opinion objective? When we're talking about our opinions ... we're all coming from a very subjective and value-ridden place, so I mean, /it's a small

31 **Bill:**   /Can I make a point?

32 **Josh:**   /it's not a small point ... it's ... I think it's an issue

33 **Bill:**   /no, it's a very big point ... but ... I think ...I'm going to propose some sort of compromise here ... I think it's a matter of each ... individual definition ...when I write down here non-biased presentation, what that means to me is that ... I will present multiple perspectives, and I will not avoid controversial issues ...

34 **Jan:**   and I won't do it my way

35 **Bill:**   Exactly, so I think it's trying to get the student to be aware...I think we're going for the same thing.

Sarah: The flow of this interaction sequence illustrates a dynamic tension typical of our team's deliberation, which haunted us throughout the process. In my original reflection paper, I described these as 'Individual vs. Communal' tensions because of the difficulty we had with negotiating a 'fixed' platform. Having to come to a negotiated consensus to produce a team product is exactly what elicited, in my view, issues that various members needed to address.

Jerri: Had I seen this transcript without knowing anything about the conflict Sarah described in her final reflection paper, I would have said that the team was struggling admirably with the inherent tensions of curriculum deliberation described in the reading –negotiating across value differences while making concrete decisions affecting 'other people's children'– and dealing with the very issue debated in the State around the curriculum framework for History and Social Studies: whose 'facts' are going to be taught to the children of Massachusetts? Ironically, Roland's use of the term 'the War of Liberation' instead of 'the War of Independence' supports Josh's point and undermines his own argument.

Sarah: Josh was arguing a valuable point with which, given the circumstances of the session, we were not prepared to engage. This instance foreshadows a dynamic of our deliberative process in which we consistently constructed Josh as 'out of the flow.'

Jerri: As a consequence, this team wasn't able to experience 'the joy'

described in Henderson & Hawthorne (1995: 18) of 'authentic dialog [that is] continuously open to the voice of the "other"' (a quote used in Josh's final reflection paper focusing on the effect of the standards movement on the learning of children in his own classroom). In her paper Sarah took 'the blame' for this situation as the group-process facilitator (see Scene II below).

Sarah: What I now see is that part of what was going on was the clash of very different expectations about what constituted the task and what constituted a good performance of that task. Four of us were working hard to come to a consensus so we could give a good presentation the following week. Josh's challenge, especially at this late hour, was seen as a block to our successful completion of the assigned task. He wanted to continue to debate the platform, while the rest of us wanted to take action by making some definite decisions about what we were going to do for our presentation. While we understood that we would not be 'assessed' on the values we presented, we believed that failing to come up with a collaboratively-generated product would constitute failing the task.

Jerri: I suspect that Josh's objection to the platform was indeed a deeply-held value emanating from a Discourse that resonated with the theme of the assigned course text, 'transformative and emancipatory curriculum,' which the class had only begun to read and assimilate at the time. As a student of political philosophy and economics, Josh had talked and written about these issues in other classes and he developed them more fully in his final paper for this course.

Sarah: Josh's serious engagement with Roland's statements about 'objective truth' in lines 15–22 is admirable. The rest of us missed this entirely, or we may have been more inclined to take up Josh's point. The issue for the other team members that I interviewed concerned 'not playing by the rules' of collaborative deliberation. This resulted in hard feelings, frustration at the process, and at least on my part, a resistance to giving Josh a fair hearing or to really consider the issues he addressed. This in turn caused him to feel marginalized by the group.

Jerri: Ironically, Josh wrestled with his inability to act on his commitment to advocacy in his final paper when talking about how his school was gripped with the standards movement. A further irony in the drama being played out here is that the team is exactly where Theresa and I hoped they would be. They are seriously engaged in the hard work of curriculum deliberation, have made important contributions to the ongoing class dialogue, and someone in the group is asking the group to think about the impact of their decisions on learners who may bring different perspectives to the curriculum. We would have interpreted Josh's contribution to the dialogue as highly relevant to the assigned task.

Scene II: Values Under Construction

Prologue: The list below is the fruit of our team's deliberations from the above transcription. Curriculum teams were scheduled to present their Platforms on the evening of October 15; the time slipped away and a few teams were rescheduled to present the next week. We were relieved that we had more time, but we still failed to make progress toward consensus. Therefore, instead of presenting a platform that represented our consensus values in a snazzy visual (as other teams had produced), we distributed the list illustrated in Figure 3.4.

VALUES-UNDER-CONSTRUCTION

equity   diversity   sensitivity to others   compassion   respect

multiple perspectives   open-mindedness   critical reflection

humor   awareness of controversial issues & conflict

Figure 3.4 Handout representing the group's platform

Sarah: During the Platform Presentations of other teams on October 15, I became increasingly dismayed by the apparent 'togetherness' and what seemed to be the polished nature of their platforms. Most had colorful, dynamic visuals to illustrate their principles/values. My *angst* grew successively with each presentation; by the end of the class I was a nervous wreck. I was vastly relieved to hear we had another week to 'improve upon' what we had prepared. As our team gathered after the presentations, it became clear that others did not share the stress I was experiencing. Only via the subsequent reflection and continued dialogue with Jerri around the experience have I come to understand what sorts of Discourses I was appropriating at that time. I was utterly unaware of their influence. As a new member of the program in her first semester of course work I did not have the 'comfortable' structure of other settings to guide me in being the 'good student' I was accustomed to being.

The co-constructed nature of the course, the allowance by Jerri and Theresa for *emergence* in both process and product in deliberating a curriculum unit, and the unconscious expectations I had for myself concerning my role as team facilitator were having a wrestling match. Visions of a finished product were dancing in my head; I didn't know what 'being a good student' constituted in this new game with unfamiliar rules. The irony here is that this dynamic reflects the Individual verses Communal tension I described above, only I had earlier ascribed it to a team mate's collaborative interaction style, and here I was unconsciously enacting it myself. This dynamic foreshadowed a collaborative breakdown at the end of the semester as we prepared our curriculum unit as a visual display for the final class meeting.

For the Platform Presentation, we did not indeed have a dynamic, colorful visual nor yet a content focus for our curriculum. What we, especially me, didn't realize is that this was just fine. Hence, the clash between prior Discourses and new ones. Before the score was always an individual accomplishment, not requiring the skills asked of us as a team. Although the process is inherently more challenging, the learning is much deeper, more transformational. In the prior game, a 'good student' was usually rewarded (and felt satisfied) with producing an 'expected' sort of project. In this new game, a 'good student' engages with new material and interacts in new ways, producing a product that is not defined, but which emerges. This happens in ways that are also not prescribed but rather co-constructed. This results in 'tensions' as well as 'results' and learning that can be intense and yet not anticipated.

Jerri: Many students have experienced the same difficulties that Sarah's team experienced. In fact, the most common suggestion is that I should give students models that explicitly describe what they are expected to do. They believe that they can avoid the anxiety they often experience when engaged in practices that differ from what they've previously encountered. My response to their requests has been to describe the process in more detail, to provide resources to help them, to articulate clearly that 'emergent' and 'in process' products are expected. As a result, the syllabus has become longer and longer (currently 10 pages) and yet students still yearn for more explicitness, aptly summed up in Sarah's description of the task as both definite and vague. The focus on explicitness undermines the goal for students to become authors rather than consumers of the Discourse of learning and teaching. I would like to shift the focus away from explicitness and towards building trust.

Sarah: Trusting the 'under-construction' part was exactly what I had trouble doing. Being 'under construction,' and not always producing polished products for a presentation may have been acceptable, but I just didn't grasp it.

Jerri: One of the certainties of the course is that the 'products' produced by most teams far exceed my expectations. They are far more subtle, imaginative and rich than my individual vision because they develop from dialogue with their team members, with the instructors, with learners in the schools, and with peers in class discussions (no doubt, their spouses/

partners have also given them feedback!). It's not that Theresa and I were against polished work. Rather, we hoped that the product would result from dialogue with stakeholders and we understand that 'emergence' takes time and is unpredictable. Nevertheless, studies of similar practices in my classroom by former doctoral students (Bailey, 1993; Hawkins, 1997; Jeannot, 1997; Zacarian, 1996) show that many students experience the same anxiety and tension experienced by Sarah when they cannot easily locate what is expected of them. In the perceived absence of explicitly-stated expectations, they fill the vacuum with expectations from previous experiences and they frequently clash over what they believe the instructor wants to see.

Most students going through the process, however, come to a better understanding of concepts and values behind the organization of the course (not that they necessarily take them up in their own practice). But the last thing I want to do is to 'inflict pain' on my students as a way to increase learning. Having the students read the reflections of former students helps some students avoid some of the anxiety, but I continue to search for ways to assure newcomers that we want students to draw on and contribute their own experiences and values to collaborative products and we expect for them to 'not meet our expectations' but to help us create new expectations. This is a hard sell since we also ask students to hold their productions up to critical scrutiny, but in a climate of trust it is possible.

Scene III: Survey on Absenteeism

Prologue: In the team's Platform Presentation, Jan had described her contemporary issues class (for whom the group was designing the curriculum), using the language frequently heard in staff rooms, which provoked a reaction from the class and instructors. She briefly commented on how her students struggled with absenteeism, and how that affected morale in the class. This prompted the class to suggest that the team find out why students might be absent, and not to make any assumptions about the reasons for it. This led to a survey that Jan composed and completed with her students. Figure 3.5 summarizes the high school students' responses collated under the appropriate survey question.

Sarah: We discovered that the students' responses to Jan's questionnaire reflected larger issues than our initially-chosen topic of absenteeism: issues around the relationships between students and the school community, a sense of alienation and disconnection ('people have better things to do [than come to school]'), issues around responsibility for engaging in the educational process, and finally issues of power (who makes the rules?).

(1) Brainstorm reasons why you feel there is a high rate of absenteeism in this school.
(a) Kids are tired from working long hours after school and some stay home to do their homework. (b) School is boring. (c) School starts too early, too long, and too strict. (d) Kids who get in trouble or have a lot of points don't come because they'll get Saturday or be suspended. (e) Kids don't like their peers. (f) Kids these days don't want to learn as much as the kids had to decades ago. Also the school system isn't as harsh as it was decades ago. Teens are spoiled these days and they don't know what the hell they want to do.

(2) How could we explore this topic school-wide?
(a) Surveys at a booth at lunch to ask why people choose to stay home; (b) Have a class meeting; (c) We could try to explore this subject, but it wouldn't do anybody any good. Teenagers won't care about it. (d) We can try to convince the teens that this is urgent and tell then what the results would be in the near future.

(3) What 'solutions' would we be looking for?
(a) How to make school enjoyable and give a little more freedom. (b) Let parents know. (c) You can't keep kids in school. (d) Change the absentee policy: Students should be responsible for making up work when they are absent. If they do, they should pass whether they've had 20 absences or none. (e) Starting school later, so we could sleep. (f) Kick troublemakers out of school!! (g) Give students a vote on the school committee. (h) I would try to find a newer solution to prevent this from expanding. I would also go around the school and ask the students what they think. I would also have a vote to see if the school committee can be more harsh about the absences.

(4) How would you present your findings to the class, administration, and school committee? (a) Make posters, write letters make presentations, have discussion. (b) Show how many kids are absent from each class. I would make charts from school with different attendance policies and # of absences on average. Show how the present policy doesn't work and how the new one will. (c) If there were enough votes from the students, I would talk to the school committee to see if they could do something about it. (d) I would tell all the teachers to talk about this subject in every class at least once a term to see if they could convince some students.

(5) How could we as a class develop a 'campaign' to help the school committee come up with an attendance policy that would be successful for both students and teachers? (a) Point reductions. (b) View all surveys, charts, petitions, etc. (c) Compare us with other schools. (d) We could try to convince the school committee that we have a pretty good chance to improve the absentees rate to go down. (e) I don't know.

Figure 3.5 Collated answers to absenteeism survey

Jan's students address a 'goodness of fit' issue, stating that schools need to address teens where they are **now,** not according to a notion of 'ideal students' of the past. Interestingly, some indicated they wanted stricter attendance policies and consistency; they were aware of the disadvantages, but also thought that other measures wouldn't result in increased attendance; 'people wouldn't care.' There were many things to tease apart in their responses to the survey on absenteeism, and a much larger and more complex picture began to emerge. Our understanding of the context broadened significantly in light of Jan's students' perspectives. Therefore, the possibilities increased for addressing relevant issues of location, power, and discourse via curriculum. Scene IV illustrates the leap from our original idea – a problem-posing unit on the issue of absenteeism – to the project we finally developed.

Jerri: This team's presentation of their platform speaks to a tension that Theresa and I were working with in designing the course. The 'work in process' presentations over the course of the semester were an experiment. Presentations take up precious class time, and they bring out the kinds of tensions that Sarah described in Scene II much earlier; we were not confident about how beneficial the new practice would be.

I had played around with the placement (and place) of team presentations in earlier versions of the course. Presentations were the culminating event – the celebration of the students' hard work and the fruit of their collaboration. The days leading up to the presentation are often filled with considerable angst on the part of the students, and on me too in the early days. Nevertheless, students are almost always amazed at the stunning displays that each team presents, which can work to repair strained relations that occurred in the process of preparation. The long parade of outstanding presentations over the years has provided me, as the instructor, with the solid faith I have that students will indeed use the tensions they experience in a constructive way.

I was not satisfied, however, with the lack of opportunity for us to reflect as a class on what had happened en route to these wonderful productions, and at what cost. Yes, students wrote reflection papers, but these were not in dialogue with one another. Consequently, I added dialogue journals and moved the presentations earlier so that we could discuss them in more depth as a group. These measures helped a little, but still we were lacking quality dialogue about the generation of products.

When Theresa suggested that teams present their 'works-in-progress' to the full class throughout the semester, I wondered how we would get through everything we needed to do. Sarah's team presentations across the semester provided the class with exactly what we were looking for – an opportunity to disrupt some of the Discourses that we were all drawing on. The picture that Jan drew of the students in her class came from a familiar Discourse: the students didn't care about school, they took the course because they considered it a 'blow-off course.' She was not going to accept low standards from them, and she was going to work on the skills they needed to succeed in life (e.g. writing summaries of newspaper articles). Jan mentioned that the district was clamping down on absenteeism and some of her students were in danger of not graduating.

The full-class discussion that followed the presentation was heated and focused almost entirely on Jan's depiction of her students and their motivation as the center of the problem. Our class began drawing alternative Discourses to ask the team about other possible reasons for the failure of Jan's students – Has anyone really investigated to find out the varied reasons for missing school or are they relying on assumptions? Have the students been brought into the dialogue about what to do? What is the school doing to make 'going to school' worthwhile for the students? Will writing summaries really prepare the students to succeed in life? What are their passions and how can the school engage them?

Scene IV: How We Got to the Handbook Project

Prologue: In the session following the implementation of the absenteeism survey, our team continued our deliberations in light of the students' responses. We brainstormed larger issues of disconnection and alienation as well as the sense of activism that was heard. We had initially conceived a project that addressed the high absentee rate and possible causes for it, and how students felt they might explore this in the school at large. The high-school students would propose solutions and then decide how to present their findings to their peers, the administration, and the school committee. Finally, they would explore how they could assist the school committee in creating a new attendance policy that would be successful for the entire school community (perhaps even the families as well). The text in Figure 3.6 contains my notes from the team deliberations in which we reviewed the survey responses.

Sarah: This scene marks a conceptual explosion as the curriculum texts finally came alive for us. We began to see in Jan's students' responses the possibilities for attempting via our/their curriculum unit to transform the Discourses that considered them already 'tracked' into lower achievement intellectually and academically. The general curricular goals we had named (critical thinking, discussing, writing, and acting) for a class that had previously been considered a 'blow-off class' were based on our platform values of respect, integrity, and critical reflection. What we heard in students' opinions about absenteeism and school in general said loudly and clearly that these were people who felt – and were positioned – on the margins of academic success for various reasons, not engaging in or being denied full participation in a climate and Discourse of education that worked neither *for* nor *with* them.

The concepts in our course readings (Henderson & Hawthorne, 1995; van Lier, 1996), which until this time had felt esoteric and somewhat elusive, suddenly took on new relevance. We began to relate them to our platform and the perspectives of Jan's students. Van Lier (1996) discusses Awareness, Achievement and Authenticity as necessary for Autonomy. We saw how Jan's students located the responsibility for 'engaging them' in others, not themselves (e.g. in the school and the teachers). Our project, as we envisaged it, could begin to empower them to take responsibility for their own engagement in learning and with the issues they articulated, investigating these issues, and acting on their findings. This in turn was *emancipatory*, a foundational notion in Henderson and Hawthorne's (1995) *Transformative Curriculum Leadership*. The project would ideally locate in the

---

11/5, Small team deliberation

– Jan did questionnaire in class for her students
    – kids think they could come up with attendance policy
        Rules: who creates them?
           students: 'boring teachers,' 'school is a jail.'
      – student-created handbook?
    – surveys for school at large
  who creates this curriculum?
        (emancipatory constructivism)

ABSENTEEISM: survey led to a huge discussion, students' questioning the whole school

Awareness – Authenticity – Autonomy

    DIALOGUE

Figure 3.6 Facilitator's notes from team discussion

students the ownership of transformative action that could directly impact their daily lives in the school context.

As we shifted our unit's focus from the specific topic of absenteeism to the issues around Discourses of power that in part determined these students' school experiences, we came up with the idea of having the students review and revise the school's *Student Handbook.* This contains the rules and regulations they had taken issue with, and is written by the school administration with no input from the student body. In our unit activities, students are responsible for identifying parts of the *Handbook* that need revising. They design strategies for undertaking action research in the school community, with their peers, the faculty, staff, school committee, and administration. They synthesize their findings, rework aspects of the Handbook, and present their analysis and recommendations to the entire school community.

It was the students' responses to the survey, together with the feedback from our course-mates, that fired up our team and pushed us to re-envision the project. One of the most exciting aspects of the unit's development was how the students themselves transformed the content of the unit, as well as our thinking about the role and efficacy of curriculum and schooling. The high-school students themselves addressed the issues that we read in our course texts and brought them alive for us in a manner that conventional study could never have done.

Jerri: As Sarah wrote these words, it became evident to me that the team had experienced the 'joy of dialogue' after all. I've seen these magic fire-works occur time and time again. There's something about the pressure of the presentation deadline, the tensions of collaborative work, continued feedback from outsiders, and the freedom to go where your ideas take you that creates the conditions for this very common conceptual explosion. The projects that have had the greatest impact on the students in this course, though, are those in which the real learners have been involved in some way, as with this one. And nothing convinces teachers about the efficacy of a practice more than seeing their own students become engaged and invested.

Theresa and I were elated at the way this team responded to the class dialogue around their first presentation. Rather than becoming defensive, which they easily could have, given the somewhat righteous tone of the discussion, the team seriously considered the feedback, sparking the conceptual explosion that Sarah describes.

Sarah: So, the ripple effect began in our platform deliberation, went out to our course-mates/instructors and returned to us (the team), then to Jan's students and back to us again. The unit as we designed it has not been carried out in full, but it has taken place in various ways at the school over the two years since the graduate course, continuing the effect. Jan herself will reflect on this in Scene VI below.

Scene V: Curriculum Faire: 'The Process Puzzle'

Prologue: Part of our task for the final display of all curriculum projects at the end of the semester was to visually represent our team's deliberative process. Our team decided on the 'Process Puzzle,' a piece of display board cut into pieces, upon which each member wrote a brief commentary on her or his individual piece (Figure 3.7). This poster was displayed together with our curriculum unit.

Sarah: This scene actually represents significant irony around team members' roles, investments and the dynamic tensions characteristic of our deliberative process discussed earlier. At the end of the semester, my investment in creating a visual display of 'high quality' resulted in my asserting influence in creating the project's display. As I struggled with allowing the 'group effort' to result in the completed display, I assumed responsibility for typing up text, creating posters, and doing other tasks. I felt that the more I did, the less some of the other team members took responsibility. One member actually came empty-handed to a team meeting in which we were to assemble the project. This I resented very much, as I felt that the effort members contributed to this part of our process was imbalanced.

At the time, I was blind to the ways in which I also co-constructed the dynamics of our interaction, and to alternative ways in which I might have chosen, rather than trying to direct or influence the outcome, to facilitate the process for all of us as a team. Because of my investment in creating and assembling the project's display boards and posters, I was so busy up until the actual Curriculum Faire that I did not have or take the time to complete my piece of the Process Puzzle. The now-humorous irony is that, together with the well-displayed curriculum unit, there was a visual representation of our team's process, lacking input (indeed, lacking the piece altogether) from the facilitator!

The ripple affecting me in this instance was the realization, months after the actual event, that I unintentionally influenced the team process in a direction that was not productive for any of us, and which landed me in a position I resented being in. The benefit of our dialogue as well as chronological distance from the experience has enabled me to better understand what occurred. It has also allowed me to better understand my interactional tendencies, perhaps unconscious as in this case, which for better or

Jan's Piece of the Puzzle

Road Blocks   *Communicative break down*

Schedule, Time   *Frustration tape recorder informative*

Different Backgrounds

PROCESS

Deliberation   *Group Discussion*

Philosophy Theories   *Multiple Perspectives*

Triple A Emancipatory Curriculum   *Roland, Josh, Sarah, Bill, Jan*

Bill's Piece of the Puzzle

In a blind stumble
we clung to ourselves
and sometimes
only sometimes
to each other

Direction ever changing
roles slow to emerge
we plodded on
and on and on
and now we're here

Sarah's Piece

Josh's Piece of the Puzzle

I think we did well in terms of devising activities that complement the transformative curriculum. I think our own group process was not always pleasant for me – sometimes it was downright dreadful! But there was beauty in the struggle I reflected on group process, turn taking, communication feedback editing, dialogue symmetry, listening skills, and other communication topics. It opened new doors for me: lots of exciting future readings.

I think our group did a fine job in terms of cultural criticism as defined by Henderson and Hawthorne. Henderson and Hawthorne's questions were central to our unit: 'Who has power over whom? What social structures maintain this dominant-subordinate relationship? Are those who are being dominated even aware that they are submitting? What would they really care if they knew? How can the power inequities be interrupted and possibly transformed?'

Figure 3.7 Reflections of each member on their group processes

Roland's Piece of the Puzzle

The Social Studies group was a rather heterogeneous group composed of people from various backgrounds. This was indeed a great asset since this diversity has generated a wide range of experiential views of how we could frame our curriculum unit. Because of this positive diversity, the group has never experienced any kind of developmental crisis, which one of our group members had witnessed in groups he participated in during the past year.

The whole group behaved as mature adults who know how and when to take turns. Every single individual paid careful attention to the sensitivity of others. Anyone who took turns was listened to with interest and great patience. Rarely has anyone been interrupted in the middle of his/her verbal contribution. People did obviously avoid that as much as possible. Very often, people wishing to step into somebody else's speech have wisely withdrawn when they saw that the speaker did not wish to get interrupted at that precise moment. But everything cannot be golden in the life of a group.

Indeed, we have often experienced some frustrations here and there. That is quite normal because we are human beings. The contrary would have surprised me a lot. We learn from contradictions and there have been a lot of contradictions that often set people on fire. But we have always been mature enough to surmount those contradictions, thus hewing stones of consensus out of mountains of heated contradictory talk. The rule has been for the individual to defer to the view of the majority. We have also experienced the exception, which is the majority deferring to the view of the individual when group cohesion was threatened with dislocation. That's why the word 'mature' is most suitable to describe our group.

As far as content is concerned, it has been supplied, shaped, and put together as a result of the global effort of the whole group. No single element of the group has been 'input-less'. Everybody has supplied something. We have strived to leave student autonomy unhindered by leaving all the initiative of the content of the curriculum unit to them. What we give students are just facilitative guidelines that will serve them as a scaffold. We have also been mindful of the notion of student awareness as argued by van Lier. The concept of absenteeism is no secret for our students. It is a topic with which they will feel at great ease since most of them have practiced absenteeism at least once. This same state of fact makes our unit authentic. It promotes students' 'with-it-ness' and full sense with ownership of the tasks and activities dealt with in class.

The concept of emancipatory constructivism has also been a constant concern that underpinned our discussions. At a certain point, we even avoided listing possible questions that students would ask during their camera survey. They have to take all those initiatives themselves. We wanted our curriculum unit to be liberating instead of oppressive. All in all, we have conceived our unit with full conscience of the new notions that we have learnt in our readings and class discussions.

worse have a strong impact on team dynamics. This in turn has caused me to be much more aware and reflective in subsequent teams, taking a step back and trying to see a larger picture and others' multiple perspectives on the situation: a lesson in listening.

Jerri: The facilitator's role in this course is a powerful location (for both facilitators and instructors) for learning about the social construction of identities and ideologies in the group, and we try to give as many students as possible an opportunity take up the role at some time during their program. Facilitators don't have to wait long before the process of positioning and alignment begins to shape their groups' deliberations and productions. Typically, when they become aware of the effects of these processes, facilitators blame their team-mates; next they blame themselves; then they blame me for not giving them an explicit method of facilitation. But eventually most begin to seriously explore how we jointly construct the Discourses that limit our ability to hear the voices of others. In the process they help all of us amplify those inaudible voices, as Sarah has done through her explorations.

Scene VI: Jan's Reflection (Spring 2000)

Prologue: As with most courses, the students went their separate ways at the end of course. Not until we began working on the article did we ask ourselves, 'What ever happened to the handbook project?' I contacted Jan and she sent us the following letter:

What happened to the project? The students didn't revise the entire handbook as our team had envisioned. It would have been difficult for a class to undertake the entire project because there was extensive material in it and the Principal at that time was not receptive. But the idea was a good one and our work inspired a number of projects in the school. There's a committee now working on revisions of the handbook. This time faculty and student input is genuinely welcomed, now that we have a new Principal. Our idea of exploring the attendance policy was a wise one, too, because it is a hot topic and one that is currently under revision. While revisions to the attendance policy did not come about because of our project, it did inspire students to begin moving for change in the school. Since September, students have been given senior privileges, a breakfast program for all students has been implemented (really a ploy to get student tardies to decrease – less Dunkin Donuts, more school!), and a senior lounge will be opened. All of these with the exception of breakfast have been because of student initiative. It goes to show that change is possible – more importantly, student-implemented change is possible.

The idea of teacher–student collaboration for change has been intriguing to me! It's not what traditional methods instructors would advocate. I know I don't remember ever having a teacher say to me 'What do you want to do for your curriculum?' 'What do you want to change?' I think it's refreshing, especially in a time and age when teenagers feel disempowered. The idea of the students investing time and energy in a project immediately gives it meaning. The students, not just the teacher, become active stakeholders too.

Teacher–student collaboration is a bit scary, though. As a teacher, you have to release control of the project to the students. I needed to act as their guide more than their project director. For me, when I want something to be successful, I tend to want to control the steps towards the outcome. Teacher–student collaboration doesn't allow for my total control, but for student autonomy. Honestly, I don't know if I would have attempted a project like this without the help and push (encouragement) of my team. They had wonderful insights and ideas. Talking out the process also helped because the project wasn't really trial and error. We discussed and anticipated what might and might not work. This also encouraged another teacher in my department [who was not taking the course] to do a similar project and she even managed to get the previous Principal to listen to the students' ideas.

It was a great lesson in risk-taking, although looking back at it now, it doesn't seem to be that big a risk. I've incorporated student-based curriculum projects in other classes besides the contemporary issues course. It's such a wonderful process to see the students' autonomy coming through. They truly are invested 100% in their products. Such pride and effort. More so than one I could develop, in most cases. All in all, a worthy learning experience for both teacher and student.

Jerri: Jan's letter foregrounds two issues for me: the timing of assessment and the predictability of outcome measures. I have always had concerns about the narrow window through which we examine and assess learning. From my own experience as a student, many lessons have stayed with me for years, shaping my ideas and forcing me to revisit my initial understandings. Others have had no impact on my thinking or my competence, even though I was able to give back perfectly what the teacher wanted to hear. The projects that engaged me in the way described in Jan's letters are the ones that had the power to engender true understanding and direct my learning. And yet, my ability to articulate those understandings at the end of a lesson, unit or course would have shown that I had not yet fully worked out my ideas. Jan's letter, the conversations with Sarah and the reflections of our Masters students at the end of their program, convince me that we have a distorted picture of how our courses affect students. We need to develop assessments that enable students to integrate, develop and articulate their learning over time, and we need to evaluate our teaching accordingly.

Sarah: I agree wholeheartedly with Jerri's description of the frequent mismatch between what is considered a successful 'outcome' or 'product' and the actual impact of a learning experience that is truly meaningful and ultimately transformative, extending well beyond the class, exam, or paper. If I had had a rubric or specific script to guide me in enacting the role of facilitator, my energies would have been largely invested in that guidance or mandate. This would have been a familiar game that would have severely limited my growth as learner and teacher, rather than engaging me on multiple levels in the process of collaborative deliberation and my ways of co-constructing dynamics with this particular group of people. The experience of this course left me with an 'itch' rather than the 'scratch' (Wiggins & McTighe, 1998) I usually experienced at the end of a course. Consequently, I returned again and again in subsequent projects and inter-actions to the issues that so fundamentally challenged my thinking in the curriculum class. For a course in ethnography of communication, I analyzed the transcript included in this chapter and interviewed team members about 'collaborative deliberation' as a 'type of talk.' For a course in action-research I explored how my tendency to take control was cutting off my students' initiative in much the same way that it did in my curriculum team. For a course in spirituality and education, I consciously stepped back when another small-group member attempted to position me as the 'leader' or 'facilitator,' integrating the growth resulting from dynamic tensions experienced in the curriculum course.

Jerri: Sarah's comments relate to my second concern – the notion of standards and outcome-based assessment. What are we losing when the curriculum developer or teacher decides in advance what it is that the learner should understand or be able to do and creates specific assessments to ensure that it is accomplished by the end of a lesson, unit or course? I was fascinated by the unpredictable and circuitous outcomes of the handbook project on Jan, Sarah and their students and colleagues. I am not suggesting that we abandon the effort to articulate what students need to learn and to assess how we are going to help them learn it. But it is important to remind ourselves that we cannot predict all that is learned or not learned. More-over, to strive for perfect alignment and predictability is to claim that we have perfect understanding to impart – a most dangerous claim. The team's project as designed did not meet their enthusiastic expectations (changing the world is a slow, unpredictable and difficult process), but the sand shifted for a lot of people as a result of their project. Once again, my expectations were far exceeded.

Conclusion

We both stand at the beginning of new endeavors, waiting for new ripples to shift the sands of our beliefs and understandings. Sarah has begun an internship teaching ESL in a public elementary school and Jerri has begun teaching a revised version of this curriculum course to a new group of students. The climate is far different now than it was just a year ago. The waves from the standards movement and high stakes testing have come crashing down on us.

Sarah: As an intern, I am experiencing Discourses of power on multiple fronts: first, the Discourse of accountability to state frameworks and standardized tests. I have noticed the slick catalogs and thick books that clearly show that preparing students for the state tests has become lucrative business opportunity, and the Discourse of marginalizing is enacted by some teachers around diverse learners, in particular bilingual students, and those who would support their full bilingual and bicultural development.

Jerri: Students in the new curriculum course that I am teaching are now reading *Understanding by Design* by Grant Wiggins and Jay McTighe, the *Massachusetts State Curriculum Frameworks,* and the TESOL *ESL Standards for Pre-K-12 Students* to help prepare them for the demands that will be made on them in the schools. Together I hope we can explore what is gained and what is lost with pre-determined standards and alignment with high-stakes assessment, especially those that have been determined by a select group rather than by consensus among stakeholders. I have heard some good arguments from the students in the class as to why explicit standards are important to them and the learners they teach. Sarah, however, was disappointed that I had replaced Henderson and Hawthorn's text because it contributed to her 'emancipation' from rigid expectations that she had come to impose on herself. Her voice ripples across the patterns that we have created through our dialogue, encouraging me to safeguard the space, time and encouragement in our instruction and assessments for unpredictability and generativity, otherwise, we cannot call ourselves educators – only gatekeepers.

Notes

1. 'Subaltern' is a 'theoretical fiction ... a necessary methodological presupposition, which enables particular kinds of analyses to begin' ... that refers to social groups further down the social scale (Moore-Gilbert, 1997: 88).
2. We used the term *learners becoming bilingual* to signal the BEM program's intentions to support students' bilingualism despite policies and programs in the State and in school districts that see bilingual education as a transitional strategy rather than as a goal.

3. Students are not required to implement their curriculum units for the course, although teachers are encouraged to use the unit whenever it is feasible to do so. Feedback from the learners is required, however. Frequently, groups try out an activity with the class followed by a feedback session.
4. In the dialogue extracts, the symbol / is used to indicate an interruption, and ... indicates a pause.

References

Bailey, F. (1993) Voice in collaborative learning: An ethnographic study of a second language methods course. Unpublished dissertation, School of Education, University of Massachusetts.

Bakhtin, M. (1981) *The Dialogic Imagination* (M. Holquist, ed.). Austin, TX: University of Texas Press.

Bakhtin, M. (1986) The problem of the text. In C. Emerson and M. Holquist (eds) (V.M. McGee, trans.) *Speech Genres and Other Late Essays*. Austin, TX: University of Texas Press.

Bhabha, H. (1996) Culture's in-between. In S. Hall and P. duGay (eds) *Questions of Cultural Identity* (pp. 53–60). Thousand Oaks, CA: Sage.

Burbules, N.C. and Rice, S. (1991) Dialogue across differences: Continuing the conversation. *Harvard Educational Review* 61 (4), 293–415.

Butler, J. (1990) *Gender Trouble: Feminism and the Subversion of Identity*. New York: Routledge.

Britzman, D. (1991) *Practice Makes Practice: A Critical Study of Learning to Teach*. Albany, NY: SUNY Press.

Cheyne, J.A. and Tarulli, D. (1999) Dialogue, difference and the 'third voice' in the Zone of Proximal Development. On WWW at http//www.arts.uwaterloo.ca/~acheyne/ZPD.html.

Escobar, A. (1995) *Encountering Development: The Making and Unmaking of the Third World*. Princeton, NJ: Princeton University Press.

Ellsworth, E. (1989) Why doesn't this feel empowering? Working through the repressive myths of critical pedagogy. *Harvard Educational Review* 59 (3), 297–324.

Fendler, L. (1999) Making trouble. In T. Popkewitz and L. Fendler (eds) *Critical Theories in Education: Changing Terrains of Knowledge and Politics*. New York: Routledge.

Foucault, M. (1972) *The Archaeology of Knowledge and the Discourse on Language* (A.M. Smith, trans.) New York: Pantheon.

Freire, P. (1993) *Pedagogy of the Oppressed* (M.B. Ramos, trans.). New York: Continuum.

Giroux, H. (1989) Schooling as a form of cultural politics: Towards a pedagogy of and for difference. In H. Giroux and P. McLaren (eds) *Critical Pedagogy, The State and Cultural Struggle*. Albany NY: SUNY Press.

Habermas, J. (1970) Towards a theory of communicative competence. *Inquiry* 13, 360–75.

Hawkins, M. (1997) Positioning, power and the construction of knowledge in group work in a graduate second language teacher education course. Unpublished dissertation, School of Education, University of Massachusetts.

Henderson, J.D. and Hawthorne, R.D. (1995) *Transformative Curriculum Leadership*. Englewood Cliffs, NJ: Prentice Hall.

Jeannot, M. (1997) Redefining classroom authority: A dance among strangers. Unpublished dissertation, School of Education, University of Massachusetts.

Kress, G. (1999) Genre and the changing contexts for English language arts. *Language Arts* 76 (6), 461–469.

Lather, P. (1992) Post-critical pedagogies. In C. Luke and J. Gore (eds) *Feminisms and Critical Pedagogy* (pp. 120–137). New York: Routledge,.

Luke, A. (1996) Text and discourse in education: An introduction to critical discourse analysis. *Review of Research in Education* 21, 3–48.

Luke, C. and Gore, J. (eds) (1992) *Feminisms and Critical Pedagogy*. New York: Routledge.

McNamee, S. and Gergen, K. (eds) (1999) *Relational Responsibility: Resources for Sustainable Dialogue*. Thousand Oaks, CA: SAGE Publications.

Moll, L.C., Amanti, C., Neff, D. and Gonzales, N. (1992) Funds of knowledge for teaching: Using a qualitative approach to connect homes and classrooms. *Theory into Practice* 31 (2), 132–141.

Moore-Gilbert, B. (1997) *Postcolonial Theory: Contexts, Practices, Politics*. New York: Verso.

Rosenberger, C. (2003) Dialogue in a school–university teacher education partnership: Critical ethnography of a 'third space.' Unpublished dissertation, School of Education, University of Massachusetts.

Sidorkin, A. (1999) *Beyond Discourse: Education, the Self, and Dialogue*. Albany, NY: SUNY Press.

Spivak, G. (1988) 'Can the subaltern speak?' In C. Nelson and L. Grossberg (eds) *Marxism and the Interpretation of Culture* (p. 272). Urbana, IL: University of Illinois Press.

Van Lier, L. (1996) *Interaction in the Language Curriculum*. New York: Longman Press.

Weedon, C. (1987) *Feminist Practice and Poststructuralist Theory*. Cambridge, MA: Blackwell.

Wiggins, G. and McTighe, J. (1998) *Understanding by Design*. Alexandria, VA: Association for Supervision and Curriculum Development.

Willett, J. (1999) Preparing to transform the Discourse of learning and teaching: It's a revolution we envision. Invited presentation at the TESOL International Conference in New York City, March 8–12.

Willett, J., Solsken, J. and Wilson-Keenan, J. (1999) The (Im)possibilities of constructing multicultural language practices in research and pedagogy. *Linguistics & Education* 10 (2), 165–218.

Wuthnow, R., Hunter, J.D., Bergesen, A. and Kurzweil, E. (eds) (1986) *Cultural Analysis: The Work of Peter L. Berger, Mary Douglas, Michel Foucault and Jürgen Habermas*. New York: Routledge & Kegan Paul.

Zacarian, D. (1996) Learning how to teach and design curriculum for the heterogeneous class: An ethnographic study of a task-based cooperative learning group of native English and English as a second language speakers in a graduate education course. Unpublished dissertation, School of Education, University of Massachusetts.

Chapter 4

Social Apprenticeships Through Mediated Learning in Language Teacher Education

MARGARET R. HAWKINS

Introduction

In this volume (and, indeed, in current social theory) we have de-stabilized and problematized concepts related to second language learning and teaching that have been historically regarded as fairly straightforward. Instead of a universal set of rules that is English, we have multiple social languages. In lieu of teachers and texts imparting the knowledge that students need to know, we see knowledge as constructed among members of learning communities (in formal and informal contexts), and we question the nature of knowledge. Who decides what information 'counts'? Whose interests and views are privileged? Which views, and voices, are not represented? And, in place of a view of learning and knowing as memorizing a specific repertoire of information, we talk about learning as apprenticeships to new discourses, and knowing as abilities to use-in-practice. These new definitions render even more visible the deep relationships between language, culture and identity, and highlight the contextualized nature of language use, and language learning and teaching. This has especially powerful implications for second (or multiple) language learning. What is it that language learners need to know? Which social language/s do/should we teach? What 'language', 'knowledge', literacies (through what representational forms) will they need to be able to recruit in order to become participating members of the communities they may wish/need to enter? And what are the consequences?

These questions have critical implications for the role of teacher education. What is it that teacher educators ought to do, and how ought they to do it? Gee (Chapter 1, this volume) suggests that language learners need to come to understand the 'cultural models' at play within specific events and activities, and within which their utterances and performances are cast.

This concept should also be applied to learning to teach. I would suggest that, approached from a sociocultural perspective, the role of teacher education is not so much to apprentice fledgling (or practicing) teachers to particular cultural models of teaching and schooling, as it is to facilitate critical understandings of the implications and consequences of the decisions they make as to what they do, and how they do it.

This chapter examines a graduate language teacher education class designed to introduce and facilitate engagement with the sorts of sociocultural perspectives taken up in this volume. The course itself was developed as a 'survey' of social, cognitive and academic/schooling issues that surround the education of students being schooled in languages/cultures other than their own. While the course covered some 'traditional' content (i.e. program design, home/community relations, role of the native language in instruction, assessment), the overarching framework, including that of the texts and articles, was on schooling, learning, and teaching as cultural, situated practices, and the implications this has for newcomers (especially those lacking access to the linguistic and cultural codes) to our schools. The ultimate goal was to scaffold a shift in perspective among these language teachers, to facilitate an ongoing engagement/reflectivity on their practice as informed by their understandings – 'knowing' as taking up and enacting understandings in practice. One norm of the class quickly became the 'so what?' question – that is, don't make a claim, hypothesis, or assertion unless you engage in analysis of the social and cultural implications it carries. We will focus particularly on an analysis of participation on a listserve that the class utilized on an extended basis, and will examine how perceptions and understandings were constructed and debated among participants in this particular learning community throughout the semester (the uptake of issues and theory) via this particular mode of communication.

Literacy Practices and Technology

On a dual level, then, this chapter explores notions of literacy practices. From the perspective of current social and critical theory, we not only have to rethink the nature of language, meaning, representation and knowledge, but our definitions of 'literacy' and 'text' as well, as an integral part of our communication systems. What is 'text' in a post-modern world, with our multiple modes and representations of meaning? What skills/abilities does it take to send, recognize and interpret messages? How do we align interpretations and meanings within situated social practices? We also bring into question definitions of 'reader' and 'writer' (individuals engaged in making meaning vs. social relationships and socially-defined activities played out, and reinforced, through texts). If our premise is that literacy is (always) a socially-situated activity, with texts as sites of meaning but also often sites of 'struggle, negotiation, and change' (Norton 1995), then interpretations of literacy events and practices must always deeply account for the contexts within which they occur, the sociocultural identities of participants, and the power and status relations being played out through such practices. These concepts formed the content of the class, and we will examine the ways in which class members engaged with this particular discourse about educational theory and practice. We will recruit these perspectives, as well, as the lens through which we examine the listserve as a mediational device for participating in the classroom discourse, and for constructing meaning from class content.

There has been much written in recent years about the use of technology in education, and the affordances and constraints of e-communication as part of classroom pedagogy. Much of this conversation has centered on notions of new global literacies and communities, and the 'new capitalism' (Gee *et al.*, 1996; Rifkin, 2000). It is argued that technology has rapidly become central to, and has led to the construction of, new global business practices, markets and economies (Castells, 1996; Kelly, 1998). It has also been argued that the rapid growth of technology has led to new and different forms of literacies and cognitions. Current schooling practices are perhaps more closely linked to traditional forms of text and communication, which will result in a future workforce that is ill prepared (DiSessa, 2000; New London Group 1996). A major, and often-cited, concern is that the new emphasis on technology heightens the divide between the 'haves' and the 'have-nots' – that those with lesser access to computers and technological skills have lesser access to the resources and forms of knowledge and communication privileged in the white-collar workplace (Warschauer, 1999, 2000; Murray, 2000; Cummins, 2000; Cummins & Sayers, 1995). This certainly makes a strong case for the inclusion of technology in education, especially for students who might have limited access in other domains. I wanted, therefore, to include the listserve in this course at least in part as a device to familiarize my students with the power of technology as a tool for instruction, and to give them the skills to incorporate computer use into their classroom practice.

I also intended the listserve to serve as a way of extending the possibilities of class discussion. This course, entitled 'Issues in ESL Education', is a graduate-level course. It is comprised of students seeking graduate degrees and/or certification in ESL, as well as graduate students from other areas, such as literacy, foreign language, linguistics. Many of the students are currently teachers (at all age/grade levels); some are international students. The purpose of the class is to promote critical engagement with the range and diversity of issues attendant on the learning and schooling of students from 'other' linguistic and cultural backgrounds. As the instructor, I tried to create an environment where active participation and discussion would be the primary class format, and where students' knowledge and experience could/would be recruited, validated, and utilized as part of the shared 'text'. Unfortunately, with 21 people in class, it is difficult for many students to speak, and/or be heard. It was difficult to discuss the multitude of issues that arose in the depth that the students wanted, to scaffold 'connections' to topics and ideas for all students, and to make time for pedagogical applications. I was hoping that the listserve would enable more extended discussions among the students, through an alternative medium.

Listserve as Mediational Tool

There has been much attention paid in recent education theory to the work of Lev Vygotsky, and in particular to his views of learning as occurring through mediated social practice (Vygotsky, 1978; Wertsch, 1991; Wertsch, 1998). Vygotsky, followed by others, defines learning as occurring through socially and culturally situated activity carried out in social interaction (Lave & Wenger, 1991; Rogoff; 1990, Scollon; 1998, etc.). According to Vygotsky, knowledge is first external, then gradually internalized. Understandings are constructed through mediating tools, or devices (see also Wertsch, 1991). Zinchenko, in discussing Vygotsky's work, explains:

> Tool-mediated action appears in two forms, external and internal. The significance of the idea of internalization is that external tool-mediated action can be transformed into internal, mental action (Zinchenko, 1985: 101)

Vygotsky focused particularly on speech/language and other semiotic devices as mediational means. '(A)s soon as speech and the uses of sign are incorporated into any action, the action becomes transformed and organized along entirely new lines' (Vygotsky, 1978: 24). This argues that the mediational tools themselves act as organizing (or sense-making) devices in and of themselves and that the characteristics and meanings that the tools carry contribute to the construction of meaning in the activities in which they are embedded (as the activities in part construct the meaning of the tools). Thus, in this instance, the listserve mediated the discourse and meanings of the class, as the class constructed the significance and content of the listserve. In discussing Vygotsky's work specifically as it relates to language classrooms, Donato claims:

First, sociocultural theory underscores the importance of conceptualizing language learning as a developmental *process mediated by semiotic resources* appropriated by the classroom (Wertsch, 1991, 1998). These semiotic resources include print materials, the physical environment, gestures, and most notably, classroom discourse. (Donato, 2000: 45)

Each component contributes to and organizes the (language) learning process, supporting the development of schema about the specific language and about language learning, as well as offering engagement and participation through differing cognitive, affective, and sensory lenses and modes. In my class, there were, of course, multiple mediating devices at work, as there are in all classrooms. My focus here, however, is on the way the listserve functioned to mediate course content, understandings, and discussions.

Recent literature on educational technology has debated definitions of computer mediated communication (CMC), as multiple forums and forms proliferate. For my purposes, I will follow the lead of Murray (2000), and use Herring's (1996: 1) definition, 'communication that takes place between human beings via the instrumentality of computers.' Analysis of computer-mediated interactions has begun to identify salient characteristics of CMC discourse. Murray, in an overview of research to date, identifies four linguistic characteristics that have emerged from research: similarity to spoken or written language; use of simplified registers; organizational structure; and mechanisms for maintaining topic cohesion (Murray, 2000: 400). Specific studies have looked at how CMC functions in terms of social and cultural relations and understandings in classrooms. As described by Kamhi-Stein:

 Research ... shows that email improves the participation of shy students (Fotos & Iwabuchi, 1998) ... reduces gender-related differences in classroom participation (Kamhi-Stein & Browne-del Mar, 1997; Tella, 1992) and promotes student–student, as opposed to teacher–student, interaction (Ady, 1999; Kern, 1996; Tella, 1991) ... (and) allows L2 speakers to improve their cross-cultural awareness (Ady, 1999; Cummins & Sayers, 1995; Kamhi-Stein & Browne-del Mar, 1997). (Kamhi-Stein, 2000: 428)

Other researchers have looked at issues such as gender (Werry, 1996), context (Baym, 1995), and the construction of identity (Lam, 2000). All of these facets are observable in the listserve discussion from this class. Certainly students who rarely spoke in class posted frequent and lengthy missives. And not only was cross-cultural awareness a direct focus of (the content of) the class, but on the list students articulated culturally-bound views, perspectives and interpretations, which were taken up directly as part of the discussion. The listserve shared and recruited some important features of class (face-to-face verbal) communication:

- same community;
- 'fed' by readings, speakers, discussions that were community events/ practice;
- 'norms' from class (i.e. members as resources, exploration of ideas, connections/schema privileged, reflectivity);
- complex environment (entries range in sophistication, style, theory/ practice focus) providing zone of proximal development(ZPD) (Vygotsky, 1978) for all;
- some specific discourse features (e.g. politeness, recognition of others, sensitivity).

On the other hand, the listserve had some unique communication features (many of which proved advantageous for participation of non-native speakers):

- no time constraints, either for writing an entry, or between posting and response (allows deeper reflection, closer articulation);
- no length constraints (allows for range: quick reactions, longer narratives, stream of consciousness, etc.)
- few stylistic constraints (postings can be informal, ungrammatical, sentence structure varies, etc.);
- multiple 'strands' occurring simultaneously (makes it easier to 're-visit' topics, make eventual connections between topics);
- no face-to-face contact (less risk-taking involved);
- allows for engagement with concepts and ideas, and simultaneously with meta-analysis.

Students in class came with varying ranges of experience with computers. Some had never had e-mail accounts, nor been on the Web. Many used e-mail, but had never been on a listserve. We never discussed 'etiquette', so this public conversation took on many of the norms of classroom discussion. Students acknowledged each other, were polite to each other, and when disagreeing tried to do so in a tactful manner. However, having all participants' contributions available to read (at a comfortable pace) and even to go back and refer to, enabled class members to listen and respond at a deeper level than class discussion allows. In oral discussion, each subsequent turn determines and constructs the course of the conversation. On the listserve, it was possible to respond to an entry that was posted several 'turns' back, allowing for parallel (and often interconnected) strands to develop simultaneously. In this way, the topic wasn't 'gone' before class members had a chance to address it. This was beneficial to English-language learners, who may have needed more time to process the language, and craft a posting. However, rather than try to illustrate how strands flowed and interconnected, I will focus on one particular strand, to illustrate how class members represented their diverse forms of engagement with the discourse (texts, topics, discussions, norms) of the class. We will see how this medium afforded access to participation, and how positions and identities were claimed and taken up by participants (for further discussion of positioning and identity, see Hawkins, 2000).

Listserve Interaction

The semester began at the end of January. An analysis of listserve postings during the first six weeks of class reveals multiple forms of usage and functions, such as:

- addressing 'settling in' issues (making sure everyone's connected, class list and phone numbers);
- providing detailed notes from class (student initiated, for those who were absent);
- concrete and practical requests for information (i.e. 'how does your school district prepare substitute teachers?');
- requests for clarification of concepts from class and/or readings (i.e. 'I was wondering what they meant between authentic and real language?') and responses;
- negotiation and debate of concepts (i.e. phonics vs. whole-language approaches to reading, assessments of programs and schools);
- questions from readings that there wasn't time for in class (i.e. 'there was an interesting point in one of the articles that I would have liked to discuss today, but we ran out of time');
- reports on books read and talks attended.

The interactions were primarily student–student, though I posed questions on two occasions in an attempt to stimulate discussion on issues I wanted to highlight, and once to recommend an article I'd just read. For the most part, the different functions of the listserve emerged from the conversations to then become reified as norms of use.

For one particular class in early April (six weeks into the semester), I had assigned three articles to be read: 'What no bedtime story means' (Heath, 1982), 'Athabaskan-English interethnic communication' (Scollon & Scollon, 1981), and 'Learning to be an American parent' (Harkness et al., 1992). My goal was to communicate just how culturally embedded language, communication, literacy practices, and cultural models are. While the class conversation had been good, I felt that there had not been enough time for the level of engagement and breadth of coverage I wanted. After class, I posted an entry on the listserve:

> We pretty thoroughly discussed No Bedtime Story in class – but didn't quite do justice, I think, to Athabaskan-English etc. I think everyone gets the difference between discourse features – so here's my question. If we buy that language is much more than vocab and structure, that different groups have significantly different language and communication practices (that lead to much cross-cultural misunderstanding), and even that our classroom language practices are situated and contextual (constrained and influenced by multiple factors, including environment, local discourse practices, and identities of learners and teachers), what does this say about what we think we're teaching, and how we'd ought to go about doing it? In other words, we've destabilized the notion of language (not one 'English'), and communication, and even of teaching – so how should we think about what we're doing? How do we make informed decisions about what to do, and why? I'd really like folks to take a crack at this – it's important. In fact, it's the very core of what we do, and who we are professionally. (Listserve posting 4/4)

This is my way to sum up the key issues from the class discussion, convert them into academic language (which class members are familiar with), and then push for pedagogical implications. As the professor, of course, I have the power to pose these sorts of questions in a more demanding way, even becoming, at the end, rather insistent that they respond. They do not speak to each other in this manner. The first response was from a Brazilian student, whose experience has been with teaching ESL to adults in Brazil. Her entry:

> Hey everyone,
>
> I would like to say again that the readings for last week's class were among the most interesting ones we read this semester, in my opinion.
>
> They address important issues that may not be explicitly related to ESL, but that are essential for the understanding of multicultural environments, cultural models that learners and they (*sic*) families bring with them to the learning environment and the extra-linguistic aspects of language, communication and language learning.
>
> The Brice-Heath article was very interesting because it made me think how important the whole socio-economical-cultural and political (why

not?) environment of the learners is to school-based learning and for the development of literacy. The ways of taking meaning from the environment, as she says, has to do with the culture in which we grow up. And these ways reflect on the whole learning process, don't they? That's where this issue is essential for us as teachers. And for me, who am primarily interested in English instruction for adults, the awareness that adults repeat aspects of the learning of literacy events they have known as children ... can lead to important insights on language acquisition patterns and learning differences, different motivations, and so on.

As for the English-Athabaskan one, in which the difference of cross-cultural discourse features is emphasized, and along with Maggie's question on this topic, I really think it is important for us to realize that the fact that we are teaching one variety of English – American English – over the others may have important political implications on learners of diverse cultural backgrounds. Bearing in mind that English is a world language, and that different varieties may have different discourse patterns, what variety is to be taken as our basis for the classroom? And if we are to teach learners English discourse features that clash with their own cultural beliefs/appropriateness of interaction, how to go about it? ... Sorry again to take so much of your time, but these are questions that have really been intriguing me lately. I would love to hear what you guys think about it. Thanks. (Listserve posting 4/5)

Note that this entry is written in a fairly formal, sophisticated style. It is both academic and analytic, consistent with her background as an advanced Masters student with an extensive background in Applied Linguistics. Yet she has claimed solidarity with her classmates, both by referring to the collective group ('us as teachers'), and by the use of informalisms ('Hey', 'you guys'). She also identifies herself as 'primarily interested in English instruction for adults.' She ends on an apologetic note, quite different from my more demanding one. She is overtly apologizing for the length of the entry (the text above is only an excerpt from the whole). But she may also be aware that she is introducing a different register, and requesting collusion in a different sort of engagement than those set by precedent (though she is enacting her understanding of what I have asked for). She has extended an invitation for a joint exploration of these issues by asking for pedagogical applications, which has been the primary focus of the listserve thus far, thus enacting 'community' norms. And she has enacted the 'politeness' norms that have become standard in both class and listserve discussions, both by her apology and her thanks.

This entry is answered by a local middle school ESL teacher. She says:

Hi All,

I read through S's message and think she has some interesting questions. Often, my Mexican/Puerto Rican students and their parents tell me about the differences in English/Spanish communication styles. The distinct Spanish communication style (which an American might consider to be like talking around in circles and perhaps never explicitly addressing the main idea or question) often carried over into the way Spanish-speaking students speak English. For example, a recent example is the way in which my students presented book talks. While most of the Korean students' book talks, for example, were short, detailed and direct (nothing fancy), many of the Mexican students' book talks were very long and expressive (rather poetic, actually). This raises some questions as to how teachers should evaluate speeches/oral projects. If we establish a rubric, certainly the criteria we set for such an assignment would be based on what we (Americans) consider to be an effective oral presentation (and generally, American teachers expect direct and detailed talks).

In regard to S's question about teaching the rules of appropriateness in one's language, I don't know that I've ever done this with my students in a formal way. It seems that when they are integrated into the culture of American classrooms, they observe and begin to learn independently the way the other American kids interact. Some of them conform while others try to keep their own cultural communication norms. Maybe it's not possible to effectively teach different cultural communication styles because one must experience them in the target culture to really gain understanding and experience. (Listserve posting 4/5)

This student speaks from her experience/identity as a middle school ESL teacher. She grounds S's theoretical discussion in concrete classroom practice, thus making connections for others and using what she knows (her students, families, and classroom practices) to make sense of new concepts. She validates and supports her classmate's posting, shares her experiences claiming a position of expertise (as a teacher), while openly engaging in exploration of new topics, and acknowledging her struggle to connect the topic with pedagogy where she feels she doesn't have the experience.

The next contributor to this conversation is a newcomer to the field. She is at the beginning of her studies in ESL, preparing to become an ESL teacher. She also has little cross-cultural experience. Here we can see where this listserve conversation has provided a ZPD for this novice:

This answer may seem to basic (*sic*) and may not really answer the question fully, but it is an extremely difficult question to answer.

I believe that the only thing that we as teachers can really do is to be open and aware of the differences among cultures. It is imperative that we become knowledgeable about the communication methods of the various cultures of the students that we are teaching. If we don't how can we teach them when we don't understand their methods of communication? While teaching students we can only help students to understand the difference. It would be unfair to try and convert students, wouldn't it? ... I am not sure if I made any points, but once again, I became aware of the complexities of teaching ESL. (Listserve posting 4/5)

The entire structure of this entry is much more simplistic than those preceding it. This student positions herself as a member of the community ('we as teachers'), but as one seeking guidance from others. It is the previous entry that has scaffolded her emergent thinking on these topics, she is directly responding to the 'teacher' posting. She presents herself as a learner authentically struggling with issues. She demonstrates a meta-reflection on her contribution and herself as a learner in her first sentence and in her final one, as she acknowledges the struggle while apologizing for it.

The next posting comes from a Korean student, who, up to this point, has been silent in class. This is the first time her voice emerges at all; it is her first listserve posting. For this, as for the others, the posting is presented as written.

Hi, all of you!

Let me contribute to the discussion about 'different discourse pattern' and 'Language as a tool to demonstrate ideas in different ways.'

Last week in class, Maggie asked if any of us had different educational experience of being lead into literacy (related to bedtime story). I felt I was one of them, who had the different way. I kind of jumped around from different culture to culture and different language community to community when I was a child, and then a adult.

So far, all of you and Maggie have been enormously supportive and patient with my 'inability' to talk actively in class or in the cyber space (via e-mail). I found out, that one of the factors that formed my 'passive' way of participating in class discussion was the absence of bedtime story in my childhood. By 'inability', I mean, the inability; to quickly form ideas and opinion, to react be relevant to the discourse, to be sure if whatever my idea would be good enough to say to the whole class, and, lastly, to find the right timing to jump into the discussion and take turns. I guess, some more and some less, even all native English speaking American student may feel the same way about class discussion. However, I think, in my case, it was from cultural biases, that my process of constructing thought were slow. It was slow mainly because, as I analyze it now myself, I was not educated to be competent in western-style discourse pattern.

Well, here is a story of mine to share with you. It is in the perspective of a child, firstly, who was a minority language speaking, and secondly, who received different educational discipline for different discourse patterns at home from parents.

I was a child without any bedtime story. I spent my childhood in Germany till I was eight years old, and, I guess, I was the only one in my Kindergarten without one, at that time. My first language was Korean and I started to speak German only after I got a chance to interact with German kids from the neighborhood ...

It was in Kindergarten, where I encounter a lot of new German culture and language. 'Apfel Kompote' (baked apple) looked 'komisch' (weird) to me. I had a totally different way of living at home. Not only was the way of living of non-western culture, but also the process of forming a discourse pattern with my parents was entirely non-western.

Rule number one for me to know when talking to my parents were that I was not supposed to ask too many questions. Usually it was acceptable till the third question, but after that a firm face of my father would usually tell me I had better stop there ... Rather than autonomy, self-determination, independence, and spontaneity, it was natural and logical for my parents to have learn how to follow the authority, which would be the main thing throughout the whole school system ...

Therefore, 'what' questions nor 'why' questions were not asked in the conversation between me and my parents. My parents usually gave orders, not questions ...

Since my parents usually were not my partner for conversation, there was nobody there who listen to my stories. Nor was there anybody leading me to further thinking: making references, asking questions, deducting some logic, etc.

... (s)o far I had realized what the Korean education did to me (= disabled me?) ... learning English was not a matter of spelling, or pieces of grammar or vocabs. It was about using English as a tool to demonstrate my ideas, that supposed to fit into the right discourse pattern. ... More or less, what I suggest as difference must be common to everybody in a certain degree. Yet, I thought, I would want to share 'my story' with all of you guys, who can, as teachers, help out those who are in similar condition as I was a child in Germany. (Listserve posting 4/7)

In Gee's terms (Chapter 1, this volume) this entry directly addresses relationships between Discourses, cultural models and learners' identities, vividly and powerfully illustrated. It provides an insider's account of the difference between 'authentic beginners' and 'false beginners.' This learner, as a Korean child in Germany, came to school '... without the sorts of early preparation, pre-alignment in terms of cultural values, and sociocultural resources that more advantaged learners at those sites have' (p. 14). She did not have the resources that might have enabled her to use the appropriate social languages and to participate appropriately in the situated social activities. The listserve in this graduate class, however, provided her an opportunity (albeit in hindsight) for critical framing – that is, an overt examination of how such practices work to include and privilege certain learners, while excluding others. And, as she has stated, this for her was the point of praxis – the point where theory, and understanding, and articulation come together and become pivotal to change.

This posting was pivotal to this learner's participation in class and on the listserve. For her, it broke the barrier, it was 'taking the plunge' and finding the waters receptive. She is quite articulate about her reasons for reticence prior to this posting, when she says that she was 'passive' (a word taken up and debated extensively in earlier listserve postings), and unable to ' ... quickly form ideas and opinion, to react be relevant to the discourse, to be sure if whatever my idea would be good enough to say to the whole class, and, lastly, to find the right timing to jump into the discussion and take turns.' Certainly she makes many grammatical errors; but the listserve has provided a 'comfort zone' for doing so. Others, native English speakers, have done so as well. The informality and non-adherence to standard forms of writing serve to enable this learner to take risks she will not in class. But, as she points out, it was more than the language itself that provided a barrier. It was the cultural patterns of discourse (all the behaviors and performances that 'count' as literate practices in this context) that must be taken into account in order to be able to assume the identity of a participant. The listserve offers opportunities to non-native speakers that are particular to this form of communication, as in the lack of stylistic and formal requirements. In addition, much of the class, including members of the majority language and culture groups, are newcomers to this discourse. They are discovering and constructing it together. They are all able to claim positions of 'expertise' through recruiting and representing multiple forms of experience and knowledge, and able, simultaneously, to assume the position of 'learner'. And this put this Korean learner on an equal footing with her classmates.

This posting can be identified as praxis for the class as well. This entry changed this student's position and identity in the class. It engendered instant respect for her from the others, and many referred to it throughout the semester. It became a common reference point in further discussions, both in class and on the list, and many students referred to it in their final papers as well. It illuminated the topics for many who were struggling, particularly through the representation of 'other' through an authentic voice. These were not just 'othered' people we were talking about, they were part of 'us'. They were part of the teaching community, and the graduate student community – part of the discussion. This was a marriage of topics; this student merged discussions of language, culture, identity, schooling and learning into one seamless narrative, thus modelling the integration of theory/theories, application to practice, and implications for learners' lives.

Analysis of Identity and Position Claims

As an additional analysis of the way students in this class claimed positions on the listserve, we will analyze the direct use of pronouns in these four postings. All four use the pronoun 'we' to position themselves in alliance with others in class as members of particular social groups, thus indicating what group identities they feel they share with classmates. They use 'I' when stating individual opinions (not representative of the groups with which they're claiming affiliation), or when specifically positioning themselves as unique. The first learner, our Brazilian teacher of ESL to adults, illustrates this. She starts by saying, 'I would like to say ... the readings were among the most interesting ...' thus articulating an individual opinion. A bit further along she says, 'us as teachers', thus acknowledging her perception of her participation in a social group characterized by the common characteristic of being teachers. She immediately follows by saying, ' ... for me, who am primarily interested in English instruction for adults', thus indicating that this feature is not common to this community, but unique to her (which was true, most of her classmates were interested in K-12 schooling). She follows this pattern consistently, with 'I really think it is important for us to realize', where 'I' represents her individual opinion, and 'us' claims solidarity as a member of the classroom community, and ' ... if we are to teach learners ... ' again showing her group identity as a teacher.

The next two entries, the middle-school ESL teacher and the novice (elementary) ESL teacher, follow these patterns. The middle-school teacher says, ' ... my Mexican/Puerto Rican students' when referring to her specific classroom and students, which of course she does not share with the rest of this class. She continues, ' ... how teachers should evaluate ... If we establish a rubric ...' using 'we' to claim an identity as a member of this community of teachers. In 'I don't know if I've ever done this ...', the first 'I' is setting up her opinion, and the second 'I' is singular because she is again referring to herself as the teacher in her own classroom, a characteristic not shared by others in the class. In fact, at the end, she is faced with a dilemma, because she wants to make an assertion that doesn't represent herself or her experiences, nor does she know if it applies to others in the class – that of someone having been immersed in another culture. She can't claim solidarity with such a community, nor even know if it exists among her classmates. So she depersonalizes it altogether by using 'one' (' ... because one must experience them in the target culture ...') . Our third student, the novice teacher, follows these patterns precisely. She says, 'I believe' to preface her own opinion, and ' ... we as teachers ... ' to claim solidarity with classmates. At the end, she says, 'I am not sure if I made any points ... ', using 'I' to refer to her particular entry, and to express doubts as to the worthiness of her contribution, thus setting herself apart from the group.

We have seen how the pronouns function to represent students' tacit views about what this community is, and their identities vis-à-vis the group. We have seen the bases on which they (fairly consistently) claim an identity as part of the group, and what they perceive as individual and unique about themselves and their positioning. This is true not only for American, native-English speaking students, but for our Brazilian student as well. Now we will contrast this with the entry from the Korean student. She begins by saying, 'Maggie asked if any of us ... ' thus initially using 'us' to connote membership in the class. However, this is the last time she uses 'us' or 'we' to refer to any identifying characteristic of this group, and/or her membership in it. She turns quickly to 'I', and an analysis of the passage reveals her deep feelings of marginalization. She says, early on, 'I felt I was one of them, who had the different way' – not only using 'I' to claim an identity unique from the group, but specifically and explicitly claiming an identity as 'one of them', the 'others' we have been discussing. She continues, using 'I' consistently, to chronicle her experiences as a child, again displaying her knowledge that these experiences are unique to her, and not shared by the group. At one point, in fact, she says, ' ... all of you, and Maggie ... ', positioning herself as having no solidarity with the class or identity as a member of the group, on the basis of her ' ... inability to talk actively in class or cyberspace.' Here we can see that the discussion format of class, and implementation of the listserve (both reflective of my desire to establish a community where students collaboratively engage in the negotiation and construction of meaning) have thus far, in fact, served to deny this learner access to membership in this community. She articulates characteristics that she sees others as having, and herself as lacking. To her, 'I' does not equal ' ... all-native English-speaking American student ... ', nor does it equal ' ... educated to be competent in western-style discourse pattern ... ' These are characteristics that our previous participants have taken for granted, tacitly assuming them as part of their identity claims. And, at the end, in marked contrast with the others, she says:

> More or less, what I suggest as difference must be common to everybody in a certain degree. Yet, I thought, I would want to share 'my story' with all of you guys, who can, as teachers, help out those who are in similar condition as I was a child in Germany.

This ending may be the most telling of all. She uses 'I', initially, to give an opinion, as have the others. She then acknowledges that perhaps her 'difference' isn't so unique to her, but ' ... must be common to everybody...'. Still, she does not use this to claim solidarity with those others; she *feels* unique, especially in this context where she is contrasting herself to others in *this* community. She refers to 'my story' – indeed, this story is uniquely hers – but says, ' ... all of you guys, who can, as teachers ... '. She, too, is a teacher. She has taught both German and English in Korea, is doing a double Masters degree here, and holds an assistantship teaching German at the University. But her feelings of alienation are so strong, based on an identity rooted in her cultural upbringing, that she feels apart, and unable to claim anything in common with the others.

These analyses afford us a close look at how members of this class speak from 'voices' specific to the identities they feel they can legitimately claim in this context. There are other identities they could claim (i.e. the Korean student as teacher). But their membership in this group, and therefore the voices they feel entitled to claim, are a co-construction of their past experiences, their understandings and interpretations as to what sort of cultural event this is and which sorts of expertise/s 'count' in this context, and even what defines 'expertise.' They position themselves, and each other, based on their cultural models of schooling, of teaching, of cultures/ cultural identities, and even of graduate school (and being a graduate student). But each of these factors carries different 'weight' for different participants as it plays out in tandem with the others. It is just these socially-situated identities that determine the content and tone of each participant's posting, just as it is the participant's individual socially-situated interpretation of the postings that help determine his or her identity in this context. And, together, they represent multiple 'meanings' taken from text, which help each student to contextualize and deepen his or her understandings; they even offer openings for students to assume a position from which they can find a voice to enter the conversation. It is, in part, the properties of the listserve that contribute to this, but only when viewed as one co-determinous factor in interaction with a host of others: the course, classroom practice, social properties and interrelations of individuals, the institutional context, etc.

Conclusion

It is time now to ask the question I hold my students responsible for (and can do no less of myself here): so what? What are the social and cultural implications of this? What difference does it make?

In a recent article, Jim Cummins (2000) argues that the debate about whether technology is a societal good or evil is misplaced. While acknowledging the divide in equitability of access, Cummins compares it to other technological innovations of the 20th century (television, cars), and argues that it is here, that it is changing society, so the question becomes not whether or not to use it, but how. Cummins, along with others who research the role of Instructional Technology (IT) in classrooms, demands that we ask serious questions as to how we can use IT to ' ... increase the linguistic power of the individual student but also to harness that power in critical and constructive ways to strengthen the social fabric of our local and global communities.' (Cummins, 2000: 539). In service of this, he asks the following questions:

> Can IT itself be harnessed to combat the social inequalities which its use reflects? Can we as language educators articulate a pedagogy within which IT plays a central role that will be effective in developing students' language and literacy abilities, and their awareness of how language and literacy are implicated in relations of power? Can we demonstrate that use of IT amplifies the impact of this pedagogy beyond what would be achieved without the use of IT? Can IT serve as a tool for promoting collaborative relations of power? (Cummins, 2000: 539)

This, then, is the 'so what.' I believe that our ultimate goal as language teachers, and as language teacher educators, is to offer our students access to the range of abilities and forms of language that will enable them to lay claim to the social identities that afford them a participant status in the social communities of their choice. Our task is not to be prescriptive, and choose for them, but to open options. And, in order to do this, we must provide not only specific language and literacy skills, but also a deep understanding of the ways in which language, literacy, and communication practices are specific to discourse communities, and the ways in which our socialization to these practices plays a large role in determining (and constraining our choices of) identities in specific social groups. This is accomplished not only through further socialization into specific discourses (which, in our language teacher education classrooms, is the traditional model of training teacher) but also through an overt focus on these issues. Gee (Chapter 1, this volume) calls for our students to become ' ... sociologists and critical theorists of Discourses in general. It is necessary that they come to understand how Discourses work to help and harm people, to include and exclude, to support and oppose other Discourses.' The listserve in this class served just that purpose; it provided a venue for students to overtly discuss and critique issues of language and culture as they relate to social equity and access in schools. And they did this through identities they were able to assume in this specific context – namely, in shared discussion via e-communication in a specific graduate-level language-teacher education course. The listserve, in answer to Cummins' questions, provided both access to identities and voices from which to speak, and an overt focus on the relations between language and literacy and relations of power. This enabled students in this class to come to deeper understandings and to connect those understandings to their specific identities and teaching practices.

As a final word, though, we need to look at what the listserve didn't do. Cummins (2000: 540) develops a framework through which to analyze the use of IT. It has three components: focus on meaning, focus on language, and focus on use. 'Meaning' has two components: making input comprehensible, and developing critical literacy. We have seen that the listserve accomplished those purposes. 'Language' has two components as well: awareness of language forms and uses, and critical analysis of language forms and uses. It is here that we begin to formulate an awareness of where the practice fell short. While the students, in becoming 'sociologists and critical theorists' (Gee, Chapter 1), did engage in discussion and critical analysis of language forms and uses, they did so only in looking at the language of others (their students), or, in the case of the Korean student, her own personal history. Warschauer (1999), in articulating research questions to be asked of IT, asks, 'How do learners pay attention to both content and form in online communication? What linguistic features do they tend to notice ... ?' Here, they engaged with content. What was lacking in this particular instantiation was an overt focus and analysis of the linguistic features and texts they were producing on the listserve in the process of construction. How much more powerful would it have been if the analysis conducted in this chapter had been conducted by the students, as an exemplar of the very topics they were discussing?

This, then, is a work in progress. It provides one way to theoretically and pedagogically think about the implications of IT for promoting language and literacy development in service of social justice and equity. However, it also points for a call for even clearer pedagogical clarity in formulating goals for IT as part of classroom instruction, and for a process of research into the specific ways the design and implementation of IT functions in service of those goals. Yes, technology is a fast-growing part of our world, and is creating new global communities and relationships, as it is creating new markets and business practices, and new pedagogies. To deny students access to technology is to deny them access to the new forms of cognition, skills, and language and communication practices that will enable them to choose their forms of participation in our changing world. In addition to the experience of using computers, though, it is possible that thoughtful applications of IT in the classroom may provide students with access to language, concepts, cultural models, identities, social relations, and critical understandings that are less available through other instructional modes. And this is well worth pursuing.

References

Ady, J. (1999) Computer-mediated communication in a high school global education curriculum: A brochure project. *Social Studies* 90, 159–164.

Baym, N.K. (1995) The emergence of community in computer-mediated communication. In S.G. Jones (ed.) *Cybersociety: Computer-mediated Communication and Community.* Thousand Oaks, CA: Sage.

Castells, M. (1996) *The Information Age: Economy, Society, and Culture* (Vol. 1): *The Rise of the Network Society.* Oxford: Blackwell.

Cummins, J. (2000) Academic language learning, transformative pedagogy, and information technology: Towards a critical balance. *TESOL Quarterly* 34 (3), 537–548.

Cummins, J. and Sayers, D. (1995) *Brave New Schools: Challenging Cultural Illiteracy Through Global Learning Networks.* New York: St. Martin's Press.

DiSessa, A. (2000) *Changing Minds: Computers, Learning, and Literacy.* Cambridge, MA: MIT Press.

Donato, R. (2000) Sociocultural contributions to understanding the foreign and second language classroom. In J. Lantolf (ed.) *Sociocultural Theory and Second Language Learning.* Oxford: Oxford University Press.

Fotos, S. and Iwabuchi, T. (1998) Using email to build EFL communicative competence. Paper presented at 32nd Annual TESOL Convention, Orlando, Florida.

Gee, J.P., Hull, G. and Lankshear, C. (1996) *The New Work Order: Behind the Language of the New Capitalism.* Boulder, CO: Westview

Harkness, S., Super, C. and Keefer, C. (1992) Learning to be an American parent. In R. D'Andrade and C. Strauss (eds) *Human Models and Cultural Interaction.* Cambridge: Cambridge University Press.

Hawkins, M. (2000) The reassertion of traditional authority in a constructivist pedagogy. *Teaching Education* 11 (3), 279–295.

Heath, S.B. (1982) What no bedtime story means: Narrative skills at home and school. *Language In Society* 11 (2), 49–76.

Herring, S.C. (1996) Two variants of an electronic message schema. In S.C. Herring (ed.) *Computer-mediated Communication: Linguistic, Social and Cross-cultural Perspectives.* Philadelphia: Benjamins.

Kamhi-Stein, L.D. (2000) Looking to the future of TESOL teacher education: Web-based bulletin board discussions in a methods course. *TESOL Quarterly* 34 (3), 423–455.

Kamhi-Stein, L.D. (2000) Integrating computer-mediated communication tools into the practicum. In K.E. Johnson (ed.) *Teacher Education.* Alexandria, VA: TESOL Press.

Kamhi-Stein, L.D. and Browne-del Mar, C. (1997) EFL teachers and email instruction: Perceived language and professional benefits. *CAELL Journal* 7 (4), 14–19.

Kelly, K. (1998) *New Rules for the New Economy: Ten Radical Strategies for a Connected World.* New York: Viking

Kern, R. (1996) Computer-mediated communication: Using email to explore personal histories in two cultures. In M. Warschauer (ed.) *Telecollaboration in Foreign Language Learning.* Honolulu: University of Hawaii Press.

Lam, W.S.E. (2000) L2 literacy and the design of the self: A case study of a teenager writing on the Internet. *TESOL Quarterly* 24 (3), 457–482.

Lave, J. and Wenger, E. (1991) *Situated Learning: Legitimate Peripheral Participation.* Cambridge: Cambridge University Press.

Murray, D.E. (2000) Protean communication: The language of computer-mediated communication. *TESOL Quarterly* 34 (3), 397–421.

New London Group (1996) A pedagogy of multiliteracies: Designing social futures. *Harvard Educational Review* 66, 60–92. [Reprinted in 1999 in B. Cope and M. Kalantzis (eds) *Multiliteracies: Literacy Learning and the Design of Social Futures* (pp. 9–37). London: Routledge.]

Norton, B. (1995) Social identity, investment, and language learning. *TESOL Quarterly* 29, 9–31.

Rifkin, J. (2000) *The Age of Access: The New Culture of Hypercapitalism Where all of Life is a Paid-For Experience.* New York: Jeremy Tarcher/Putnam.

Rogoff, B. (1990) *Apprenticeship in Thinking: Cognitive Development in Social Context.* New York, NY: Oxford University Press.

Scollon, R. (1998) *Mediated Discourse as Social Interaction.* London: Longman.

Scollon, R. and Scollon, S. (1981) *Narrative, Literacy and Face in Interethnic Communication.* NJ: Ablex.

Tella, S. (1991) Introducing international communications networks and electronic mail into foreign language classrooms: A case study in Finnish Senior Secondary Schools. *Research Report #95.* Helsinki, Finland: University of Helsinki.

Tella, S. (1992) Boys, girls and email: A case study in Finnish senior secondary schools. *Research Report #110.* Helsinki Finland: University of Helsinki, Department of Teacher Education.

Vygotsky, L.S. (1978) *Mind and Society.* Cambridge, MA: Harvard University Press.

Warschauer. M. (1999) *Electronic Literacies: Language, Culture, and Power in Online Education.* Mahwah, NJ: Lawrence Erlbaum Associates, Inc.

Warschauer, M. (2000) The changing global economy and the future of English teaching. *TESOL Quarterly* 34 (3), 511–535.

Werry, C.C. (1996) Linguistic and interactional features of Internet relay chat. In S.C. Herring (ed.) *Computer-mediated Communication: Linguistic, Social and Cross-cultural Perspectives.* Amsterdam: Benjamins.

Wertsch, J.V. (1991) *Voices of the Mind: A Sociocultural Approach to Mediated Interaction.* Cambridge, MA: Harvard University Press.

Wertsch, J.V. (1998) *Mind as Action.* Oxford: Oxford University Press.

Zinchenko, V.P. (1985) Vygotsky's ideas about units for analysis of minds. In J. Wertsch (ed.) *Culture Communication and Cognition.* Cambridge: Cambridge University Press.

Part 4

The Uptake of Sociocultural Approaches in Language Education

Chapter 5

Social Languages and Schooling: The Uptake of Sociocultural Perspectives in School

JENNIFER MILLER

Introduction

The emergence of sociocultural perspectives of language, typified by notions of situated meanings within repertoires of social practices, indicates a powerful new direction for theorists and practitioners in the field of second language acquisition and use. In this chapter I have set myself two tasks. First I want to look at how the theoretical framings provided in this book may both inform and transform what teachers and students do in schools. What are the implications of such framing for how we teach ESL, for institutional practices, and for curriculum? What shifts might teachers, administrators and indeed students need to make to accommodate and benefit from these insights? But secondly, I wish to interrogate the 'fit' between sociocultural theory and English as a Second Language (ESL) practice, that is, to look at convergences and tensions between second language acquisition (SLA) theory and practice on the one hand, and the transformational directions offered by social discourse theorists such as Gee, Kress, Fairclough and others. As I see it, the challenge for schools is to establish a balance between a focus on the contextual and the sociocultural, and what might be considered more traditional principles of language acquisition – a balance in which teaching and learning strategies derive from a synthesis of the two. Gee suggests that our students should become not merely consumers of Discourse, but players of the game, themselves 'sociologists and critical theorists.' I want to situate these propositions within the practices of schools in relation to non-English speaking background (NESB) students.

For my purposes in this chapter, I will draw heavily on my own experience as an ESL teacher working with recently-arrived migrant and refugee students in high schools in Queensland (Australia). I work both at the

University of Queensland in the TESOL field and in an intensive English language reception centre for high school migrants and refugees, Milpera State High School. This school will provide a practical real-life setting for many of the ideas I wish to explore here. I will also draw on my research on the English language acquisition and social identities of some of these students (see Miller, 2003).

Before turning to a description of Milpera High, it is important to recapitulate the specific ways in which sociocultural theory has already transformed the field of SLA. This is because I cannot begin to think about my school or ESL in a way that is divorced from an understanding of languages as social practice. In what follows, I outline some of the moves inherent in putting the social back into language education. In broad terms, these include shifts towards notions of discourse acquisition rather than language learning, insights into the political nature of the conditions of production, and the importance of socially-situated identities in all linguistic interactions.

From Second Language Acquisition to Discourse Acquisition

The process of acquiring new linguistic, social and cultural practices has been described by Pavlenko (1998) as a 'self-translation' – a transformation of self through discourse necessary for discursive assimilation, in which one is heard and read by others. A number of researchers working in language-related fields, including Gee (1996), Firth & Wagner (1997), Lippi-Green (1997), Norton (1997), Rampton (1995), Leung *et al.* (1997) and Toohey (1998), have suggested a reconceptualization of second language acquisition research, which would incorporate newer understandings of language as socially and culturally constituted. It is helpful to arrange some of the concepts underlying recent sociocultural discourse approaches as a set of contrasts with concepts inherent in SLA. Although the oppositions in Table 5.1 are more complex than a simple binary suggests (they are not either/or propositions), they illustrate the incorporation into second language research of insights from other fields and disciplines.[1] The contrasts open up a new set of questions and new ways to think about language education.

It can be seen that from these 'oppositions' (which are actually dimensions or continua), that the conceptual shift from language to discourse involves moving away from a 'stick figure' notion of the learner (implied by the left side of the table) towards a conceptualization in which all social language users are implicated. SLA research has continued to seek out models of teaching and learning which stress the role and responsibility of

Table 5.1 Concepts underlying SLA and language as discourse

SLA	*Language as discourse*
'decodable' meanings	situated, contextualized, and negotiated meanings
cognitivist and mentalist orientations	social and contextual orientation
focus on individual competence	focus on competence realized socially through interaction
native speaker as an idealized source of perfectly realized competence	competence realized by all speakers to varying degrees in a range of social contexts
native/non-native binary	collaboration of native speaker and nonnative speaker in discourse
standardized language as the goal	standardized language as a myth
neutral communicative contexts	ideologically laden contexts with real consequences for participants
focus on formal learning environments	focus on discourse in a range of settings or social fields
learner as 'subject'	speaker as a social identity, enacted in particular social situations
search for generalizable rules and methods	understanding of the contingency of local contexts
lack of an emic perspective	centrality of participant perspectives
focus on development of communicative competence	focus on contextual and interactional dimensions of language use
good language learners can learn	'authentic' and 'false' beginners are parts of social hierarchies that impinge on learning
difficulties predominate in studies	consideration of communicative successes; problems viewed as contingent social phenomena
learner as defective communicator	learner/speaker drawing on resources in an interactional context
misunderstandings common in native/ non-native communication	misunderstandings common in all communication
interlanguage, fossilization & foreigner talk as key concepts	language use, identities and social context as key concepts

the individual learner. As Nunan, (1995: 55) puts it, 'In the final analysis ... it is the learner who must remain at the centre of the process, for no matter how much energy and effort we expend, it is the learner who has to do the learning.' However commonsensical the appeal of such a statement, it accords insufficient weight to social and contextual factors, and expresses a skewed perspective on language learning and use, which does not incorporate an understanding of how discourses work, or how language is related to issues of social representation and identity. It reduces teaching to what Bourdieu (1991: 34) might call, along with structuralist linguistics, 'the charm of a game devoid of consequences.'

Importantly for ESL teachers and schools generally, the shifts in Table 5.1 also highlight a questioning of the traditional native-speaker/non-native speaker binary, and assumptions within notions such as 'standard English.' Lippi-Green (1997) reminds us that standard language and non-accent are abstractions, idealizations that do not really exist. She argues that the opposite of standard appears to be non-standard or substandard, and that 'these terms automatically bring with them a uni-directionality and subordination which is counterproductive to a discussion of language variation in linguistic terms' (Lippi-Green, 1997: 60). Lippi-Green also draws attention to the ideological aspects of standard language, 'a bias toward an abstracted, idealized, homogenous spoken language which is imposed by dominant bloc institutions and which names as its model the written language of the upper middle class' (1997: 64).

As an alternative to the blunt notion of native speaker competence, Rampton (1995) and Leung *et al.* (1997) propose the concepts of language expertise, language affiliation and language inheritance. Language expertise refers to what you know about language(s), including linguistic and cultural knowledge; language affiliation refers to an attachment, allegiance and identification with the language, and therefore focuses on connections between people or groups; language inheritance constitutes one's language background, and is to do with continuity between groups. Leung *et al.* point out that, for many, there may be limited allegiance to the language inheritance, and a blurring of and within the conventional categories of native and nonnative. This work is particularly relevant to the language competence of migrant students, whose language expertise, affiliation and inheritance in the first language is likely to be disrupted on acquiring discourses in their second or third language. These ideas also highlight the socially-situated identities of speakers.

The notion of the discursive construction of identity has recently been incorporated into other work on second language acquisition, notably by Norton Peirce (1995), Norton (1997) and Siegal (1996). Norton Peirce (1995) draws on the work of Bourdieu and Weedon in her theory of social identity and language acquisition. She writes:

> It is through language that a person negotiates a sense of self within and across different sites at different points in time, and it is through language that a person gains access to – or is denied access to – powerful social networks that give learners the opportunities to speak. (Norton Peirce, 1995: 13)

As a refinement of the idea of motivation in learning, Norton Peirce proposes the idea of investment in language learning and use. She claims that investment is better than motivation as a signal of the socially and historically constructed relationship between language learner and target language, as well as the ambivalent attitudes towards practising and using the language. The influence of Bourdieu is evident in her comment that 'if learners invest in a second language, they do so with the understanding that they will acquire a wider range of symbolic and material resources, which will in turn increase the value of their cultural capital' (Norton Peirce, 1995: 17). This is related to what Gee describes as cultural models, socially and ideologically situated images and theories that must be acquired by both body and mind. But is it acquisition or learning? Are they different?

Acquisition vs. Learning

There is considerable tension between the positions often taken by SLA theorists and practitioners (who focus on the conditions surrounding the production of individual learners) and Gee's (1996) position that users of Discourses must be the 'right who' doing the 'right what,' as they enact socially situated identities. For me, the critical point about a Discourses view is the vital implication in production of the hearer. If speaking is primarily a social activity, then ways of hearing are part of that activity. This is integral to any understanding of how discourses work, or how language is related to issues of social representation and identity. Norton Peirce (1995) sums up the contrasting position from SLA in the following way:

> Theories of the good language learner have been developed on the premise that language learners can choose under what conditions they will interact with members of the target language community and that the learner's access to the target language community is a function of the learner's motivation. (Norton Peirce, 1995: 12)

The implication is that not all learners can choose the social conditions surrounding their language production, nor the responses of the target language community (users of the dominant Discourses). This view is in direct contrast to that of Nunan, for whom the burden of learning resides with the learner, irrespective of conditions that may obtain. Rampton (1987: 49) reminds us that for too long, SLA research has run 'the risk of remaining restrictively preoccupied with the space between the speaker and his [*sic*] grammar, rather than with the relationship between speakers and the world around them.' This relationship is to do with Discourses (languages in use), rather than language or second language per se. It is to do with the way speakers speak, and hearers hear, or as Gee reminds us, the way language users are recognized by other users in any social situation.

To further unravel this problem of acquisition or learning of languages, I wish to turn briefly to Gee's (1996) *Social Linguistics and Literacies*, in which he suggests a relationship between the concepts of first and second languages on the one hand, and primary and secondary Discourses on the other. Primary Discourses, acquired in informal settings through face-to-face interaction, are the basis of one's first social identity. At school they are implicated in being, and in locating, 'authentic' and 'false' beginners. Secondary Discourses are developed in a more conscious way through apprenticeship to institutions and other groups. In these terms, school is a 'public sphere of secondary Discourse,' with literacy being defined as 'mastery of the secondary Discourse' (Gee, 1996: 143). The acquisition/ learning distinction is pivotal, and Gee draws a convincing analogy between Discourse acquisition and learning, and first and second language acquisition and learning.

Gee (1996) illustrates the analogy between the disparate fields of discourse and SLA research with a number of comparisons. For brevity I refer to first and second language as L1/L2, and primary and secondary Discourses as D1/D2. The examples offered by Gee include:

- interference, or the transfer of aspects of the L1/D1 (such as grammatical or phonological features) to the L2/D2;
- the filtering of aspects of the L2/D2 back into the L1/D1;
- the simplification of the L2/D2 by those who are acquiring these;
- the use of the L1/D1 as a fall-back position in circumstances of stress.

It seems highly likely that other parallels could also be drawn between secondary Discourse and second language.

The dilemma that Gee (1996: 144) presents is that Discourses are acquired 'in natural, meaningful, and functional settings' rather than learned through overt teaching. Central to this notion is Gee's claim that Discourses are mastered 'by enculturation (apprenticeship) into social practices through scaffolded and supported interaction with people who have already mastered the Discourse' (Gee, 1996: 139). Knowing 'about' the language is therefore not knowing how to 'do' the language. In Gee's terms, knowing 'about' the language is what can be taught and learned, as opposed to acquired. He argues, however, that good teaching should lead to meta-knowledge about the interrelationships of the primary and secondary Discourses to each other, to the self and to society. That is, good teaching facilitates learning to critically frame and reframe knowledge.

What is not elaborated by Gee is that good classrooms can also be 'natural, meaningful and functional settings,' where teachers create the conditions for acquisition, via apprenticeship. They also assist students to gain the metaknowledge necessary to process the second language and relate it to their first, inflecting new Discourses with elements of those already present. A site where students spend at least 1600 hours a year can hardly be termed 'unnatural' or inauthentic. This is not to underestimate the difficulty of such a task for both teachers and learners in schools. As Gee (1996: 146) writes, 'Non-mainstream students and teachers are in a bind. One is not in a Discourse unless one has mastered it and mastery comes about through acquisition not learning.' Implied here is the notion that the conditions most favoring acquisition lie in a range of sites and contexts beyond the formal classroom.

In relation to second language acquisition and use, Spolsky's (1989) notion of natural acquisition contexts for language learning are worthy of mention. Natural acquisition contexts, according to Spolsky, include learning for communication, unmodified language input, and being surrounded by native speakers. Such contexts provide a real-world social context for learning, along with a primary focus on meaning. Non-English speaking background (NESB) students in Australia or the United States, who are learning English in an English-speaking country are presumably in a natural acquisition context, as opposed to a formal learning situation, where students are instructed in a foreign language. These students travel on buses and trains, go shopping, use the Web, see movies, talk to other students, field phone calls – all in the second language. There are presumably ample opportunities for multiple interactions and practice, which Spolsky stresses are essential for acquisition.

However, it should be added that in the initial phases of their schooling, NESB students are often in an intensive language centre offering a formal language learning program, where different conditions obtain. In the early phases of language learning, the teacher may be the only one in the classroom fluent in the target language; there may be limited access to native speakers; the language input is highly modified; and there is much controlled practice of forms. These students are using transport, shopping and talking to friends, yet their classroom experiences may more resemble those of a foreign language classroom than a natural acquisition context, and their outside opportunities for practicing the target Discourses may be limited (see Norton & Toohey, 2001; Sharkey & Layzer, 2000).

As Gee points out, ESL learners and their teachers are in a bind. If Discourses are acquired rather than learned, what are teachers to teach? How can authentic beginners and marginalized learners be 'given' the power to transform practice with texts and Discourses, and to critically frame what they know and what they are learning? Bourdieu (1991: 37) suggests that language must be viewed not as 'an object of contemplation,' but as 'an instrument of action and power.' As a practitioner, it seems to me essential to believe that teachers and schools can make a difference. If we can't use these insights to teach and to empower our students, then the value of teaching as practice and as a way of life is in question. Knowing in advance that Discourses are ideologically loaded, and that among the multiliteracies suggested by Luke some are more prized than others in schools, and that some identities are more valued than others, is itself important knowledge for teachers and students. Before turning to a specific school setting, it is useful to recall some salient points about school literacies and Discourses.

The Value of School English

It has long been recognized that schools reward specific types of language knowledge and use, forms that stem from the norms of the white middle class (Bourdieu, 1993; Gee, 1996; Heath, 1983; Heller, 1994; Lippi-Green, 1997; Luke, 1996). For some students (those Gee calls 'false beginners'), the discourses of school are very close to what they know already, and participation in spoken and written texts poses little problem. For others, it is difficult to gain access to what may appear as 'very foreign ways of talking and acting' (Ballenger, 1997: 1). Dominant groups decide what is valued literate knowledge, which then becomes entrenched within the hegemonic curriculum. Implicated in these decisions are cultural values and social hierarchies (Hymes, 1996).

Part of the knowledge valued by school is a knowledge of what is assumed to be standard English and its forms, an institutional language competence which is the linguistic capital required by the academic market. Lippi-Green (1997: 65) writes, 'The process of assimilation to an abstracted standard is cast as a natural one, necessary and positive for the greater social good.' This abstracted standard features grammatical and discourse competence, and the forms of written English. Writing is privileged over speaking at school, argues Lippi-Green, because it's hard to learn and is associated with particular sociocultural contexts. In terms of both spoken and written language use, she lifts a veil on standard English as an abstract idealization imposed by those with vested interests in its institutional maintenance. She also points out that there is a vast difference between communicative effectiveness and grammaticality. In regard to the US context, she claims further, 'Teachers are for the most part firm believers in a standard language ideology which rejects or marginalizes those varieties of US English which are markedly non-middle class' (Lippi-Green, 1997: 131). Similar beliefs are still entrenched within Australian institutions via assessment and in regard to tertiary entrance, via external examinations in which linguistic minority students find it notoriously difficult to excel.

We have long known in SLA that an overt focus on rules is unhelpful for many aspects of language learning (Lightbown & Spada, 1999). Persistent error correction, for example, has little impact on the learner's internalization of structures. Although students may not learn much from the corrections on their work, the sad fact is that for many students those red marks locate exactly where their writing will be found wanting, by the teacher and by others. Even within a frame of literacy that is socially constructed and institutionally located, a level of grammatical accuracy continues to be what teachers and examiners target. Gee (1996) problematizes this situation in the following terms:

> These non-mainstream students often fail to fully master school-based dominant Discourses, especially the 'superficialities of form and correctness' that serve as such good gates given their imperviousness to late acquisition in classrooms without community support. (Gee, 1996: 146)

Perhaps we need to see the 'superficialities of form and correctness' as one of the many Discourses that linguistic minority students must acquire.

With increasing emphasis on oral presentations in school, speaking, as well as writing, becomes a vital part of school English. Lippi-Green (1997) claims accent becomes a litmus test for exclusion, but also that certain accents are less stigmatized than others. Light European accents, for example, are heard differently from Asian accents. This is also the case in Australia, where French accents are found charming and used in TV advertisements, but Vietnamese accents are heard as 'hard to understand.' Along with accent, we could also argue that non-standard forms and dialects, and even the use of other languages, are also motives for exclusion in schools.

In relation to linguistic minority students at school, I have suggested that there is some tension in the arguments about acquisition and learning. It is likely that the problem is not as simple as the summary 'languages are learned, while Discourses are acquired,' but this may be a useful platform to work from. I have then argued that school requires specific forms of Discourse that potentially disadvantage minority students. Literacy, claims Gee (1996), has historically played the dual roles of both liberator and weapon. The metaphor might presumably be extended to Discourses. The acquisition and use of English is essential for students wishing to participate in social and institutional practices, and in the wider society. However the notion of a standard English discourse, or school English, may be used as a weapon against those from language minorities (and of course others), who are outsiders to the Discourse(s).

It seems clear that we cannot view the competence of the speaker in isolation from social practices, speaking in isolation from hearing, Discourse in isolation from relationships of power. These are all interrelated in the social languages, activities and practices of schools. Let us turn now to an example of one school where a diversity of social languages, cultures and practices is a defining characteristic.

Milpera State High School

Milpera State High School, an intensive English language reception centre for high school age migrants and refugees, is special in many ways. Although now an administrator at Milpera, I have worked as an ESL teacher at this school intermittently for over a decade, and always found it the least stressful and most interesting and rewarding school teaching I have experienced. Comprising approximately 170 students aged 12 to 18, of 20 to 30 nationalities, it offers an intensive ESL program to students for six months on average, the time spent at Milpera depending on student needs and levels of English. Students then move to ESL Support Units in regular high schools where there is progressive integration into mainstream classes, and then finally to full mainstream integration.

Although it is just one of a number of centres providing on-arrival programs throughout Australia, Milpera is the only purpose-built school for migrants and refugees in the country. The Milpera school population varies a great deal over time, depending on patterns of migration and humanitarian programs responding to various international crises. At the beginning of 2003 the largest group of students is from the Horn of Africa, but there are also substantial groups from Taiwan, Mainland China, the Middle East, former Yugoslavia, and Vietnam. A snapshot of the school population in March 2003 reveals a total of 165 students, with the following nationality profile:

Sudanese	57
Taiwanese	23
Iraqi	21
Chinese	16
Vietnamese	12
Afghani	9
Thai	5

In addition there were between 1 and 4 children from each of the following countries: Korea, Japan, Iran, Eritrea, Ethiopia, the Philippines, Indonesia, Cambodia, Liberia, Malaysia, Russia, Western Samoa, East Timor and Belgium. Note also that the 57 Sudanese students speak an array of tribal languages, often in addition to Arabic.

There is a great diversity of ages, ethnic backgrounds, languages, cultures, socioeconomic status and circumstances of migration. The one common factor is that students arrive at the school with limited or no English. Milpera State does not fit easily therefore into the definition of a speech community developed by Gumperz and Hymes (1986: 54), that is, a community sharing rules for the conduct and interpretation of speech, and rules for the interpretation of at least one linguistic variety. The only linguistic variety in common for these students is English, which they are all busy acquiring, along with the rules for interpreting it. English functions therefore as a lingua franca, in which there are naturally vast differences among the 150 students in terms of proficiency. Some students need just a few weeks at the school to start using English in a range of social and academic contexts. Others, who have had almost no schooling or inter-rupted schooling in their country of origin, or have learning difficulties, tend to stay a year or more. Lack of L1 literacy, particularly for some African and Iraqi students, is a huge hurdle. And even in a specialized school such as Milpera, the range of sociocultural backgrounds means that some students are, in Gee's terms, false beginners to the Discourses of English, while others are authentic beginners.

Milpera State is like a collection of imported speech communities in one site, as well as being an integrating community in which nascent English skills are practised and developed, while 20 or so other languages continue to be spoken for a number of classroom and social purposes. For many, English is the third or even fourth language learned. Many students are indeed 'global kids': from Somalia via Sudan and Egypt, speaking Tigrinia, Amharic and Arabic, from Afghanistan via Pakistan, speaking Hindi, Urdu and Persian, from Bosnia via Germany or Austria, bilingual in Serbo-Croatian and German. Sometimes students speak their first language intentionally to other students who don't understand. In this case, the first language (L1) acts to exclude (or include other members who may be nearby), and may function as a source of humor or even of abuse. I have on occasion witnessed a torrent of derision in a language unknown by the interlocutor, resulting in a sense of powerlessness that is almost tangible. Even when the L1 is spoken in this way for a humorous motive, the effect can be discomforting. However, the overwhelming impression of the interactions between Milpera State students is one of multicultural and multilingual harmony. Students are often interested in each other's languages – at pains to learn and teach greetings and swear words in several languages. Walking around the school at lunchtime one notes that the majority are in their first-language groups, but others are engaged in interethnic cross-cultural interactions in English – on the basketball courts and soccer fields, in the library, on the computers, or just sitting in groups around the grounds.

Many features of Milpera State are expressly designed to smooth the way for students to feel they belong to the school's diverse community:

- the school provides a strong positive model of interculturalism;
- several teachers speak another language; the guidance officer is Chinese;
- teachers are ESL specialists and tend to find the work very rewarding;
- there is a strong emphasis on pastoral care in the first language and providing access to community and government services for students and their families;
- there are low teacher–pupil ratios;
- there is also the pervasive and much-valued presence of numerous bilingual teacher aides, including speakers of Spanish, Serbo-Croatian, Vietnamese, Chinese, French and German. Interpreter services are frequently used for other languages.

Students arrive at the school to enroll virtually every day of the week and all year round. There is a brief assessment of their spoken and written English, and they are placed in one of eleven classes, depending on their English language proficiency. The beginners' classes are therefore multiage, with students aged between 12 and 19. After the Beginner level, students are placed in age-appropriate groups. Students with little or no English spend on average five weeks at the Beginner level, five weeks at the Post-Beginner level, and then 15 weeks at Year 8/9 or Year 9/10/11 level, depending on age. Every five weeks a class moves on to the high school ESL units, and there is a staff meeting to determine if individual students in any class should be moved into a more or less demanding level. The progress of individuals is discussed at special meetings to ensure all students are placed appropriately. Case meetings are held for specific students who seem at risk. There is therefore a constant spiralling towards exit and adjustment to the students' needs and rate of progress.

Milpera State also plays a significant role in providing images of 'Australian' identities and social practices to students. There are excursions and outings, sports and swimming carnivals, three-day camps in the bush, and visits from students from other schools and members of the community. The students receive intensive language-focused tuition in English, mathematics, science, and physical education, but there is no formal summative assessment in any subject. The emphasis is on learning the discourses of these subjects as intensively as possible, but in a non-competitive and very supportive climate, the object being to provide enough English for students to cope with the tasks and language demands of the high school mainstream. In addition, many practices of regular high schools are modelled, such as daily classroom administrative routines, an afternoon of sport or electives, the canteen (needed for practising language forms as much as for food), and the access to sports fields, the library and computers at lunch time. Predictably perhaps, the sports field and basketball courts look similar to mainstream versions in terms of gender participation. I recently noted 32 boys playing basketball, 16 boys playing soccer, and not a single girl playing either.

As mentioned above, the school runs on five-week cycles. Every five weeks, a class or two moves on to high school, and a new beginners' class is officially begun, in spite of the continuous enrolments. There is a small assembly to mark the exit of classes moving to high school, and to acknowledge students' achievements in the reception program. At a recent exit assembly I attended, the leavers performed a presentation to their teachers and 150 peers, at least 20 of whom had just arrived in Australia and at the school. The assembly began with a short performance by an Aboriginal community member, who played the didgeridoo and then donated the hand-painted instrument to the school. At Milpera State High School, reconciliation and the study of indigenous peoples are a strong focus in the curriculum. The exiting students then performed, presenting posters of their 'life images' in small groups and pairs, outlining their dreams and aspirations, their problems and strengths. They performed in English, using a microphone, and then summarized the talk in their first languages. I was part of an audience that sat in rapt attention, listening to English, Bosnian, Vietnamese, Mandarin, Tagalog, Indonesian, Samoan and Somali. I was part of an audience that saw and heard this as utterly unremarkable in terms of its linguistic plurality. Here was a performance, and a hearing that seemed in marked contrast to what I had observed at other high school assemblies. The assembly finished with a large group of former Yugoslavian students, a united group of Bosnians, Serbian and Croatian students, singing 'Twist and Shout' in Bosnian. The audience clapped along.

Like any school, Milpera is a complex mixture of social identities and hierarchies enacted within a range of micro-environments. Its linguistic, ethnic and cultural diversity are part of this complexity. For the migrant and refugee students, it constitutes the on-arrival program, in which language acquisition and settlement needs are urgent priorities. The institutional practices, curriculum, and methodological approaches of Milpera reflect in a number of ways the sociocultural perspectives presented in this book. But I do not wish to represent the school as an idealized environment, from which contradictions, conflicts and limitations are absent. Significant conceptual shifts such as those indicated in Table 5.1 necessitate ongoing work within institutions. For any school, including Milpera, these are new shifts involving new practices. In the following description and discussion, I will use aspects of Gee's vision for teaching and learning social languages, but I will ground this discussion within the context of Milpera and the high school ESL centres that follow the Milpera program.

If we use a vocabulary that includes situated meanings, cultural models, the representation of identities, social languages and Discourses in social contexts, we soon realize that each term is interwoven with all the others. Meanings are situated in the course of enacting identities, while using particular social languages framed by certain cultural models. As a practitioner and as an administrator, I cannot separate social identities from social language use, or the Discourse game from differentially powerful cultural models. But what does this mean on the ground in terms of curriculum choices and decisions?

Curriculum and Pedagogical Shifts

At Milpera, there is no English language textbook. As a former teacher of French and German, initially I found this disconcerting. Surely there was a core of essential English language knowledge for the beginner? What about basic grammar, vocabulary, dialogues? Some of the students, particularly those from a Confucian tradition, also feel the loss of a textbook at times, and the security of knowing what it is that must be learned. Instead of 'a textbook,' students engage with a multiplicity of texts – class sets of books on geography, science, mathematics, social issues; graded readers; magazines; the Internet; high school textbooks from a range of subject areas; other students' writing; poetry; visual texts; films; CD Rom; grammars in context; spoken discourse; newspapers; reference books.

When I returned to teach briefly at the school a year ago, my starting point in the classroom was an audio-recording of an interview I'd done with a former Milpera student (who was by then at high school), along with a transcript of this interview. To illustrate, here is a brief excerpt (all names used are pseudonyms):

Me: OK. If you can think back to, what was it like at first, arriving here with no English, almost no English. Can you remember?

Neta: Well it was really weird, but when you came, when, when you come to Milpera, you see all the people that don't really speak English, so you just become part of them, and you know ... But when you come to high school, it's really difficult, it's... you think you know English when you're at Milpera, or if you're getting really good, but when you come to high school, you just, you're just lost. And then if you find some fre..., if you're lucky enough to find some friends, like who are gonna be with you and you know, who like to be with people who are from different backgrounds, then it's really good cause because then you can practice English better and like, be competing better.

This example of spoken discourse provided 'the way in' to many important insights and 'learnings' for the students:

- it showed the differences between spoken and written grammar;
- it highlighted the feelings and experiences of someone like themselves;
- it linked directly to their present life and school experience;
- it reflected some of the fears they had about high school;
- it showed the leaps that were possible in terms of language acquisition, yet was in itself a model of the hybridities inherent in the early phases of acquisition.

Once we had listened carefully to the tape several times, the transcript itself became the basis for reading comprehension, vocabulary and grammar activities, including an activity focusing on cohesion in sentence structure. Students then transformed the genre into a personalized written account, and finally they conducted similar interviews with other students. I leave it to the reader to see other possibilities using the type of text above. Within the discourse of the brief excerpt above, Neta is seen enacting the identity of 'former Milpera student,' and commentates on her on-arrival experience and the social memberships available to her at Milpera. Neta contrasts these with the memberships on offer initially at high school, and the need to find students 'who like to be with people who are from different backgrounds.' Such people, she suggests, open up opportunities for practising and competing. These are important insights that are part of the 'language value' and cultural models of the text. Yet the pedagogy I used with this text also drew on established principles of communicative methodology – from text in context, through reception, guided practice in reception and production towards less guided production using the identities of the students.

The curriculum at Milpera takes as its point of departure the notion that the classroom is not 'a space for formal learning,' but a natural language acquisition context, where meaningful and purposeful social activity negotiated in a range of social languages takes place. Like many ESL teachers in Australia, a number of Milpera teachers have studied functional grammar deriving from Halliday, and use the vocabulary of functional grammar in their teaching. Central to the curriculum are the written and spoken genres required by the mainstream high school English syllabus. Mainstream syllabuses in mathematics, science and health and physical education are also used as the basis for Milpera's program in these subject areas.

There are other practices within the curriculum that help students move towards an understanding of what Gee would call situated meanings and cultural models. I used above an example from a classroom English lesson. But clearly the learning of multiple Discourses occurs in a range of sites, both within and beyond school. In terms of identity, it is useful to think of these as sites of identity representation. This notion is one that throws into relief the textualized and contextualized nature of the Discourses of identity. As we move from one site to another, encountering different partners in interaction, we invoke different representations of our identity, and draw on different linguistic resources. Within regular high schools there are, for example, many sites one could observe – visualize the ESL classroom, the mainstream English classroom, the school assembly, the handball court, the canteen queue, a corridor, the administration lobby, the manual arts centre, the music block, the place under B block where the in-crowd sits, the mathematics staffroom, the bus stop outside the school. As your eye roams like some wild hand-held camera, you hear the different Discourses, and take note of their dissonances. Each of these sites affords linguistic minority students different opportunities, constraints and conditions to use social languages, and to represent themselves through language use. Beyond the school, other sites present other possibilities, constraints and conditions. This understanding relates directly to curriculum issues.

The notions of situated meanings and cultural models are central to these curriculum considerations. If meanings were not situated and negotiated through social activity and communicative interaction, then a dictionary would suffice to learn another language. To expand their repertoires of social practices and language use, Milpera students go on frequent excursions, which are then used as the basis for the development of classroom Discourses. Three-day camps to the bush or to the rainforest also serve this purpose. I recently attended one of these camps to a rainforest area with a group of mainly former Yugoslav and Chinese students, and observed the intensification of learning that took place. For some students, it was the first time away from home and family. The camp focused on an environmental education program, and the cultural models offered by the environmentalist camp leaders were a revelation to some of the students. The language work was situated in its real-life contexts. A spontaneous and informative talk on the camp's resident carpet snake occurred as it draped itself alluringly around the shoulders of the bravest students. Discourses on forest animals and animal habitats took place while baiting observation traps, then freeing the animals next morning. Students then wrote up these experiences in their journals. With regard to these activities, it is impossible to avoid the question of which language is in use. Within each site there are microcontexts of first-language use, sites of second- and third-language use, and sites where these overlap and intersect. This is seen as normal, inevitable, and as part of the learning process for Milpera students. On the bus journey to the camp, former Yugoslav students played pop music in their language over the loudspeaker. On the bus on the way home, the Bosnian students sang the pop songs, then invited other students to sing in their own languages, which they did. This may seem a small move, but for me it was symbolic and significant. It could not have occurred before they had spent the three days together.

As well as the students' going out to the community, the community comes into Milpera. More than 30 volunteers, including retired and unemployed teachers, work on a regular basis at the school, working in the Support-a Reader program, helping with speaking and conversation activities, and assisting in classrooms for collaborative group and individual work. Along with the school's 12 teacher aides (7 of whom are bilingual), these volunteers, from a range of backgrounds and age groups, provide valuable language models and partners for the students, as they work on written and spoken Discourses.

In addition to these Discourses, there is a strong focus at the school on technology, centred on a classroom with 20 networked computers. This presents a huge cultural shift for some students, although the appeal of the computers is universal. A week ago, I enrolled two Iraqi sisters, who had lived with their parents illegally in Turkey for nine years, and had no schooling for this entire period. The younger one had never been to school, but seemed bright and well-adjusted in the interview, which was conducted through an interpreter. She had taught herself to read and write Turkish (a matter I confirmed by asking her to do a writing task, which was then read by the interpreter), and to understand and speak Turkish from television. After nine years without school, within weeks she and her sister will be word-processing, researching topics using CD-ROM databases and programs, downloading information from the Internet, importing graphics and generally finding their way around the information technology Discourses now highlighted in Australian schools.

The Discourse of Personal Narrative

I have described above a range of Discourses, activities and social languages open to students at Milpera. One curriculum practice at the school, in my view, is an activity that opens up a range of discursive practices to students, while allowing them to use their previous Discourses and identities and to renegotiate, to translate and to transform these Discourses and identities. This practice is journal writing, which is begun in the Post-Beginner phase of the program (6–10 weeks after arrival for students with literacy) and continues until exit.

The evolution of the personal journals, and the insights they provide to the writers and to the teachers, are critical for several reasons.

(1) The act of writing provides a very different communication context from face-to-face spoken interaction. It is a mode that takes the heat off the speaker. There is no waiting for responses, no awkward long pauses, no pressure to respond, no agonizing search for an unknown or forgotten word. Students can formulate in their own time what they want to say.

(2) The Discourse of journal writing may be, but is often not overtly shaped by the teacher. The students themselves customize meanings in contexts of their own choosing.

(3) As an ESL practitioner and also researcher, I had observed how linguistic minority students are often made voiceless in school contexts. Journals, particularly for the silenced Chinese speakers in my own research, provided a means of expression and validation simply not available in day-to-day social or classroom encounters, and also provided the freedom to include personal insights of a reflective nature. Some students also have a greater facility in writing than in speaking English, often due to the nature of their prior language learning.

(4) The use of journals opens up the possibility for students to use narra-

tive accounts, a form that, while not particularly valued as a school genre, allows the student creative freedom in the discourse. In narrative, experience and responses are constructed and located in text, and provide a resource for the display of identity (Schiffrin, 1996).

(5) For the teachers, the diaries are instances of the phenomena they are engaged with, namely the teaching and learning of the Discourses of English. Teachers can read and observe the extent to which the writing clarifies, supports, extends, contextualizes or contradicts evidence from classroom language use. They also make decisions about what kind of feedback they will provide to students, whether this relates to spelling, syntax, paragraph structure or other features of the writing, to content, or to personal problems raised by the student.

In second language acquisition research, journals have often been used to document an individual student's language acquisition and student teacher reactions to their courses and practice (Bailey, 1990; Long, 1983; Nunan, 1992). In research framed by sociocultural understandings, and indeed in teaching, they can be a tool for capturing students' own representations of second language learning, identity and social interactions. Here is a brief example from a Chinese girl's school journal:

> Today we had lecture about 'book talk.' I very worried. In front of the students and teachers I very nervous. Before I stayed home recite from memory to my father. That's very fluent. But at critical moment I all the forget. So I got C+. I very feel unwell. (Class diary, 29 November 96)

Delivering oral presentations in front of the class is an integral part of the curriculum in many subjects, and ESL teachers try to prepare their students with experience in what is for many an unfamiliar genre at school. Such practice begins at Milpera. The writer of this excerpt, Nora, had told me that speaking English in class at Milpera was facilitated by two conditions. First, she said that no one spoke English perfectly, and secondly, because everyone was a language learner, students were unafraid of making mistakes. However there is a marked difference between answering a question or speaking informally in class, and the stress of speaking in front of a group in the sustained and structured way implied by the oral presentation genre. The latter is a different Discourse and is nerve-racking for most students, including Nora. From this excerpt, we note that what makes her nervous is in part the thought of being physically in front of the students and teachers who are watching and listening. Her practice run recited by heart to her father was 'very fluent,' but how well she describes the real thing: 'at critical moment I all the forget.' Nora's talk was an assessment item, for which she got a C+. She took this personally, that is, she, not her talk, got C+, and she felt ill. There is much one could analyze in the small journal entry above, but teachers of course don't have time for micro-linguistic analyses of text. However the text provides clear feedback to the teacher on Nora's feelings, her strategy for learning at home, her anxiety and her response to the C+. There is also some use of Mandarin word order, although this does not interfere with meaning. What I am suggesting is that Nora's text helps her language acquisition and provides her teachers with valuable information. There is considerable evidence in the literature that texts valued by school encompass discourses which require students to reproduce 'particular forms of cultural logic and social identity under the guise of the transmission of neutral skills and techniques of authorship' (Luke, 1995–6: 33; see also Heller, 1994). Central to these neutral skills and techniques are expository genres and grammatical accuracy. Student journal writing is neither 'admissible' nor valued in this sense. In fact at high school, there is little call for the type of text that Nora, for example, does best, namely the dramatic and creative narratives that fill her journal, everyday stories which, as Gee (1996: 103) suggests, 'often make 'deep sense' in quite literary ways.' Such stories are prized at Milpera, and I will argue later that they need to be more valued in regular high schools.

Identity Shifts

At the start of Gee's chapter in this book, he reminds us that using social languages and enacting social identities entails being recognized by others in doing so. This is a crucial part of using Discourses effectively, and indeed in using a second or third language. Before looking at ways in which ESL students enact and represent their identities, I want to consider briefly how speakers are legitimized in their use of Discourses by hearers. It is worth noting here Bourdieu's conception of linguistic practice, in which cultural context and the social conditions of production and reception are intrinsic to language use. In simple terms, Bourdieu argues that linguistic relations = social relations = power relations. They occur within particular contexts or social fields, in which symmetries and asymmetries of status and symbolic capital are always inherent.

What Bourdieu calls the 'linguistic habitus' is therefore realized through a process of legitimation, entailing a set of social relations or an institution and the joint participation of speaker and listener. The right to speak and the power to impose reception are intrinsic to this (Bourdieu, 1977). In Bourdieu's (1993) terms, this participation is between the authorized speaker and the believing listener. That is, a speaker must possess the authority to speak, part of which is derived from the listener, an idea also stressed by Gee in *Social Linguistics and Literacies* (1996).

What does this mean for the ESL speaker, struggling to enact her identity through the Discourses of a third language? In his introduction to Bourdieu's *Language and Symbolic Power* (1991), Thompson reminds us that in Bourdieu's terms:

> ... differences in terms of accent, grammar and vocabulary – the very differences overlooked by formal linguistics – are indices of the social positions of speakers and reflections of the quantities of linguistic capital (and other capital) which they possess (Bourdieu, 1991: 18)

Such differences are therefore indices to the listener about the speaker. Lippi-Green (1997: 73) observes that accent, for example, often functions as 'the last back door to discrimination.' In the dominant discourse, the manner of speaking is integral to the legitimizing process, as shown by Bourdieu's (1993: 66) statement, 'One of the political effects of the dominant language is this: "He says it so well it must be true."' The implication is that the reverse may also be applied to those subjected to the dominant discourse. The hearer may therefore tacitly accept or deny the authority of the speaker to speak, and if symbolic capital is not recognized as such, it is not capital. That is, if you have the 'wrong accent,' non-standard pronunciation or faulty syntax, you may also lack credibility, and the affirmatory role of the believing listener. It is not enough to be seen and heard in language interactions. As Gee (1996: 127) puts it, the speaker must also be authorized, recognized and accepted as a group member, having 'word-deed-value combinations' acknowledged as legitimate by others. In this way one is apprenticed to the Discourses and social practices of the group. For this to happen, the speaker must be heard as a user of the group's language, understood and acknowledged as a legitimate speaker of that language. We could say that, for the purposes of integration of migrant students into the mainstream, being visibly different is sometimes less important than being audibly similar. A Year 11 Taiwanese student in a regular high school recently summed this up in the following way:

> If your English is as fluent as Australian students, the Australian students do not really see you that much differently. I saw them talking to those Asian students whose English is good in the same way as they would to other Australian students.

In other words, if you sound alike, you are not seen as different. 'Good English' frames you as someone worth talking to, as capable of being talked with, and as a member of the group. Some minority speakers understand very well that how you sound affects how you are seen and heard, where you can go, whom you can speak or be with, how you are treated, and how you can influence events and those around you.

In a school such as Milpera, there are many believing and legitimizing listeners. These include, as Neta suggested above, 'all the people that don't really speak English,' the bilingual teacher aides, the administrators, the home liaison officer, and the ESL teachers, who listen in particular ways, with what I have often called 'ESL ears.' That is, they are sympathetic skilled listeners who are both supportive and non-judgmental. ESL teachers are experienced in modifying their talk and their listening, during which they often seem to be able to screen out effects of accent or soft volume, to mentally rearrange the syntax, to use non-verbal signposts to derive intended meanings, and to encourage the speaker with simple questions, along with 'all the right noises.' They also use a range of strategies described by Wagner (1996) such as requesting clarification, and checking for comprehension by asking for confirmation. As an illustration of this kind of listening, here are two small examples[2] taken from my talks (as researcher, but also as ESL teacher) with students who had left Milpera to go to high school.

Example A

A:	Ah, at the first time, I felt, ah, like (pause) I was apart, you know, from Milpera? Cause I was the oldest.
Me:	You were apart ((a part? I wasn't sure how to interpret this.))
A:	Yeah
Me:	You're different. ((I opt for this interpretation.))
A:	Yeah. I felt like that. Because I was 20 (..)19. I feel apart, because you know I have to do things like, uh, little boys () you know, get into a group...

Example B

Me:	What's your new school like Bun Tan?
Bun Tan:	Not bad miss.
Me:	Yeah. What's not bad?
Bun Tan:	I don't know.
Me:	What about the uniform?
Bun Tan:	It's not good like ah, at Waverly High School (.) it's very nice than Sandford.
Me:	What does Sandford uniform look like?
Bun Tan:	Like a leaf, you know?

Me: Green
Bun Tan: Yeah, green and white. And the pants is grey, short pants.

In example A, I was unsure whether I had heard 'apart' or 'a part,' and sought to clarify by using a paraphrase of one possible meaning – 'you're different.' The message about having 'to do things like, little boys, you know, get into a group' was then clear enough. In example B, the interview format replicates the elicitation techniques that ESL teachers carry out routinely, generating questions to keep the discourse flowing. To the question about school uniform, Bun Tan said that his uniform was 'like a leaf.' I interpreted this immediately as 'green' and he confirmed my interpretation in his last turn. These are the kind of small but automatic conversational moves made by ESL teachers a hundred times a day.

The problem for the students is that the public at large does not have 'an ESL teacher's ear,' and many people are simply not prepared to do the intense listening work required to understand varieties of English that are heard as non-standard (see Lippi-Green, 1997). Normally in spoken interactions, the responsibility for keeping the communication alive is shared. In speaking another language, or speaking English with an accent, or in ways that are heard as non-standard, there are often serious consequences for the speaker. In cases where the speaker is not fluent in English or has an accent, speakers and listeners sometimes have to work hard to foster mutual intelligibility, which requires both an effort of will and a degree of social acceptance. However, Lippi-Green points out that at times the dominant speaker may refuse to carry any responsibility for the communicative act. What she calls 'language ideology filters' come into play whenever an accent or a hesitant 'non-standard' voice is heard, causing the listener to reject 'the communicative burden' (Lippi-Green, 1997: 70).

For ESL students in high schools, those who reject the communicative burden often include the other students at school. Here is what one ex-Milpera student (T) said in conversation with a Mandarin-speaking research assistant (F):

T: After I came to this school, I seldom talk (..) speak English.
              Before, when in Milpera, there were some friends from, not
              Australian – there was a chance, sometimes to speak
              English, but now, here, no.
F: Is that because there are so many Taiwanese students or ...
T: Yeah, and the Australian classmates won't actively talk to
              me, so I won't go to talk to them.

Neta, the Bosnian student from an earlier excerpt, made a similar comment about high school:

> We came to the school and like (.) I didn't have, I didn't have many friends, or most of the time I just stayed up here, up in ESL, because there was no people who spoke my language then. It was only me (...) So all these Australian people, they are nice but like, now they really won't, you know (...) talk to you. Now, when I know English, I was so confident in myself and everything. I can be with anyone I want. But then when I came, like, no one really didn't care, like you just (...) you're just by yourself. Most of the time I spent in ESL here. () It was really hard on you then.

In terms of identity and social language use, the key phrase here for me is, 'I can be with anyone I want.' Identities are about being, and being recognized by others while 'being.' As Neta describes it here, it was she who made the move to accommodate the Australian students; it was she who appropriated their Discourses. As things stand, the full burden of acquiring the discourse and sociocultural rules, that is, of acquiring audibility in English (Miller, 1999), or what Kelly Hall (1995) terms 'interactive resources,' falls on the migrant students themselves. It is they who must adjust to the social and linguistic conditions and practices present in schools. By implication, their identities as speakers of Vietnamese, Samoan, Tigrinia, Bosnian and Mandarin are not assigned value within schools.

Contrast this with the experience of a recent group of Bosnian Milpera students, who had all spent a number of years in Germany or Austria before coming to Australia under the Special Humanitarian program. After some Milpera students were invited to another school's 'multicultural celebration' it was discovered that Milpera had a considerable resource in its quasi-native German speakers. A group of 15 German-speaking former Yugoslav students was then invited back to the school to participate with the senior Anglo-Australian students of German. This resulted in a further reciprocal invitation from Milpera. This was a validation of the Milpera students' linguistic competence, their identities as fluent speakers of German, and their own sense of worth. It was socially and linguistically a valuable learning experience for both groups, a chance to juxtapose Discourses (the inviting school was an expensive girls' private school) and languages. Both groups of students are keen to continue the liaison. For this to occur more often, there must be in schools more recognition of the need to reinscribe linguistic minority students as competent in a variety of ways, and to place a positive value on these competences.

Critical Framing and Transformed Practice

I have suggested so far that, in a conception of language use that incorporates a knowledge of Discourses and sociocultural competences, a number of transformations are implicated. These include a move from SLA acquisition principles to understandings about Discourse acquisition, a questioning of the acquisition-learning binary, a view of classrooms as natural acquisition contexts, a valuing of diversity and alternative Discourses within the curriculum that should also incorporate Gee's concepts of situated meanings and cultural models, and finally the recognition that within Discourse, legitimization by the hearer has powerful consequences for the speaker. What further transformations might be necessary for institutional practices in schools to better represent sociocultural perspectives? In my view as ESL teacher and administrator, there are two moves that are essential, and seemingly contradictory – but contradictions are not new to social situations or schools. On the one hand, teachers need to problematize their own practices (for example what they accept as right and wrong in students' work) and, on the other hand, students' development of critical multiliteracies must include mastery of standardized forms of the Discourse of school English. That is, to move towards what Gee calls a critical framing of Discourses, both teachers and students need to shift their conceptions and practices. To begin to unravel this further, let's consider two texts, one by a student and one by a teacher.

Student Shifts ... Teacher Shifts

In the following text by Nora, a Chinese student from Shanghai, we read her journal entry in which she recounts 'a bad day' at her high school. Nora had been in Australia just one year when she wrote this piece, and had arrived with very little English. She spoke Mandarin, Shanghainese, and understood some Cantonese. She had spent six months at Milpera and was, at the time of the journal entry in a high school, attending both ESL and mainstream classes. Her use of the word 'foreigner' needs explanation, and can be understood from a previous interview interchange.

F: Do you get to talk with Australian kids?
N: Yeah, at mainstream, they are all foreigners, so I speak English to them.

The tables are endearingly turned in this quintessentially Chinese perspective, in which all those not from the middle kingdom, but specifically in this context Australians, were outsiders, or foreigners.

Student text

Here is the excerpt from Nora's journal (once again, double brackets are my insertions):

Oh! I very to be out of luck!

From this morning, when I caught the bus, I'm discovered my bus ticket was finished and I forgot to change the bus ticket, so I paid for that bus, and that driver was very ferocious. I don't like he, I don't want see he again.

In the first period I very carefully listen to the teacher.... Teacher let us do some work, I done very well (I think) A person she copied at me, when I readed it out, teacher said 'good.' She didn't said anything ((else)). But that people copied at me, she readed it out, My teacher Yelled: 'Excellent! That was excellent!' And said many good words of she. I'm very set ((sad/upset)). I thinks the teacher was very equitable, she just like foreigners, and every she always think the foreigners are getting better. Foreigners are best! For example: last time a foreigner written a science report, she copied my other classmate, when she gave this one to the teacher, somethings were wrong, but the teacher still mark she's right, and gave her full mark. My classmate got lower marks than that foreigner. so I think all the teachers are not equitable.

In this afternoon, a foreigner just asked me somethings about that video. When I answered her, teacher said 'Nora, shout up!' I very unhappy all the day.

Before the Tina told me some thing about the teachers likes the foreigners. I don't believe she, now I realize that. I just don't know why the teachers always likes fornigner, they always like white skin, gold hairs?

In world was cares never equitable, not equitable at the all. (17 June 97)

Even without a detailed text analysis of this journal entry, you will recognize immediately some features typical of narrative structure, as suggested by Labov (1972). These include the opening statement of the general theme, orientation to the events and description of the events themselves, and the inclusion of one or more complications, followed by a resolution of sorts and a coda. In her first line, Nora provides the abstract of her story, with 'Oh! I very to be out of luck!' This is Chinese word order, and it seems likely that, having forgotten the verb 'am,' she looked up the Chinese verb, which is always unconjugated, and found 'to be.' In the first three paragraphs Nora then describes four incidents that are instances of the bad luck theme. The fourth paragraph contains her moral evaluation of the instances described, in which she concludes teachers are guilty of discriminating against Asian students. The final line constitutes the coda to the narrative. In spite of its anomalous syntax, it conveys the clear message that the world is not a fair place. This is a structure very typical of Nora's entries in her journal. The final coda is a common feature in her writing, in which she seems to draw on a discourse of cultural aphorisms in order to provide philosophical commentary on what she is experiencing. A Chinese teacher also suggested to me that the concluding homily is a generic feature of many texts presented to primary students in Chinese schools. A story is followed by a moral, and Nora is therefore drawing on this cultural resource, or cultural model of narrative.

The text reveals a number of other features very typical of Nora's writing.

(1) There is evidence of her use of her electronic dictionary, possibly for the verb 'to be' in the first line, but certainly for vocabulary such as 'ferocious,' 'equitable' and 'realize.' The use of the term 'foreigners' speaks also to her sense of identity as Chinese, and her membership of the category that is not 'white skin, gold hairs.'

(2) Nora heightens the impact of her narrative by including reported speech three times on each occasion to convey the teacher's voice.

(3) Although there are numerous grammatical errors in the text, and certainly inconsistencies in the grammar and spelling, they do not impede meaning, apart perhaps from the word 'set' used for upset/ sad.

(4) There is a dramatic quality to the writing, enhanced by the conscious injection of Nora's emotional responses to the events she is describing.

Within the narrative, she develops an argument, to which there is a moral conclusion, namely that the world is not equitable. Who could argue with her?

As an English teacher for many years, I can see why a teacher might find this writing a little strange, but I have seen many texts written by native English speakers with far more grammatical anomalies, and fewer points of interest. Here, for me, is a text that makes 'deep sense' in quite literary ways (Gee, 1996: 103). Let's turn now to a teacher text.

Teacher text

The task described by the teacher below was a written draft of an oral presentation, in which students were to present the marketing strategy for an imaginary product, complete with visual aid. The speaker is in fact Nora's high school ESL teacher, who commentates on the writing of Nora and her Chinese friend Alicia.

When she showed me her script I thought oh my god where do I start? If I fix it and make it perfect it's no longer theirs, but we took the most glaringly obvious expressions, we talked about how to express various bits. Even though their language was, you know, what are they trying to say here? (...) they had all the right features of adverts. They understand what they're supposed to do, and some of the subtleties of what they're trying to produce and it's the language that's their biggest problem.

Although the task is basically an oral, current practice for students is that the text is first drafted in written form, and in full. This creates anomalies for all students in regard to the nature of spoken discourse as opposed to, say, an essay, but places particular pressure on ESL students, who must show mastery of standard grammatical forms in the written draft. The oral is in essence another written task, an uncomfortable fusion of oral and literate practice. In other words, the expository talk is a contrived situation in which students must sound like a book (Baker & Freebody, 1993; Gee, 1996). There was no acknowledgment that these girls were operating in their third language. In fact, while the teacher stated that the girls understood the generic features of advertisements ('they had all the right features of adverts'), their use of 'the language' (English) was constructed as 'their biggest problem.' The teacher's impulse was to take their idiosyncratic discourse, and to 'fix it and make it perfect.' Another teacher had described Nora's writing as 'all back to front and twisted – unmarkable stuff.'

What is there to say about these two texts in juxtaposition? To begin with, there are several points to make about teaching:

(1) Nora's text is of a type that is underused and undervalued in high school. In the Queensland English curriculum, the narrative has receded in importance to become merely one of a multitude of genres covered by the English syllabus. Journal writing inhabits an even more obscure place, yet clearly it offers students the opportunity to use their identities, to juxtapose and to experiment with Discourses, and to reflect on their metaknowledge of the learning process, and the social practices surrounding them. In the acquisition of the Discourses of school literacy, it deserves to be more widely used.

(2) Teachers need to see themselves as more than the gatekeepers or arbiters of 'the language,' by which they mean 'proper English,' as if there were only one language. The perspective of social languages highlights for teachers that there are social language users, using Discourses in context for a variety of social purposes, drawing on their identities and linguistic resources in diverse ways, not just correct or defective uses of language.

(3) It is worth noting that communicative effectiveness is only partially determined by grammaticality. It would be easy to construct a text like Nora's that is 100% grammatical in school English terms, but which lacked the literariness, colour, immediacy and emotion of Nora's journal entry. Furthermore, expectations of unreasonably high levels of grammatical accuracy from students who have been here, in Nora's case, for less than two years, defies what we know about the time needed by most students to acquire academic proficiency in another language (Cummins & Swain, 1986).

Having said that grammaticality needs to be put in perspective by teachers, for linguistic minority students the development of grammatical competence nevertheless needs to be constructed as a priority because it lies at the core of the ways these students are heard and read by dominant language users. And is a key element in the subordination and denigration of non-dominant varieties of English. If we acknowledge the ideological hierarchies inherent in Discourses, whether we call something 'situated practice' or 'communicative competence,' the legitimization principle is the same. We cannot view the competence of the speaker in isolation from the linguistic market, language in isolation from social practices, speaking in isolation from hearing. To underplay the need to 'get it right' in grammatical as well as Discourse terms is to fool ourselves and to dis-empower those acquiring the Discourses. I am not advocating a return to grammar-based methods, and I am aware of the tensions in this argument. However, there is no easy resolution for students or teachers in schools. Teachers need to broaden their understanding and acceptance of a wider range of social language uses, especially by those who are acquiring the dominant Discourses – and students need to continue to work on grammatical as well as sociocultural and Discourse competences. A critical framing of Discourses, and transformed practice depend on it.

Conclusion

Schools have a moral responsibility to provide conditions that challenge the marginalization of minority groups, particularly for those for whom the dominant language is not the first language (Auerbach, 1995). But enabling and empowering marginalized learners remains an ongoing challenge for teachers, administrators and schools. I have not tried in this chapter to provide easy answers, but to open up new ways of looking at some of the time-honoured dilemmas of teaching English as a second (or third or fourth) language. After 20 years in language classrooms at school and at university, after many years of reading and research, I am convinced there is no sure-fire winning formula, no magic recipe for teaching and learning language that will enfranchise all learners to dominant Discourses. What I do believe is that sociocultural understandings, including a knowledge of Discourses, identity theory, and an awareness of the political nature of social languages, all offer teachers and students a new and wonderful chance to transform their practices for the better. It does not entail ditching communicative approaches based on SLA pedagogical principles that work, but rather expanding the repertoires that are possible within these approaches. From the inevitable complexities raised here and elsewhere in this book, it is possible to distill particular insights and directions that seem desirable for teachers, students and schools using a sociocultural framing of language acquisition and use. A sociocultural view of language acquisition implies various practices. Here are some of them.

(1) *Institutional practices*:
  • that value the languages and cultures of linguistic minority students in ways that are both symbolic and tangible, reinscribing them as linguistically and socially competent;
  • that maximize the opportunities for students to use the target language and Discourses. Savignon (1991) is unequivocal in her claim that language learning results from participation in communicative events. To acquire the majority language, students must have a voice in classrooms and need to participate in as many social interactions as possible outside classrooms;
  • that recognize and acknowledge the powerful links between social language use and identity, and the ways in which Discourses are implicated in processes of discrimination and subordination;
  • that avoid labels such as ESL or NESB that may simultaneously enable and stigmatize learners (Thesen, 1997) .

(2) *A curriculum*:
  • that aims to develop multiliteracies using multiple text types, including spoken Discourse and technology as bases for language practice and development;
  • that reflects the social lives of the students, embedding language tasks within activities that connect students to their own linguistic and cultural backgrounds, and using their primary Discourses, identities and languages as resources for learning and teaching others;
  • that incorporates a focus on metaknowledge about language learning;

- that takes the students out into the community and brings the community into the school;
- that values a range of genres and Discourses, including the personal narratives and visual texts of the students;
- that acknowledges and teaches that ways of hearing and reading are part of discursive practice which can help or constrain second language development. An enlightened and enlightening goal would be for more teachers and students to hear 'with ESL ears.'

(3) *Pedagogical practices:*
- that combine the many fine aspects of communicative language teaching with a sociocultural framing of social language use;
- that do not privilege hegemonic Discourses over the diverse social languages present within classrooms;
- that provide the conditions for minority language students to speak and to be heard
- that enable students to develop sociocultural, Discourse and grammatical competences that will empower them to participate more fully in their education;
- that incorporate and value a multiplicity of texts and technologies;
- that can discriminate between authentic and fake beginners, so as to cater appropriately for both groups, and to avoid setting the linguistic high jump bar at a level that real beginners can never clear;
- that explicitly teach the generic features and structures of texts.

To become, as Gee proposes, real players of the Discourse game, Discourse theorists in their own right; to become skilled in critical multi-literacies minority language speakers need to acquire the many competences of an effective Dominant language user. They also need to be let into the game, and to be heard as emergent users of the Discourses (see Miller, 2000). Within the institution of school as a social field, the conditions of reception often work against a hearing for minority speakers. Schools must be aware that, where English-speaking students do not talk or even try to talk to linguistic minority students, discriminatory and racializing practices are implicated. It is a case where silence speaks volumes to the acceptance of segregated school communities, and the denial to one group of the right to participate fully in their education. While students cannot be forced to mix (Ryan, 1997), there are sound reasons for drawing to all students' attention the consequences of certain groups remaining socially and linguistically unheard and separate.

This is first because even small and apparently inconsequential interactions help trace how the world is socially constructed, and are an index to cultural understandings, that is, everyday interactions are part of the doing of social identity. These interactions are essential for the acquisition of discourse and sociocultural rules, and the building of language resources. This applies equally to students for whom English is a first language as it does to migrant students, but linguistic minority speakers need the chance to acquire the subset of dispositions used in English, which are needed to succeed in school. Second, access to a range of communicative and social roles is access to social power (van Dijk, 1996), its converse being equally true. The effective marginalization of linguistic minority students poses a risk to all members of the school community, which Cummins (1996) has suggested can be challenged only by the affirmation not of difference, but of diversity, in which the negotiation of identity is a key. This entails a shift in perception in relation to the identity of linguistic minority students. Instead of viewing students who have lived on two continents and speak three languages as having a language problem, such an affirmation of diversity reframes these students as competent and productive members of the school community, which can only benefit from their inclusion as members. Hearing and acknowledging these speakers opens up for them the possibilities of self-representation and ongoing Discourse and identity work in their new country. For the hearers, the focus on reception opens up a terrain where diversity may be heard as normal and valuable. Such a focus is vital in a broader, more heteroglossic approach to understanding language acquisition and use as social phenomena, and language itself as an instrument of action and power.

Notes

1. A recent form of this table appears in Miller (2003). This version is published with permission from Multilingual Matters.
2. In the transcripts of conversations, double brackets ((like these)) indicate the author's own comments, (.) (..) and (...) indicate pauses of varying lengths, and empty brackets () indicate unintelligible speech.

References

Auerbach, E. (1995) The politics of the ESL classroom: Issues of power in pedagogical choices. In J.W. Tollefson (ed.) *Power and Inequality in Language Education* (pp. 9–33). Cambridge: Cambridge University Press.
Bailey, K. (1990) The use of diary studies in teacher education programs. In J.C. Richards and D. Nunan (eds) *Second Language Teacher Education* (pp. 215–226). Cambridge: Cambridge University Press.
Baker, C. and Freebody, P. (1993) The crediting of literate competence in classroom talk. *Australian Journal of Language and Literacy* 16, 279–294.

Ballenger, C. (1997) Social identities, moral narratives, scientific argumentation: Science talk in a bilingual classroom. *Language and Education* 11 (1), 1–11.

Bourdieu, P. (1977) The economics of linguistic exchanges. *Social Science Information* 16, 645–668.

Bourdieu, P. (1991) *Language and Symbolic Power*. Oxford: Polity Press.

Bourdieu, P. (1993) *Sociology in Question*. London: Sage Publications.

Cummins, J. (1996) *Negotiating Identities: Education for Empowerment in a Diverse Society*. Ontario: California Association for Bilingual Education.

Cummins, J. and Swain, M. (1986) *Bilingualism in Education*. London: Longman.

Firth, A. and Wagner, J. (1997) On discourse, communication, and (some) fundamental concepts in SLA research. *Modern Language Journal* 81, 285–300.

Gee, J.P. (1996) *Social Linguistics and Literacies: Ideologies in Discourses* (2nd edn). London: Taylor & Francis.

Gumperz, J. and Hymes, D. (1986) *Directions in Sociolinguistics* (2nd edn). Oxford: Basil Blackwell.

Heath, S.B. (1983) *Ways with Words*. Cambridge: Cambridge University Press.

Heller, M. (1994) *Crosswords: Language, Education and Ethnicity in French Ontario*. Berlin: Mouton de Gruyter.

Hymes, D. (1996) *Ethnography, Linguistics, Narrative Inequality: Toward an Understanding of Voice*. London: Taylor and Francis.

Kelly Hall, J. (1995) (Re)creating our world with words: A sociohistorical perspective of face-to-face interaction. *Applied Linguistics* 16 (2), 206–232.

Labov, W. (1972) *Language in the Inner City*. Philadelphia: University of Pennsylvania Press.

Leung, C., Harris, R. and Rampton, B. (1997) The idealized native speaker, reified ethnicities, and classroom realities. *TESOL Quarterly* 31, 543–560.

Lightbown, P.M. and Spada, N. (1999) *How Languages are Learned* (rev. edn). Oxford: Oxford University Press.

Lippi-Green, R. (1997) *English With an Accent: Language, Ideology and Discrimination in the United States*. London: Routledge.

Long, M. (1983) Inside the 'black box': Methodological issues in classroom research on language learning. In H.W. Seliger and M. Long (eds) *Classroom Oriented Research in Second Language Acquisition* (pp. 3–35). Rowley, MA: Newbury House.

Luke, A. (1995–6) Text and discourse in education: An introduction to critical discourse analysis. In M. Apple (ed.) *Review of Research in Education* 21 (pp. 3–48). Washington: American Educational Research Association.

Luke, A. (1996) Genres of power? Literacy education and the production of capital. In R. Hasan and G. Williams (eds) *Literacy in Society* (pp. 308–37). London: Longman.

Miller, J. (1999) Becoming audible: Social identity and second language use. *Journal of Intercultural Studies* 20 (2), 149–165.

Miller, J. (2000) Language use, identity and social interaction: Migrant students in Australia. *Research on Language and Social Interaction* 33 (1), 69–11.

Miller, J. (2003) *ESL and Social Identity in Schools*. Clevedon: Multilingual Matters.

Norton, B. (1997) Language, identity and the ownership of English. *TESOL Quarterly* 31, 409–429.

Norton Peirce, B. (1995) Social identity, investment, and language learning. *TESOL Quarterly* 29, 9–32.

Norton, B. and Toohey, K. (2001) Changing perspectives on good language learners. *TESOL Quarterly* 35 (2), 307–322.

Nunan, D. (1992) *Research Methods in Language Learning*. Cambridge: Cambridge University Press.

Nunan, D. (1995) Closing the gap between learning and instruction. *TESOL Quarterly* 29, 133–158.

Pavlenko, A. (1998) Late bilingualism: Reconstruction of identity and 'discursive assimilation.' Paper presented at the 6th International Pragmatics Conference, Reims, France, July.

Rampton, B. (1987) Stylistic variability and not speaking 'normal' English. In R. Ellis (ed.) *Second Language Acquisition in Context* (pp. 47–58). Oxford: Pergamon.

Rampton, B. (1995) *Crossings*. London: Longman.

Ryan, J. (1997) Student communities in a culturally diverse school setting: Identity, representation and association. *Discourse: Studies in the Cultural Politics of Education* 18 (1), 37–53.

Savignon, S. (1991) Communicative language teaching: State of the art. *TESOL Quarterly* 25, 261–277.

Schiffrin, D. (1996) Narrative as self-portrait: Sociolinguistic constructions of identity. *Language in Society* 25, 167–203.

Sharkey, J. and Layzer, C. (2000) Whose definition of success? Identifying factors that affect English language learners' access to academic success and resources. *TESOL Quarterly* 34 (2), 352–368.

Spolsky, B. (1989) *Conditions for Second Language Learning*. Oxford: Oxford University Press.

Thesen, L. (1997) Voices, discourse, and transition: In search of new categories in EAP. *TESOL Quarterly* 31, 487–512.

Toohey, K. (1998) 'Breaking them up, taking them away': ESL students in Grade 1. *TESOL Quarterly* 32, 61–84.

Van Dijk, T. (1996) Discourse, access and power. In C. Caldas-Coulthard and M. Coulthard (eds) *Texts and Practices: Readings in Critical Discourse Analysis* (pp. 84–106). London: Routledge.

Wagner, J. (1996) Foreign language acquisition through interaction: A critical review of research on conversational adjustments. *Journal of Pragmatics* 26, 215–235.

Chapter 6

Tinker, Tailor, Teacher, Text: Using a Multiliteracies Approach to Remediate Reading

ALISON BEYNON

Introduction

In this chapter, I present a case study discussion of an alternative literacy pedagogy used to help non-reading adolescents 'break through' to literacy. The case study examines the pedagogy-in-process over a period of a year within a multilingual, multicultural classroom in a school for disadvantaged children in Johannesburg. The pedagogy used is based on the Multiliteracies approach initially designed and advocated by the New London Group (Cope & Kalantzis, 2000). In this study, I show how the Multiliteracies approach provides access to the learning of literacy skills for children who have found mainstream school literacy practices impenetrable. Multiliteracies refers to an extension of the idea of literacy beyond its traditional associations with the word, the text, the page. Rather, it advocates a multiplicity of channels for the making of meaning. These channels, or modalities, include the use of language in its spoken and written forms, sound, images, gestures and action. All forms of communication are multimodal (Kress, 2000; Kress & Van Leeuwen, 2001). A particular mode can dominate in a text, for example, written language is foregrounded in a piece of writing. However, in a performance piece, many modes are operating simultaneously or at different points in the performance: in this sense, a performance is a good example of a multimodal ensemble. A pedagogy based on the Multiliteracies framework would actively expand and vary its methodology to include these modalities in the acquisition and production of literacy.

The Multiliteracies approach opens up literacy pedagogy to a wider range of resources for learning and for teaching. I will argue that different modalities engage individual children differently in the learning process, and therefore differ in the effectiveness with which they deliver literacy skills at individual levels. My description will include observations of the shifting levels of motivation and emotions that accompany the use of different modalities with individual children. It will demonstrate how 'changing the channel' can bring a significant intensification in the way a child engages cognitively with learning material. By acknowledging diversity in learning modes and exploiting it, the New London Group's Multiliteracies pedagogy has an emancipatory purpose, providing opportunities for the democratizing of education in contexts where literacy is unequally acquired. I believe that it is precisely because of this perceived capacity for providing redress that the approach has been taken up at a variety of educational levels and contexts within Johannesburg (Newfield & Stein, 2001).

The Multiliteracies approach, informed in part by Gardner's (1993) theory of multiple intelligences, shows how children with strong verbal intelligence are privileged by traditional practices that favour verbal modalities. In contrast, children with strengths in other areas are deprived of the opportunity to learn through modalities that suit their particular and individual profile of intelligence. As their school histories proceed, their lack of success is interpreted as a personal deficit rather than as a pedagogic shortcoming. The concept of remediation is usually ensnared within this deficit model of literacy learning. Cole and Griffin (1986) expose the intransigence of the teaching profession when methods that have clearly failed to develop literacy and understanding of text are then used more intensively in school remedial programs. I would like to demonstrate how a Multiliteracies approach provides a range of modalities that teachers can exploit to design individual literacy pathways for individual children. There is a sense in which the word 'remediation' is then given new meaning: the revision or revisioning of literacy learning through the mediation of its expression across a range of modalities, in order to facilitate access to literacy for each individual learner. As I proceed, I will show that this creative selection and design process, in which the teacher, in response to the needs of learners, becomes the architect of customized learning programs, can be extended to include the learners' choice, design and execution of their own learning project. I will argue that the theoretical framework of Multiliteracies supports a more flexible approach to remediation, and allows more agency both for learner and teacher in the learning process.

A second strand I will develop is an observed outcome of using modalities to suit individual children. It is the pleasure and the intensity of engagement that seem to accompany communicative and literacy acts that are natural and comfortable for the individual. I will argue that the increase in engagement brings with it an increase in intellectual or cognitive function. Contrary to the long-held belief that cognition is a 'cool' affair, research from various quarters is now suggesting that desire, intensity of feeling, or Eros (hooks, 1994) fuel cognition, and 'cognition and affect are indissolubly linked in reading' (Mathewson, 1985). The importance of affect in the development of reading has been a central value in the whole language movement, and has been extensively explicated in the work of Rosenblatt (1978, 1994) on motivating reading. I draw on many of these values and principles in my own pedagogy. Perhaps the most significant of these in my work in remediation is the need for the learner to be active in the construction of meaning. However, the urgency of the problem facing adolescents who still do not read means that every strategy that can support literacy learning is crucial. The more technical aspects of a phonics-based approach also form a part of our remediation program. In line with the recent trend towards a balance between the more holistic approach of whole-language and the more technical approach of phonics-based methods, our remedial program has evolved a dynamic interweaving between the two.

The concept of extensively 'mediating' one's practice to accommodate the individual learner has been developed in the New London Group's notion of 'situated practice' in relation to their reconceptualization of meaning making as different forms of designing and redesigning (New London Group, 1996). This is the third strand that I will pull through the fabric of my argument. Situated practice eschews the blueprint, the universal model, in favour of the particular, the tailor-made. It takes into account the temporal and the local, the idiosyncrasies of the here and now, the personal pedagogic history of each child. To respond in this way, the teacher needs to 'tailor' the curriculum, fitting and refitting, continuously adjusting and adapting instruction, to meet the needs of the full range of difference in her class.

But the mediation of situated practice works outward towards the larger social context as well as inward towards the need of the individual. The concept includes the idea of mediating practice so that it is also congruent with the social context and culture of the learner. Learning is always situated within a sociocultural context, and mastery of skills comes about through membership in a community of learners immersed in practices that are relevant to their life world, or primary Discourses, as well as relevant to pedagogic goals, or secondary Discourses (Gee, 1996). Congruence between the Discourses of school and community confers easier access to literacy and knowledge, as framed by the curriculum. Where membership in a Discourse gives access to status or power, that Discourse becomes dominant.

During the apartheid era in South Africa, the education system was a primary axis for the conferring of power, privilege and knowledge to a minority group. The enormous gap thus created between the educationally privileged and the educationally disadvantaged has been very difficult to narrow, in spite of this being the focus of the current emancipatory programs in education. A major feature of post-apartheid educational restructuring has been the introduction of a civic-orientated, outcomes-based curriculum that has sought to align the discourse of schooling more closely with the cultures and values of the composite population of its classrooms (Department of Education, 2002). Yet old paradigms persist as teachers struggle to free themselves from transmission-style models of language teaching that support a dominant discourse to the exclusion of other values. Reading pedagogy in schools around Johannesburg has been characterized by 'the rigidity of the surrounding practices' that focus on class/individual reading aloud of 'official' texts. These are followed by comprehension exercises that assess knowledge of the text, rather than understanding and response (Granville, 1997; Mkhabela, 1999). Institutional power over both the content and the modes of expression used in school literacy processes serve the school and the teacher in terms of convenience and control. They do not necessarily serve the project of delivering literacy to all our children. In schooling patterns such as these, notions of language use are constrained and narrowed, defining learning within very narrow bands.

My own observations of literacy practices within historically disadvantaged schools in the Johannesburg area suggest that teachers mostly rely on methodologies from their own schooling years. The endless recycling of familiar but often unproductive methods has been aptly named 'procedural display' (Bloome, 1994). Such procedures, which retain legitimacy only because of their familiarity, are particularly dangerous with arrested readers, because they endlessly put off the day of reckoning till it is clear that the child or children in question can no longer function in the schooling system. Failure to attend to the problem then directly contributes to the high dropout rate of High School students, as well as to our endemically poor Matric results each year. An example of such 'procedural display' is the prototype for reading lessons in schools I have visited in Alexandra, a township in the middle of Johannesburg that is inhabited by low-income or unemployed families. Reading lessons at Middle School level, for instance, mostly take the form of individual children reading aloud in turn for a minute or two from a text, which is approached 'cold' with no prior discussion of the topic or story. Weak readers suffer humiliation as their incompetence is exposed and as they incur the irritation of both teacher and class. Alternatively, their incompetence is concealed with a mix of help from friends nearby and excessive prompting from the teacher. Some teachers collude in the systematic camouflage of weak readers by ignoring their presence, or always asking for volunteers to read. Needless to say, strong readers come forward and weak readers lie low. The result is that large numbers of learners proceed to High School, barely able to use their text-books. It is in the context of the urgent need for a reappraisal of literacy teaching in South Africa that I offer the following view of a literacy peda-gogy that radically accelerated the process of becoming literate for three adolescent 'authentic beginners' (Gee, 1999).

Continuities and Discontinuities

The methodology that I use, of 'situated practice' using a multiplicity of literacies, requires a very different use of space and a very different under-standing of the possibilities of the classroom.

(1) The movement and performance that is so crucial requires the class-room to double up as a studio-cum-theatre where there is room for the unexpected, the watcher who enters the scene, the performer who stands back to watch. Learners become actively involved in the process of cultural and communal production. They are not just users of the culture and language but also makers of culture.

(2) The use of a variety of modalities to represent meaning generates a 'workshop' feel to the classroom. The classroom hums with community 'business'.

(3) The agency that children begin to exercise depends upon the forum-like nature of such a classroom, inviting negotiation, sharing and interpreta-tion of meanings. Real-life dramas unfold, important decisions are taken, emotions are aroused, expressed, validated, contained. In such a space, new possibilities arise for the relationship between learner and learned.

Many of the individual histories that children bring of their encounters with literacy include histories of loss, shame and envy (Stein, 1998). Loss, anger, disappointment, anxiety, boredom and alienation are to my mind weightier obstacles in a child's journey into literacy than whether he has reversals of 'b' and 'd'. Yet there is a potential for very powerful learning entangled in these difficult emotions, and in the spectrum of more 'posi-tive' feelings that will emerge later in the year, such as excitement, pride, pleasure and joy. By the same token, there are deep impulses towards learning that are often marginalized in mainstream schools because they may seem culturally disjunctive with the norms of school discourse. Signif-icant learning can at times be messy, noisy, frustrating, explosive, or even maddeningly slow. What my pupils and I discover together in our theatre of possibility is that there are many 'ways in' to literacy, if one can only let go of some of its stereotypical forms.

Early Days: February 1999

To gain a sense of the process that emerging readers go through in this particular class, I need to take you back to the start of the scholastic year. In the first few weeks we 'do reading and writing' much like any other school, with paper, pen and text. I use this period to get a sense of where individuals are on the road and what they need. I also try to establish the classroom as a community of learners who will assist and encourage each other. We bring reading problems out from the wings to centre stage. Many non-readers feel guilty at not having learned the rules of the game after all this time. Usually no explanation has been given to them for their failure. They make their own deductions, which are usually self-deprecatory. So we talk about the fact that there are many paths to learning and that it is my responsibility as teacher to help them find a fit. I talk about our relationship: I am a tailor, working with them to measure, match and construct a garment for learning that is comfortable and their own. It is their responsibility to actively possess their garment, to wear it with conviction, to shape and reshape it if necessary, and then to begin the apprenticeship in the tailoring of their own literacy career.

We begin to form collaborative groups as a context for our literacy practices. These groups are mixed-ability groups of four or five students so that children with better-developed skills can assist those with less skill. For all the children in my class, collaborative work is a new experience. They have previously been taught in large amorphous classes, where it is a case of the survival of the quickest. Anonymity and loneliness in learning have been their constant companions. I find it very moving to witness the relief they feel at being part of a small intimate group in which they can each explain, copy, mimic, joke, demonstrate, compare and even correct one another's efforts. And sometimes compete! This sense of Ubuntu (the Zulu word for community spirit) takes shape slowly over the months of the one academic year I have in which to effect change.

In this particular year I have six Angolan children from three separate families, all at different levels of proficiency in English. One child as yet speaks no English. So it makes sense to cluster these children over two groups so that they can interpret for each other, but also benefit from hearing and speaking English and our other indigenous languages.

Literacy Project One

I use the oral retelling of story as a bridge into literacy work for varied reasons, particularly for the engagement that narrative can stimulate, but also for the many benefits to second language learners. These include the immersion in the sentence patterns of the target language it provides, the firm framework for practising correct language, the spur to fluency when the learner is responsible for delivering the narrative to a waiting audience. Storytelling also allows children to draw on multimodality in their perform-ance, through the use of gestures, sound effects, and audience interaction. The story we begin with is a traditional African fable about intelligence, from the Anansi collection. It tells how Anansi seems to be the man most 'gifted' with intelligence in his village until his growing arrogance persuades him to store it for safe keeping from envious robbers. His wife makes him a storage pot and the intelligence is squeezed in. He ties the pot to his chest and attempts to climb a tree to conceal it in the top branches. He of course makes little progress. Unbeknown to him, his son is watching, and suggests that he tie the pot on his back for easier ascent. In an epiphanic flash Anansi 'sees' the true nature of intelligence as an attitude, not a commodity. He throws the pot to the ground with a laugh. It shatters and the intelligence escapes to enter all.

This is a wonderful story to begin with, as its satire helps us as a group to explode the myths that intelligence is the prerogative of some, a gift, or a fixed entity that cannot be altered. This is vital for these learners, most of whom have come to believe that they are stupid. We realize that Anansi's son really looked carefully at what was before him. He saw the pot, the fat stomach of his father, the tree, the struggle. He saw in his imagination that it could be a different configuration. This is one way we can solve problems, by re-imagining other possible ways to do things. We talk about the mind and how it makes images. We use the word 'imagination'. I suggest that it is like a stage in the mind where anything is possible, where rearrangements of what exists can be made. Ideas about intelligence, identity, possibility and agency are being loosened up.

We end by acting out the story in small groups with whatever props are to hand or can be invented, i.e. imagined, and with a traditional drum to augment Anansi's boasting around town. In the art lesson, we have worked with the modes of image and language, having made a backdrop showing the landscape of the story, with a few bare words of the text attached, announcing the village, the forest and the tallest tree. A few of the children, unused to activity in the classroom, horse around for a while before attempting the task. Others make a valiant effort. One enterprising group conceives of the pot in this way: three children sit on their bottoms holding hands in a circle with their feet pressed together. They lean back and spin round in a circle 'on the potter's wheel' as Anansi's wife makes the pot. Another group gets the giggles as they stuff imaginary brain matter into their pot. One boy vigorously shakes his head over the pot and then tugs an obstinate piece of grey matter out of the recesses of his skull. Their amusement shows me that the satirical point of the story has been well made. At least two of the four groups are 'playing with the possible'.

I have rewritten the story at three levels. The first level is the barest of text, but already the words that will appear in the text are known, felt and enfolded into experience. My beginner readers will be assisted through peer encouragement and contextual support to manage words such as intelligence, village, jealous and tree. No banal and patronizing basal-ese for them. As children master their level they know that they are free to move up to the next level of text complexity as soon as they feel ready. The story is the same, only the detail, the vocabulary range and the syntax of the text differ.

Three first-level readers stand out for observation. Of these, two don't read at all, and one reads haltingly at Grade 2 level. Let's look at them more closely.

On the margins of literacy

Thami

Thami is already 12 years old, but reads at the level of a second grade child. He is slight in build and taut with contained anger. He hardly speaks and when he does so, it is the bare minimum, so as not to appear rude. He often resists doing tasks, and deflects attention away from his resistance by busily doing complex drawings. They are very accomplished drawings, full of detail, and the vigour that is missing in his interactions with others. The other children have selected to ignore his alienation and accept his silent presence alongside them without comment. Occasionally they do comment on his beautiful pictures.

Thami has reason to be angry. For the last six years, like thousands upon thousands of South African schoolchildren, he has been in classes so large that he has been barely known to his teacher, a name on a long list with an 'F' for 'failed' next to Reading and Writing. His reading difficulties have gone unattended to, till it has become clear that a rescue mission is required before he can go any further with education. Thami's mother has brought him to our school in the hope that we can make something happen. We must and we will. Perhaps his drawing will be the way in to literacy.

Nininho

For Nininho, who is 10, school is a great adventure in the joyful enterprise of living. He and his three sisters have been brought to Johannesburg to escape the war in Angola and to ensure that their education is not interrupted any further. Their home-language is Portuguese. English is relatively new to them, but they are acquiring it very quickly. Nininho's sisters had begun the process of learning to read, back in Angola, in spite of 'school in, school out' because of the war. But Nininho is 'the lazy one', according to his sisters.

Yet Nininho has a gift for learning. He is intensely alive, passionate and curious about the world around him. He can explain to you how dolphins communicate, and how elephants raise their ears before charging. He can act out a demonstration of how leopards 'stalk', 'sprint' and then 'pounce' with exquisite grace and mimetic skill. He loves to participate in our circle discussions, confidently sharing his reflections on friendship, or on learning, or on how to handle bullies. But he will not read! 'My father is going to beat Nini when he comes to visit next month', says his sister, Faema. 'Please Miss, you must teach him quickly, before my father comes'. Yes, indeed I must. But there is a mystery here which I must unravel first.

I watch for the signs that communicate individual need, and the individual path. I think the sign that Nini is giving me is that he needs things up close and personal. He needs text to be present to him in the way that his body is present. I think for Nininho the way in to literacy will be through a sensory mode, either bodily performance or visual or tactile representation.

Mpho

Mpho's problem is perhaps the most initially daunting in my class. For Mpho is 15 and can read and write only his name. He has been at school for at least seven years. In that time I should imagine that thousands of flashcards have been flashed at him, hundreds of phonics worksheets have passed on and off his desk and dozens and dozens of pencils have been sharpened and worn, sharpened and worn, in the ongoing enterprise called learning literacy. Yet he has gathered no skills in this area other than a dogged belief that the system is right; so he must be wrong, defective, stupid and unworthy. It is in cases like these that one becomes sharply aware of the hollowness of 'procedural display', and the urgent need in our schools for literacy methodologies that 'deliver' rather than withhold.

Mpho is a tall, heavy boy with a stoop, which I guess must come from trying not to stand out quite so obviously in the junior classes in which he has been retained. His face is mostly closed and expressionless, yet there is an air of resigned dignity about him. I think he must be relieved to find himself in this hybrid class with its mix of cultures, languages and ages. At least he is only one year older than the next oldest child. And at least there are others who also struggle with reading.

Does he dare to hope that this time round he can learn to crack the code? His face gives nothing away. Woodenly, he goes through the motions of the preliminary pen-and-paper literacy tasks we carry out. For Mpho, with as yet almost no knowledge of letters or sounds this means copying in perfect cursive the nearest words into the empty spaces. But I can see that there is no doubt in his mind that these procedures are 'the correct way to do things'. When we go on to use gesture to flesh out word meaning, or act out our understanding of a story, he is unconvinced, and doesn't participate. And when we embed text in the body of a drawing to support understanding, he becomes disgruntled. I can see he feels we are spoiling the pictures. That 'stuff' is not literacy as he understands it. Literacy is paper, pen, print. Even if it doesn't work for him. How will we make it work for him?

Mpho has learnt to collude in his own failure. Thami and Nininho provide me with the leverage of a resistance to the forms of literacy that they cannot use. This presses us forward in the search for a way in. But Mpho is so conditioned by the ideology of schooling that he will accept no help unless it comes in the form he can recognize as legitimate literacy practice. I will probably have to help him on these restricted terms, at least initially. A word pops into my head. Scaffolding. I will try meticulous inch-by-inch scaffolding.

Crossing the threshold

Each group performs the Anansi story with varying degrees of expressiveness, understanding, ingenuity and hilarity. Mpho chooses to sit out, and watches from the sidelines. I assure him that we are making certain that we know and understand all the words in the story text before trying to read it. He is not convinced that this could be worthwhile. So I give him the very simple version of the text to peruse while he is watching. We find and circle the words 'man', 'pot' and 'forest' because these begin with sounds he knows from his first name and surname. During the performances his eyes dart anxiously between the real story unfolding in action and the story captured on paper. He is an outsider to both worlds.

Thami, on the other hand, has put a foot over the threshold. He has made a major contribution to the painting of the backdrop. And dissatisfied with the starkness of the black koki text that I have added on the landscape, he meticulously rewrites it in forest-green, village-ochre and tall-tree-brown and sticks these over my text. The acting is another matter. He will not perform, but acts as a sort of set-dresser and props person for his group. This is the first time that I have seen him participate in a group activity. Silently, of course.

Nininho comes into his own. He is the most pompous and braggardly of Anansis, and prolongs the first scene with a sure sense of satire as he struts about the village boasting of his accomplishments. His audience is hugely entertained. He deftly threads bits and pieces of other stories he knows into the narrative: ' ... and you know I can make ladder to the moon, yes I can! Wife, bring me telescope. Today I am looking the moon.' In the pot-making episode, he extemporizes, ordering yet larger and larger pots, but always dissatisfied. It suddenly occurs to him to exploit the synonyms for big that we have recently learnt and he introduces these in increasing order of magnitude. 'No, it must be huge.' – 'Take it away, I want it enormous.' – 'But this is not gigantic for me.'

His struggle with the pot on trying to climb the tree is an inspired piece of mime, and his interaction with his son beautifully timed, convincing us all of Anansi's change of heart. In the denouement of the story he very sweetly hands each of the members of his audience a piece of the intelligence from the shattered pot: 'for you, and you, and you.' I am struck by the intensity with which he has felt his way into the narrative, the understanding he shows of its moral point and the power with which he has shared this with the other children. They are caught up in a somber, post-narrative silence. Then like the talented griot (storyteller) he is, he shifts the mood by approaching me and saying: 'I give a little bit for you, Miss.' We all burst out laughing.

In the days that follow, we move on to a more technical approach to complement our meaning-based approach. We render the story into the squiggles and curves and dots that make it text. The words we need for reading the story are learnt off flashcards, are printed in dough, are written in chalk on the paving and walked, are felt in our own form of braille, and are then finally BINGO'd in a word-matching game. These strategies are a form of 'back-to-basics', ensuring that learners are developing automaticity with the 'currency' of literacy. Yet they utilize a range of modalities that appeal to learners who have developed resistances to the academic associations of words on paper. There is a sensory, bodily pleasure in rolling the shapes of words. Such pleasure helps to change the learner's relationship with literacy. There is a heightened sense of the shape of words when they are three-dimensional that sharpens awareness of the details. With an increase in pleasure and awareness comes an increase in mastery.

I try to make the methods we use transparent to the children. For instance, in word-recognition skills we talk about taking a photo of the word that will stay in memory. To this end we play with the words we are learning, examine their innards through a magnifying glass, feel their contours, take them apart, put them together. But at the same time we examine their phonic features. Why is the soft 'j' sound in intelligent and jealous made in different ways? These procedures give the children a grip on the slippery slope of orthography. But they don't give them a reason to climb the mountain. It is the involvement with narrative that does that.

The fact that the words we are learning to read have already been encountered in the story gives them a 'potential energy'. They are part of a web of words that interweave to make up the narrative. So although the process in this phase is analytic rather than synthetic, the components of the text we are preparing to read have become highly charged for the children. They form part of the matrix of meaning that is the story, so they are learned with a sense of purpose. Assivaewe screws up her face as she reads the word 'jealous'. Ahmed reads the word 'shatters' with relish as he remembers the climax of the story.

Mpho, now that we are dealing with print on paper is very determined. But his concentration is jeopardized by the paralysis that grips him when facing text. He stares at the word on the flashcard:

'man'

He remembers there was some connection with his name. He turns to me and says 'Mpho'. I nod. It is difficult for him to separate the initial sound from the rest. It is an enormous feat of aural analysis. I notice he is breathing heavily. He tries 'mmm' and then the connection happens. 'man'. When we get to:

'forest'

the connection with the f in his surname breaks down for him. He is momentarily floored. Suddenly he gets up and walks quickly to the cupboard. I am taken by surprise. Mpho very seldom gives himself permission to initiate an action in the classroom. Now he takes the Anansi backdrop out of the cupboard and unrolls it. Then hesitating a little, he puts the flashcard under the word on the landscape and says 'forest'. I am amazed, as I had thought he had hardly looked at the scenery during the performances. He too, is amazed. He shuffles the flashcards as he has seen me do and begins to read them off again, with an almost zealous fervour as though he were afraid the words in his head might slip away from him. He can read seven words consistently. This means that he will be able to read at least a word or two from each of the sentences as we do our paired reading.

Before the paired reading, the class reads the story together. The preparation period has meant that at least in this micro-experience of reading, the children are fluent and read with feeling. They savour this experience. I can see residual actions passing through their limbs as they read, Anansi's swaggering shoulders here, a memory of the swirling pot there, the feet under the tables working away at the tree as Anansi struggles to climb. Thabo cannot resist recreating the birdcall he had used in his performance, as the class reads: 'He went to the forest.'

I believe that it is in their immersion in the active and lived experience of the story that children develop the capacity to carry the meaning over into the more abstract form of the text. The performance has been a multimodal, 'situated' experience. Through different forms of embodied engagement with meaning making, these children are beginning to enter the world of literacy. For some children, a particular modality has been preferred above others. For Thami, it is the visual. For Nininho, it is the gestural. Some children, like Thabo, have worked simultaneously at several modes, in an accomplished display of what Kress (1997) calls synaesthesia. But for each, there has been a repertoire of modalities to draw on, to transform and to use for utterance. The process of shifting from the preferred modality (e.g. acting or drawing) to a less familiar modality (e.g. reading) is not so daunting because meaning and engagement are in place. This shift is a creative act of transformation, or more precisely, transduction (Kress, 1997).

For some children, reading this story has been their first experience of reading fluently and with confidence. Most of the children manage most of the very restricted text. Not Nininho. Nininho is resting on his laurels and hardly looks at the page, but joins in joyfully, telling rather than reading the story. He seems oblivious of the pressing matter of his father's arrival! Mpho joins in here and there in his deep adolescent voice. He has meticulously underlined the words he knows and pounces on them a split second after they appear in the reading. There is a very powerful drive in him to learn that is at last beginning to find its channel. It is wonderful to watch. Thami follows silently, his lips moving imperceptibly as he processes the words. He doesn't waver from the text for a moment. I believe the theme of this story is important to him at a deep and abiding level.

Five months on: July

It is five months and many stories later. The class is becoming a community. The groups re-constitute themselves, as friendships shift and needs change. Thami has begun to participate in class discussions. Within his own group he still prefers to keep a low profile, but I notice that he is comfortable and contained within it and won't give up his place to a new boy. The details in his story illustrations show that he understands what he reads very well. Although he reads aloud rather mechanically, the sensitivity of expression is evident in his illustrations.

Nininho's father has come and gone. Nininho's reading is still minimal, so no doubt he had his 'beating'. He will take a stab at a word here and there but will not read sentences or extended text. As a result of the storytelling we do, his oral fluency is greatly developed considering that last year he knew almost no English. Of all the children in my class, he is the most in love with new and interesting words. He enjoys introducing them into his everyday speech. But his relationship with print on the page is still a very distant one. We need to find a strategy for bringing the spoken word and the printed word together in a way that will move him forward towards reading.

I have worked on various hunches, but unsuccessfully so far. Here is one dead-end I came up against. A month or two ago we were studying dolphins. This was a highlight for Nininho, who is fascinated with their ability to communicate at a distance. He was able to tell the class a stirring story he had seen on television about a boy who befriends a dolphin, and saves its life by warning it of danger. Years later the dolphin returns the favour when the boy falls from a trawler. Nininho told the story to the class with his usual panache, using words like 'communicate', 'rescue' and 'distance' with ease. I wrote the story out at a very accessible level and served it up to the class as our next story text. I titled it 'Nininho's Story' and put his copy on his desk, enticing him to try to read it. But he would have none of it. With a half apologetic, half wry smile he just said: 'No, Miss'.

Mpho walks tall and has become a 'character' in the class, with a bit of style in the way he does things. Gone is the grey spell that school had cast on him. He loves the mechanics of reading, the BINGO, the flashcard drill, the feel of the playdough in his hands as he rolls it out and prints out his spelling words for the week. He will even lower himself to do 'walking the chalk'. His commitment means that he manages to keep up with first level texts in each new story event. His dream is to move up to second level texts, and this is imminent. Because of the many years he stood at the door waiting, to be inside is especially sweet for him. But what will we do with Nininho?

Literacy Project Two

Our current story is from the San tradition and is part of a larger project we are doing on San hunter-gatherer communities still living in the Kalahari desert. We have learnt in detail what the daily routines of gathering consist of. We have acted out a hunt in silence, using the hand signals that designate the different animals in the bush. We have studied those animals and know their habits and how they can help us survive – particularly the extraordinary ostrich whose shells we will use in our art lesson for making decorative San-style beads. We have puzzled over the meanings of the rock art that is our heritage. We are ready to hear a tale by the fireside.

The story we begin with is a culture-hero story that tells how fire was brought to the San people. Later we will contrast this story with the Prometheus legend. The San story tells how in early times only Ostrich cooked his food, hiding his burning log under his wing when not in use. Mantis, the culture-hero, tricks Ostrich out of the log by enticing him high up into a plum tree, for a plum feast. Clumsy Ostrich has to lift his wings to balance, as he straddles the branch on long legs. The log falls out and Mantis is waiting to catch it and pass it on to the San. This is the story we are learning to retell from memory.

Language immersion through storytelling

A central feature of the approach we use is the evolution of storytelling into storyreading. I use the word evolution to stress its gradual quality. This is not just a textual follow-up to an oral experience of a story. It is a lingering within the story – a fully multimodal and saturated experiencing of it before venturing into its symbolic representation in text. The art of storytelling, which has been very much part of the culture of Southern African communities, opens up possibilities for the child to exploit the many modalities available to him, that are usually excised from pen and paper literacy. Storytelling calls on aural, gestural and performative modalities. It also creates a space for the infusion of meaning and feeling into the textual form. So much of our conventionalized literacy practice severs form from affect, and thereby renders text hollow and lifeless.

The task I have set for this story is that each child should be able to tell the story from memory to the rest of the class, using at least two modalities. Some children will tell the story with accompanying gesture. Some will use shadow puppets to tell the story with sound effects. Some will dance the story and sing it. To prepare for the memory aspect of the task, together we work out a graphic mnemonic device that acts as a summary and also as a visual trigger. We break down each sentence into a bare minimum of signs, pictures and words, almost like a rebus story, but even more condensed. For instance the opening sentence of the story is, 'Long ago, people did not cook their food'.

A great deal of discussion goes into the choice of a symbol. Ideas for showing 'long ago' range from an arrow going backwards to a clock face with an arrow. Several children point out that a clock is inappropriate in a San story. How would the San measure time? Some children think of showing a series of moons. The words people, cook and food can easily be suggested pictorially, but the possessive adjective their is problematic. Its meaning is less graphic. A few children realize that it is relational and suggest an arrow tying the word food to the stick figures. Some opt to just print the word 'their'. I stipulate that children may use any symbol they think makes sense in the context, as long as they can read it back to themselves. An important criterion is economy.

In this way we work our way through the story, rendering it into graphic representation. When all else fails, we just use the original word. 'What is the point of all this?' you may ask. The point of all this is to establish for the child the relationships between sign and meaning, and their embeddedness in social interaction. By actually constructing the sign system themselves, children get to see that sign systems are constructed within speech communities. It is the meaning that can be rendered from the sign that is foregrounded, rather than the form of the sign. The more formal and given quality of the alphabetic system they must learn is to some extent demystified, and it becomes easier for the learner to 'possess' the communication system she or he inherits.

The children are busy working out their rebus summaries. They are intrigued at the ease with which verbal meaning can be earthed in picture form. This will be a natural entry point for looking at the history of writing, hieroglyphics, pictograms and the alphabet. They discuss the variations they are coming up with and take pride in being different from each other. They compete with each other in the speed with which they can decode. They argue about how to represent the word 'only' in the second sentence. No one wants to take the easy way out and just use the word. It makes for an interesting investigation of what work words do. What actually is conveyed by the word 'only'? We try the word out in different contexts until it is clear that it both excludes and isolates. Do Zulu or Sotho or Portuguese have pointer words like this? We are building up a meta-awareness of how different languages achieve the same effects.

When the children finish, they begin reading off the story and committing it to memory. For some, the act of making the story concrete, turning the verbal into image has been virtually enough to store it in memory. For others some practice is needed. But they all enjoy this exercise immensely. I have made it clear that these devices are only a frame for the artful telling of a story. They are free to elaborate and add their own details, or tweak and twist the story if they wish, but knowing the basic frame gives confidence.

We talk about versions of a story and how stories shift and change, expand and contract from community to community, from storyteller to storyteller. I want them to feel that there is space for them to individualize the story, but they can only do this if they are thoroughly inside it. One could say they are learning to play the game, but also 'to call the game' (Gee, 1999). Later, as we progress towards the complexities of writing, we will rewrite the story with a different set of creatures and a different 'trick'. The goal is a sense of agency, the development of the individual voice.

The way in

When the children are ready, they choose the modalities they will use and begin practicing. Two of the girls choose to sing and dance their story. They begin making seed rattles for the occasion. Thami will try the shadow-puppets and Mpho will do a series of drawings to hold up for each section of the story. Nininho will tell his story in his favourite way, with gesture. I ask him if he doesn't want to try something new. We are all familiar with his talent for acting. But, I point out, others are taking risks with things they haven't done before. It would be lovely if he could surprise the class. He looks intrigued. 'Something new, Miss?' I nod. He walks back to his table, thoughtful. He opens his book where his story text and his graphic text face each other on a double page. He begins reading off his graphic text with ease. He, after all, had constructed or encoded it, and so the task of decoding is a breeze. Then he turns to the verbal text. Some of the words are known to him through spelling exercises, through his half-hearted attention with flashcard drill, through the text we embed in our pictures. But the sheer density of words on the page in wave after wave of arbitrary squiggles and strokes has always been overwhelming to Nininho. These signs he has not constructed or negotiated himself. I can see the resistance and the fear that grips him! But there is also desire ... desire to show that he too can take risks, and the desire to understand the connection between the two parallel but contrasting codes staring up at him from the double page.

He looks at the first sentence in the verbal text. The proximity of the icons that he so meticulously drew in the graphic text must be activating a process that he has not experienced before. He begins reading aloud, with his finger under each word. At first he reads haltingly, then with increasing confidence. Here and there he refers back to what is his home ground, the graphic text, looking for the image that is the root of the word. Here and there he makes an intelligent guess. But he keeps going. Once or twice he finds a word that he knows well and he savours it. Like the word plums. We had had much fun in our spelling with the word plum because if you add the final e that lengthens the vowel you get plumes, which you will find on the ostrich's tail. It became a class joke to say that you eat plumes, or that the ostrich has plums on his tail. Now Nininho with a giggle reads:

'He invited Ostrich to eat plumes off a plume tree.'

He knows that story from its inside. So he navigates his way through the maze of words all the way to the climax. He looks up at me to see if I have taken this in, that he is actually reading. I am transfixed. So are his ever-watchful sisters. Faema, the eldest, is standing over him grinning broadly. He gets to the end:

'Mantis ran off and cooked his food with the burning log. Then he gave it to us, the San people, so we can cook our food.'

Others have gathered around, and burst into applause. Faema hugs Nininho and rocks him, so proud and so relieved. Later, her skepticism will induce her to test him on individual words, to ensure that this is not just rote learning. He will be able to convince her that a substantial number of the words are now recognizable to him, even out of context. Meanwhile, Weza shouts, 'Nini is reading. Nini is reading!' Nininho disentangles himself from Faema's embrace and, beaming, begins again, with a power-ful confident voice:

'Long ago ...'

It is now October and we have begun to tell and write our own stories, both personal and imaginary. Nininho and his sisters have been whisked off rather abruptly to a boarding school in Angola. Thami has taken Faema's place as a catalyst for learning in his group. He uses his new reading skills to scout for text that intrigues him. He enjoys the connections that reading gives him. In fact he has become our hypertext man. If I mention lemurs, he knows where to find a picture, and will offer it up to the class in a jiffy. Mpho on the other hand enjoys being a regular guy who can read like everyone else.

Conclusion

In the above teacher narrative, I have tried to demonstrate how certain features of a Multiliteracies pedagogy can be applied to developing literacy skills in children who have found mainstream school literacy pedagogies impenetrable. Through its key concept of pedagogy as a multimodal, situ-ated practice within specific cultural and social contexts, Multiliteracies offers literacy and teachers a way forward for thinking about classrooms as multi-semiotic textual environments, in which all participants, together, engage in the designing of meanings. Such pedagogies make the process and practice of literacy learning more inclusive, while strengthening and enriching personhood and community. In the same way that a tailor designs a garment to 'fit' the particular shape and body of the wearer, so can a teacher, building on what she knows and understands about each child, design a curriculum that is tailored to 'fit' the needs of individual children. Children are then at liberty to reshape this garment, transforming it into their own through their own powers of agency, creativity and skill. Through the possibilities it offers of engaging with multiple literacies and cultural practices, Multiliteracies provides new entry points for revitalizing literacy pedagogy for those children who have been excluded, marginalized or silenced by the narrowness of literacy pedagogy in mainstream South African classrooms.

References

Bloome, D. (1994) Reading as a social process in middle school classes. In D. Graddol, J. Maybin and B. Stierer (eds) *Researching Language and Literature in Social Context*. Clevedon: Multilingual Matters.

Cole, M. and Griffin, P. (1986) A sociohistorical approach to remediation. In S. de Castell, A. Luke and K. Egan (eds) *Literacy, Society and Schooling: A Reader*. Cambridge: Cambridge University Press.

Cope, B. and Kalantzis, M. (eds) (2000) *Multiliteracies: Literacy Learning and the Design of Social Futures*. London: Routledge.

Department of Education (2002) *Revised National Curriculum Statement Grades R-9 (Schools): Policy Overview*. Pretoria: Department of Education.

Gardner, H.E. (1993) *Frames of Mind: The Theory of Multiple Intelligences*. New York, Basic Books.

Gee, J.P. (1996) *Social Linguistics and Literacies: Ideology in Discourses* (2nd edn). London: Taylor and Francis.

Gee, J.P. (1999) Learning language as a matter of learning social languages within Discourses. Paper presented at TESOL Conference, New York, March.

Granville, S. (1997) Transforming literacy practice: Surviving collisions and making connections. *Teacher Development* 1 (3): 465–479.

hooks, b. (1994) *Teaching to Transgress*. New York: Routledge.

Kress, G. (1997) *Before Writing: Rethinking the Paths to Literacy*. London: Routledge.

Kress, G. (2000) Multimodality. In B. Cope and M. Kalantzis (eds) *Multiliteracies: Literacy Learning and the Design of Social Futures*. London: Routledge.

Kress, G. and van Leeuwen, T. (2001) *Multimodal Discourse: The Modes and Media of Contemporary Communication*. London: Oxford University Press.

Mathewson, G. (1985) Models of attitude influence upon reading and learning to read. In R. Ruddell, M. Ruddell and H. Singer (eds) *Theoretical Models and Processes of Reading* (4th edn). Newark: International Reading Association.

Mkhabela, T. (1999) An investigation into foundation phase educators' attitudes: Classroom practice in relation to Curriculum 2005, Masters research report, University of the Witwatersrand, Johannesburg.

New London Group (1996) A pedagogy of multiliteracies: Designing social futures. *Harvard Educational Review* 66, 60–97.

Newfield, D., Stein, P. and the Wits Multiliteracies Group. (2001) Exploding the monolith: Multiliteracies in South Africa. In B. Cope and M. Kalantzis (eds) *Transformations in Language and Learning: Perspectives on Multiliteracies.* Australia: Common Ground Publishing.

Rosenblatt, L. (1978) *The Reader, the Text, the Poem.* Carbondale, IL: Southern Illinois University Press.

Rosenblatt, L. (1994) The transactional theory of reading and writing. In R. Ruddell, M. Ruddell and H. Singer (eds) *Theoretical Models and Processes of Reading* (4th edn). Newark: International Reading Association.

Stein, P. (1998) Reconfiguring the past and present: Performing literacy histories in a Johannesburg classroom. *TESOL Quarterly* 32 (3), 517–528.

Part 5

Implications of Sociocultural Perspectives for Language Teacher Education

Chapter 7

Language, Sociocultural Theory, and L2 Teacher Education: Examining the Technology of Subject Matter and the Architecture of Instruction

DONALD FREEMAN

'Technology', 'Architecture', and 'Re-sourcing'

Language has always been something that we know, we know how to use, and (perhaps) we know how to teach to others. But what if language isn't what we think it is? What if we literally don't know what we're talking about? In this chapter, I want to examine how defining language as a sociocultural practice destabilizes much of what we 'know' in second language teaching and in second language teacher education. In second language teaching, we generally think of language in terms of its structural properties rather than the identities it creates. In this familiar view, language is more about grammar than about individual or social capacity. So we pay more attention to the forms of language than to its uses (Larsen-Freeman, 2003). Approaching language as a sociocultural practice (Gee, 1996; Lantolf, 2000) challenges that thinking, however. It forces us to think about *who* – as contrasted with *what* – the particular language is, about *how* that language makes an identity, as contrasted with how the language itself is put together. This view challenges – or at least rearranges – how we think about what goes on in second language teaching, and it redefines the status quo in how we prepare people to be second language teachers. Thus I would argue that taking language from a sociocultural perspective can drive deep changes in the operating system of second language teacher education – and indeed teacher education more broadly – which will be very productive.

I want to build on the foundation of the preceding chapters, each of which examines the usefulness of working with language as a sociocultural practice. Notions of the complexity of language as a social resource are well explored, from the initial conceptual framework that Gee presents very cogently in Chapter 1, through the three accounts relating to teacher education: Stein's presentation of 're-sourcing' (Chapter 2), Willett and Miller's account of a transformative teacher education program (Chapter 3), and Hawkins' analysis of social apprenticeships in an on-line environment (Chapter 4). The two chapters that follow – Miller's chapter about language teaching and learning in a newcomers' center (Chapter 5) and Beynon's chapter about middle school remedial literacy (Chapter 6) – take the theory from how new teachers learn to how they use it in the language classroom. Left to be explored, then, is how classroom practice and teacher preparation fit together. What is it in our conventional approach to teacher education that is rocked so profoundly by this understanding that language creates who we are?

In this closing chapter, I examine how the theoretical framework, as presented in Chapter 1, and the different accounts of practice that follow it, can reshape thinking about second language teacher education more broadly. There is much that could be said; however, I will focus on what I see as the core argument for how the sociocultural view of language destabilizes – ultimately can reconstitute – teacher education in second languages and other subjects as well. This argument has three parts as I see it:

(1)   The relation between teacher education and the classroom, in any subject area, depends on a stable concept of *what* is being taught. I call this concept '*the technology of subject matter.*'

(2)   Teachers are taught – and more deeply they are socialized into – a 'packaging view' of content based on the equation that *content plus method equals teaching*. I refer to this equation as '*the architecture of instruction.*'

(3)   To reshape teacher education, we must re-examine these first two propositions about stability and packaging. We have to rethink how teaching creates content and the central role that language plays – no matter what the subject matter – in the process of creating content in the classroom. To talk about this process, I borrow Stein's image of '*re-sourcing content.*'

In outlining this argument, I want to argue that these three ideas – of technology, architecture and re-sourcing – have the capacity to recast how we think about, and indeed what we do in, second language classrooms and in the preparation of second language teachers.

Before moving on, let me say a word about the terms I am using. In this chapter, I use 'language teachers' (in the singular and in the plural) to refer to teachers who perceive themselves, and are perceived by others, as being primarily responsible for developing their students' adequate knowledge and use of English as a new language. Because these teachers may work in so-called '*English as a* ... "second," "additional," or "foreign" *language*' settings, it seems more parsimonious to refer to them in this way. Similarly, I use the term 'second language teacher education' to refer to the professional preparation and the continuing professional development of these teachers. Thus, for me, the terms 'teacher education' and 'teacher preparation' are largely interchangeable.

Finally, to add one further qualification: Since all teachers teach in and through language, arguably any teacher is to some degree a 'language teacher.' In fact, in this line of thinking, the difference between a math teacher and an ESL teacher may be a matter of foreground and background, in which the math teacher foregrounds the mathematics content and backgrounds the language used to convey it, while the ESL teacher would do the reverse. Thus, arguably, the discussions here will pertain to all teachers, as they are – and have the potential to be – language teachers.[1]

Challenging the 'Technology of Subject Matter'

More than many other forms of teacher preparation, second language teacher education has always been anchored in its content. We have defined what we do in second language teacher education in terms of the content we deliver. This approach is a logical and a comfortable one since it readily distinguishes what we do from our counterparts in mathematics or science or social studies, for example. Our work as second language teacher educators is to prepare teachers whose students need to learn and use second languages. In the content areas, their work is to prepare those who will teach students to learn and use mathematical or biological or historical knowledge and skills. Thus the stability of these enterprises depends on these discipline-based definitions of content. It is a stability that extends to (and is reinforced by) the structure of higher education, in which teachers are prepared, and to schools in which they teach.

However, this stability leads to a false sense of clarity: namely that content is key. Getting the content 'right' (whatever that means) will lead to effective student learning. Thus teachers are tested on their 'content knowledge.' Educational materials are refashioned to better 'introduce' content, and classroom assessment systems focus on students' 'mastery' of content. Taken together, I refer to this focus on content as 'technology of subject matter.' I use 'technology' here in the broad sense, that it enables things to get done in education in ways that are generally accepted as being efficient and effective. The question is: does this technology of subject matter truly fit the nature of the content as teachers teach it and as students learn it? Is it an accurate and faithful view of learning? Or is it a facilitating mirage? Clearly, there is no question that content matters in teaching and learning. The question here is: How do we define and understand content, particularly in language teaching?

Content has several dimensions, which is part of the difficulty. There is the content *(A)* that comes from the subject area or discipline. Let's take biology as an example. This first content *(A)* would be biology as the scientific field including biologists' knowledge-base, practices, ways of thinking or habits of mind.

There is the content *(B)* that is taught in the classroom. In this example, it would be 'high school biology' or perhaps 'middle school science', or 'Advanced Placement "AP" biology'.

And there is the content *(C)* that is conveyed in the act of teaching as in the 'second period biology class' last Tuesday in this example. So we can map these three contents in the biology example in the following way:

A *biology* $^{(content\ A)}$ teacher teaching *9th grade biology* $^{(content\ B)}$ to her *second period biology class* $^{(content\ C)}$.

(There is still a fourth content, the students' perception of biology; a point to which I will return later in the chapter.) Keeping these contents straight is the role of the technology of subject matter.

The problem is that any content – whether it is biology, math, or history – exists in language. Language is the form these contents assume in classrooms; it is the vessel, the vehicle, or the medium, depending on the image you choose, by which it is conveyed. Language is the medium through which these subjects, to use Caleb Gattegno's apt phrase, are 'put into circulation.' It is the Discourse, to use Gee's term, in which these contents exist. Language provides the key tool in the sociocultural practice of the discipline/subject-matter.

This contention – that language *is* content – is well documented in research, not only on the classroom talk and the participation structures in elementary classrooms (e.g. Cazden, 1998; Mehan, 1979; Gee, 1999) but also in different subjects including math and science (e.g. Lemke, 1988) and social studies (e.g. Short, 2002). In most classroom teaching, the point seems to be that language blurs the distinctions between the three levels of content outlined above and, in doing so, calls into question the stable notion of the technology of subject matter. In second language (L2) teaching, however, the stable image of content seems to hold – perhaps because, in these L2 classrooms, it is hard to see what besides language is being taught. In a biology class, for example, the medium and the content seem distinct – there is the biology and the language in which it is taught. In a second language classroom, language provides both the content (*what* is taught) and the medium (*how* it is taught). In second language teaching, the duality of language as content and medium ranges from situations in which content and medium are isomorphic (as, for example, in English taught in English to non-English-speaking students) to situations in which content and medium are schizophrenic (as, for example, in French taught primarily in English to non-French speaking students).

To unpack this relationship between the different dimensions of content in language teaching, Karen Johnson and I proposed a heuristic. We suggested a distinction between 'subject matter' and 'content' in language classrooms in which 'subject matter' would equate to content *(A)* above (e.g. biology/biologists' practices, etc.), while 'content' would equate to content *(B)* (e.g. high school biology). We defined the distinction as follows:

> ... we suggest that it may be useful to distinguish between content, which we define as the teachers' and students' *perceptions* of what is being taught in a lesson or course, and subject matter, which is the professional or disciplinary *perception*. (Freeman & Johnson, 1998: 410; italics added)

We went on to note that, 'content and subject matter are distinct yet convergent versions of the same phenomenon' (Freeman & Johnson, 1998: 410); they differ largely in who is doing the looking – as we noted in using the word 'perception'. This content/subject matter distinction, we argued, could provide a way to sort out these conceptual issues of content in which second language teaching and teacher education seemed to be mired. While teacher educators in many other disciplines were acknowledging the interconnection between the various levels, or instantiations, of content, in second language teacher education we seem mired in lumping language-as-content together with disciplinary knowledge of language, principally from applied linguistics.[2]

While the conceptual debates may be interesting, it is arguably more important to see if and how this heuristic of separating content and subject matter can be useful in understanding classrooms. I believe it can be, and so I turn here to an example from Jennifer Miller's chapter (Chapter 5), and her description of using student journals. Here Miller provides a very brief excerpt of an entry by Nora, a 'Chinese girl,' to illustrate how 'journaling' can provide access to students' perceptions of classroom learning. In the passage from her journal, Nora describes her experience of preparing for and giving a 'book talk', or an oral book report. Nora, the student, writes:

Today we had lecture about 'book talk.' I very worried. In front of the students and teachers I get very nervous. Before I stayed home recite from memory to my father. That's very fluent. But at critical moment I all forget. So I got C+. I very feel unwell. (Class diary, 29 November 96)

From what she writes, Nora seems to have prepared for the assignment by writing out her report, memorizing it, and then rehearsing it in front of her father. As the lesson unfolds, she is to give the oral report 'in front of the students and teachers'. She becomes quite understandably nervous and she freezes – 'at critical moment I all forget.' The content of this lesson is oral reporting on the books the students have read – the 'book talk'. However, Nora's perception of that content is framed by a self-reported perception of failure: 'So I got C+. I very feel unwell.'

To contrast the view of content in this instance, let us imagine that the assignment had been to 'write a book report.' Let's further imagine that in the lesson the teacher had students, Nora included, read each other's book reports, perhaps in groups; then maybe the teacher had them discuss what they had read and report on what they had learned to the whole class. Now admittedly we have no way of knowing what Nora's perception and experience might have been in such a lesson, but that is not the issue here. The point in this thought experiment is that this contrasting lesson imagines a very different content from the one that Nora describes in her journal entry. In this imagined lesson, the content is written text and group discussion with follow-up informal reporting. In Table 7.1, I try to capture the contrast in the two lessons. On the left is the actual lesson as reported in Nora's journal; by way of contrast, on the right is the lesson imagined in this thought experiment.

Table 7.1 How the same subject matter is instantiated as two different contents

How the same	Lesson from Nora's journal	Imagined contrasting lesson (thought experiment)
subject matter	Curricular concept of	'doing book reports'
is instantiated	*doing = talking*	*doing = writing*
as two different *contents*	Students give book talk/ oral book report in front of class	Students read written book reports to peers and then discuss.

As suggested in Table 7.1, the same curricular concept or subject matter ('doing book reports') can be instantiated in quite different ways in the classroom. Further, these different instantiations can lead to different student experiences, and ultimately probably to learning different things. It is important to underscore that this illustration is not about 'good' or 'bad' lessons or teaching; rather the contrast is meant to show how the 'same' subject matter ('doing book reports') becomes two very distinct 'contents' in these two lessons, one reported by Nora in her journal and the other imagined through the thought experiment.

Teaching children to 'do book reports' is a curricular concept that is part of the subject matter in most English-medium middle schools around the world. As I argued earlier, the general view of lesson planning and curriculum sees the subject matter, in this example doing book reports, as a 'what' that can be 'packaged' in different ways (or genres as Miller calls them). Table 7.1 illustrates two different ways of packaging the same curricular concept. In Nora's case, the concept becomes an oral book report or book talk, while in the imagined lesson it becomes a written text that is read and discussed by students. So there is one form of packaging as an *oral* book *talk* and another as a *written* book *report* and discussion. However, this is where the technology of subject matter comes in. The underlying assumption is that the subject matter is the same; it is stable and is simply being packaged differently. It is this principle of stability that undergirds the technology of subject matter.

Enter the fourth content touched on earlier: namely the students' expectations and experience. From the student's perception, the two forms of packaging can be quite different. Consider Figure 7.1 as a curriculum map of Nora's experience.

The map suggests that the teacher planned for and organized the class instruction according to the upper row (following the arrows left to right), while Nora, as she writes in her journal, prepared for the lower row (following the arrows right to left). As captured in the middle column

	Subject matter →	Enactment →	Content
Teacher's perception	Doing book reports →	Talk, oral report →	Students give oral reports
Student's perception	Giving a book report ←	Memorize written text ←	

Figure 7.1 Nora's experience – a curriculum map

(enactment) the written book report was something Nora knew and could manage ahead of time, but she felt ill prepared for the other (the oral book talk), in spite of her preparation. So in a sense both teacher and student thought they were participating in the same lesson, but it turns out that they had quite different perceptions. In this way, the heuristic of content/ subject matter can help to unpack the vying perceptions and experiences of the teacher and the student about what is being taught and learned.

Let us pull back to the more general question: What does this potential complexity of content mean for second language teaching? In this field, the technology of subject matter has been firmly established over time. Teaching languages through grammar translation depended on a stable defined view of subject matter that allowed translation from one language to the other. It was probably the post-Sputnik ascendancy of audio-lingualism in the 1960s that firmly established the technology of subject matter and the notion of language as structure in second/foreign language instruction. Through Audio-Lingual Method (ALM) patterns, the subject matter of grammar translation became stable classroom content. Since the 1960s, there have been various countervailing approaches and descriptions of language, including among others Wilkins' (1976) notional–functional syllabuses, the work on language genres (Hyon, 1996), systemic linguistics (Halliday, 1978), or multiliteracies (New London Group, 1996). Interest-ingly, each of these moves has attempted to make the connection between language as structure and its community of users more prominent in their analyses. Their aggregate success has been to make the notion of *who* is using the language and *how* it is being used more central in understanding *what* language is. However, as persuasive and useful as these alternatives are and have been, they have not dislodged the overall focus on language as structure and form – a focus that continues to drive classroom instruction, curricula and materials and most forms of assessment, as well as the prepa-ration of language teachers.

Language teaching is hardly alone in this tension between needing (or wanting) a stable image of subject matter (which I have called here a tech-nology of subject matter), and recognizing the community that uses that subject matter in the world at large (from whence the subject matter actu-ally comes). Similar patterns emerge in other subjects. In the teaching of first and second language writing, for example, 'process views' of writing as composing (e.g. Calkins, 1986) have chafed against conventional views of writing as mastering structural features of the language by moving from sentence to paragraph to the five-paragraph essay. Likewise, in mathe-matics instruction, views of mathematics as a thinking process have run counter to those of math as arithmetic manipulation (e.g. Lampert & Ball,

1998). In both these instances, the educational innovation has involved moving the subject matter closer to the way in which it seems to function in the world at large. This has involved fashioning an instructional version of the particular content from the subject matter as it is used by that user-community. So process writing aims to emulate writers as they compose. Its proponents argue that writers do not simply organize words into sentences, sentences into paragraphs, and paragraphs into extended prose; rather they write through a process of creation, refinement, and revision. Similarly, those who work with mathematics education argue that mathematical thinkers in the world don't just apply memorized tables and algorithms. These educators want classroom mathematics teaching to reflect use of mathematical habits of mind to think and solve problems: to 'mathematize' as do math users in the world.

These competing views of subject matter (writing as manipulating sentences vs. writing as composing; math as arithmetic vs. math as mathematizing; language as structure vs. language as it is used in and by communities) raise a basic tension in education. On the one hand, there is a dominant archetype that portrays a subject matter atomistically, as made up of discrete, structural pieces that translate easily into classroom content. In these examples, this would be subject matter as manipulating sentences, math as arithmetic, or language as structure. Countering this view are alternative approaches that frame subject matter in terms of the thought processes, uses, and identities it creates and defines in a particular community of users – be they writers (writing as composing), mathematicians (math as mathematizing), or language users (language as 'languaging,' to use Larsen-Freeman's term (Larsen-Freeman, 2003). These alternative user-process views translate into classroom contents that emphasize learning as discovery, interaction, and the creation, among learners, of new personae as competent practitioners.

So why has this archetype of stability so dominated our work in classroom teaching and teacher education? Why do we persist in presenting students in classrooms and teachers in teacher education programs with these images of content as stable form instead of presenting content as the fluidity of user processes (as in composing, mathematizing, or languaging)? There are many reasons evidently, well beyond the scope of this chapter. However three points are worth noting here.

(1) Language teaching is not alone in adhering to the archetype.
(2) The archetype is deeply embedded at the level of instruction, in the way classrooms operate, in the way curricula, materials, and assessments are designed and undertaken, and in what learners and their

teachers expect to do in teaching and learning (e.g. Sizer, 1992). At an institutional level, the archetype is equally embedded in the way that schools are organized and operate – from the practice of age-grading, for example, to the structure of academic departments in secondary schools, to practices and policies of passing vs. retaining students in grade, and so on (e.g. Tyack & Cuban, 1995).

(3) The archetype of stable subject matter is fundamentally social. Students are socialized into it from the start of schooling; 'good' students excel at it through tests; parents expect it of their children (from 'knowing the multiplication tables' to being able to 'sound out words'); and teachers know that it is their job.

To capture all of these dynamics in this archetypal view, I refer to them as the *'technology of subject matter.'*

Unpacking 'The Architecture of Instruction'

The various ways in which the technology of subject matter drives the preparation of teachers are key to its socializing power. They shape the expectations and practices of what individuals must learn in order to *be* teachers and to *do* teaching. In other words, they are at the heart of the Discourse of being a teacher. Perhaps the key assumption, one that translates widely into expectations and practices in teacher education, is what I referred to earlier as the 'packaging view' of teaching, namely that 'content plus method equals teaching.' In language teaching for example, a grammar point (the present perfect) will be 'packaged' in a classroom activity ('Ask your partner if s/he has ever seen an elephant') in order to practice and learn language. Because this image of packaging seems both unidirectional – as the teacher 'packages' the content for the students – and perhaps two dimensional, I have expanded this assumption to a spatial image: *'the architecture of instruction.'*

In the idea of architecture, I want to capture the notion that someone *designs* instruction, that the teacher *builds a representation* of the content from which the activity of teaching and learning operate. The complex interrelationship of content (what is taught in a classroom) and instruction (how it is taught) has been the focus of much thinking and research in education since the mid-1980s. As I said previously, part of the issue lies in the ways in which language, as a medium or vehicle, portrays or carries content. But part of it lies with teachers, how they understand the content themselves, and how they represent that content to students. These are all key building blocks in this architecture of instruction.

Teachers as Architects

If we think of teachers as the primary architects of instruction, several key ideas emerge. Certainly the 'site' of that architecture – the classroom, school, community, and participants – all shape what can be built. So too do the 'materials,' the students' prior knowledge and experience as well as the curricular materials and expectations, and the 'architectural program' or vision of what is to be built, as expressed explicitly by instructional standards, curricular goals and tacitly by community norms and expectations. Operating within these elements, however, is the teacher. She works both as mediator of these various expectations and demands and as a force in her own right: how she understands the subject matter, how she manages it as content, is central.

It is relatively recent to see teachers' perceptions and understanding as central to the classroom enterprise (Freeman, 1996). In focusing on teachers' understandings of what they are teaching, Shulman (1987) proposed the concept of 'pedagogical content knowledge,' suggesting that teachers act in the classroom from a blend of local, teaching knowledge (known as *pedagogical knowledge*) and disciplinary or *content* knowledge. The resulting *pedagogical content knowledge* (or PCK) framework outlined an integration of these two knowledge sources so that *how* and *what* are synthesized in classroom practice. Grossman describes the process as follows:

> Teachers must draw on both their knowledge of subject matter to select appropriate topics and their knowledge of students' prior knowledge and conceptions to formulate appropriate and provocative representations of the content to be learned. (Grossman, 1990: 8)

When it was first proposed, and as it has been worked with as a heuristic concept, PCK created a stark contrast with the prevailing view that teachers simply 'packaged' subject matter as content in teaching methods to convey it to learners. In PCK, the teacher was not just a translator of content into classroom activity, but someone whose thinking about and understanding of what she was teaching allowed for a range of learning possibilities (whether extensive or limited) on which she drew to create what happened for her students with that content. From the student perspective, this more complicated view of what is being taught has sometimes been referred to as 'subject-matter representation'. This research (e.g. Reynolds, 1989) asserts that how teachers '(re)present' subject matter as content in lessons shapes students' experiences and their conceptions of its broader importance, meaning, and implications.

All of which brings us back to Nora, and the illustration in which the two lessons – the book talk and the book report – (re)present the subject matter as two different contents (see Table 7.1 and Figure 7.1). In fact the Nora illustration highlights the dilemma of how we understand what is being taught: Is it stable material that can be 'packaged' in various ways? Or does the material differ according to circumstances in which it is presented and experienced in a particular classroom instance? I am arguing for the latter view, which I believe is amplified and supported by the sociocultural view of language. Simply put, the notion of a constant and stable subject matter is a fiction; stability is an artifact of an artificial 'third point' that allows us to compare two instances of teaching and learning by saying that they are lessons about the 'same' content. If teaching is understood as 'packaging' subject matter into activities, then the oral performance and written report are conceived as two potentially interchangeable (re)presentations of the same subject matter or curricular concept – 'doing a book report.'

There are at least two shortcomings with this line of thinking of teaching as 'packaging' subject matter into activities. Conceptually, the packaging view has to create or assume this third reference point that defines the subject matter. It is the third point – subject matter – that allows for the seemingly isomorphic relationship between the two contents, as in Figure 7.2 below.

In this example, if there were no curricular concept of a book report, or meta-language with which to label it, there would be no way of connecting the oral book talk with the written book report. This third reference point, the subject matter concept of doing book reports can be (re)presented in these two different forms. Empirically then, the packaging view runs into trouble when it is tested against students' experiences, as Nora's case illustrates so well. Although we have no data to confirm it because the contrast is in essence a thought experiment, one might well say that the oral

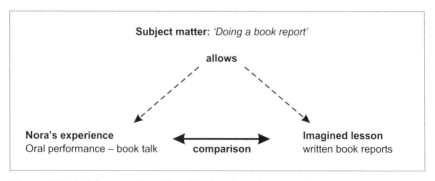

Figure 7.2 Subject matter: The third point of comparison

(book talk) and the written (book report) versions of the subject matter (doing book reports) are isomorphic, they are not in the student, Nora's, experience.

These arguments – of pedagogical content knowledge, subject matter (re)presentation, and of distinguishing subject matter and content – call into question the notion that there is a singular content in language teaching. Part of the challenge lies in the twin notions of singular meaning and stable language structure as the third point(s) of comparison that can drive teaching and curriculum in language classes. Gee's analysis in Chapter 1 addresses this same issue, when he argues straight out that there is no single, unitary English: 'Teaching and learning language and literacy is not about teaching and learning 'English', but teaching and learning specific social languages.' Gee's argument goes well beyond a geo-political view of language diversity, as in the notion of World Englishes (Kachru, 1990), as he notes, quite accurately, that social class, gender, ethnicity, as well as geo-political histories and settings all contribute to and shape the diversity of social languages.

Just as language is not singular, neither is meaning, as Gee points out: '... at the level of social languages, *there is no such thing as meaning*.' (Chapter 1, original emphasis) In the wonderful example of 'spilling the coffee' that – depending on the physical form of the coffee – could require either a mop or a broom to clean up, Gee points out that words do not have singular meanings. Rather, he contends that the general meanings we sense in words are a function of the cultural models that we associate with (and which are triggered by) them. So in these two moves, Gee undoes key assumptions about the nature of what is taught in the language classroom and the third point of comparison that provides much of the foundation for the architecture of instruction in second language teaching. There is no language; there are diverse social languages. And there is no meaning, but words that are situated entities triggering and referring to what Gee calls cultural 'story lines' or mental movies or theories shared by members of the club that uses them. These contentions of sociocultural theory take head-on the technology of subject matter and with it the architecture of instruction: that teachers can design and teach comparable lessons based on a stable, fictional third point.

This analysis is invaluable and much needed because it challenges the assumptions about the apparent singularity and stability of subject matter on which most classrooms (and indeed most teacher education) are based. To see language as social languages, as Discourses, challenges archetypes and it calls into question the technology of subject matter in language teaching and in other subjects. Then from a pedagogical point of view, we have constructed an architecture of instruction that depends in large measure on a stable subject matter that is 'English' and on pedagogies that teach students the meaning of words. Consider the notion of standardized curricula, for example. How can textbooks be produced for use in classrooms as different as Japan, Brazil, and Spain if there is no English as a singular subject matter? Or consider standardized testing programs: how can standard assessments of proficiency work if there are not stable meanings and uses of language against which students are judged?

In a curious double bind, these devices simultaneously work and do not work. They 'work' because the course book or the test carries some generalized meaning, parallel to the sense of 'coffee' in Gee's example, that is picked up and given meaning in and by a local community of users, a particular class or group of test takers. Thus 'coffee' becomes either coffee the liquid or coffee the powdered grounds depending on the circumstances. At the same time, one can argue that these standardized devices do not work because their designers can never know or predict with certainty how they will be interpreted in diverse settings, whether the 'coffee' will be liquid or grounds in a particular spill. This is both because of and in spite of what language is: a group of social understandings, positions, and identities that can be portrayed as a set of forms and structures. Like the particle and the wave in physics, language may be both of these things.

It is important to realize, however, that inventing stability for subject matter in language teaching is largely a technological undertaking that involves creating and sustaining a singular view of language and a stable view of meaning. Curricula, materials, testing, indeed the leveled structure of instruction, are all by-products of this central assumption that there is *an* English (or a French, or a Japanese, or a Xhosa). To a great extent, the educational enterprise is designed and built through an architecture of instruction that depends on this secure view of language as having a single grammar and a stable lexicon, both of which are used for diverse communicative purposes. But if, as Gee and sociocultural theorists argue, this singularity is a fiction, then the stability itself becomes a technological device, and the architecture of instruction is on shifting grounds.

Some Cracks in the Architecture of Instruction

Although we may not engage directly and fully with the implications, I think we recognize these fictions on a daily basis. We know, on some level, that when we think and act as if language were a stable system of meanings, we are ignoring the community of people who are using and constantly changing it. In fact, I would argue that the tension that is created between these fictions of stability and singularity and lived experience pushes innovation in everyday classroom practices. So we refashion, or update, teaching practices in an effort to reduce the tension in this unreal view of content. What is interesting then, is how these efforts introduce cracks in the architecture of instruction as we try to redesign in response to this tension.

To illustrate how these redesign efforts work to justify the archetype of stability even as they accommodate the experience of language as a socio-cultural practice, I turn to three examples from second language teaching. These are the concepts of communicative language teaching, of learning styles and learner training and autonomy, and of linguicism – or the assumption that one version of a language is somehow 'native' and there-fore superior to others. Each of these ideas constitutes what I would call efforts to redesign the architecture of instruction. Perhaps not coinciden-tally, these innovations developed during the decade of the 1990s, during which time the work of Wertsch (1998, 1991), Gee (1996), and other socio-cultural theorists was a growing influence on the field of second language teaching. Examined closely, each innovation reveals what I would call 'cracks' in an architecture of instruction in the second language classroom, an architecture that is based on the concept of a singular and stable subject matter and a view of the teaching that packages content in methods and materials to present it to learners.

Communicative language teaching (CLT)

In many ways, the broad-based movement in favor of communicative language teaching (CLT) (Richards & Rodgers, 1986), which gained wide-spread acceptance throughout the 1990s, revealed an evolving recognition of the socially-constructed nature of language. In CLT, there is an implicit orien-tation towards the user(s) of the language through an explicit emphasis on accomplishing purposes through language. In trying to accomplish their purposes with the language, learner-users seek, to paraphrase Gee's terms, to tailor the 'design' of the language to their 'identities' and the 'activities' in which they will engage in that language. When these notions of flexibility and use meet the technology of subject-matter stability, especially in pub-lished materials, something has to give. CLT accomplishes this 'give' by organizing content in a sort of hub-and-spoke design. Students encounter 'the basics of the language' as the hub, which they then elaborate for their 'own purposes' through the spokes of activities, specific lexicon, and register.

Figure 7.3 shows an example taken from a widely used CLT text *East-West Basics* (Graves & Rice, 1994). Here the hub language, the verb 'live' and

SPEAKING

1 Asking where someone lives: *Where do you live?*

Do you **live** around here?	Yes, I do.	Where do you **live?**	I **live**	in San Francisco.
	No, I don't.			on Pine Street.
	do not → **don't.**			near Chinatown.

1. *Pair work.* Complete the conversation and practice it.

A: <u>Do</u> you live around here?
B: No, I ____. I ____ in New York.
A: Really? Where in New York?
B: In Manhattan, near Washington Square. How about you?
Where ____ you ____?
A: I ____ in Texas.
B: Really? Where in Texas?
A: In Richardson. It's near Dallas.

**Now talk about where you live.
Use the questions in the box.**

> Do you live around here?
>
> Where do you live?
>
> Where in ____?

2. *Class activity.* Interview your classmates.
Find someone who lives near you.

28

Figure 7.3 An example of a CLT text
From Graves & Rice (1994: 27–28)

'yes/no questions', is introduced through a series of three so-called vertical dialogues. This design allows students to meet the language much as they would in a classic audio-lingual textbook. Thus the language, which is here portrayed as a series of interactions, is cast in terms of the notions of stability and singularity discussed earlier: this is what you say and how you say it in this situation. The activity that follows creates a different image of the content:

Now talk about where you live
Class activity: Interview your classmates.
Find someone who lives near you.

Here the language is organized more flexibly and loosely, asking students to work in pairs or groups to personalize the content by using it to talk about themselves, their locales, and their experiences. In this design, which is common in CLT materials, the dialogue provides the hub, while the activities that follow offer various spokes through which students appropriate the language for their own scaffolded uses.

What is striking in this hub/spoke approach is its ingenuity. Faced with the broader theoretical rationale that 'The target language is a vehicle for classroom communication, not just an object of study' and 'Students should be given an opportunity to express their ideas and opinions' (Larsen-Freeman, 1986: 128–129), materials and curricula could quite logically have become wholly localized. Each teacher might develop lessons for her own students. Materials would evolve in each class through its interactions. Yet such an approach would be unrealistic on many fronts, including the lack of resources and time available to most teachers to do so, the interests of schools and school systems to provide comparable education across classrooms, the concern of learners to connect what they are learning to the wider subject matter and the economics of materials design and publishing. So the question is how to maintain the stability of the content, which allows for technological efficiencies as I have argued earlier, while encouraging this new view of flexibility and localization? In CLT, with the hub of stable language and the spokes of classroom activity, both ends seem to have been achieved. In this way, the architecture of instruction can be maintained, even as more pluralistic views of language 'identity' and 'design' are encouraged.

Learner autonomy and learning styles

It is probably no coincidence that, while CLT promoted a view of language that gradually decoupled it from the strictly structural approach of audio-lingualism, a different view of learners was also evolving. In the same time period, in many circles, the passion for learner autonomy and learner training was also building, spearheaded by work on learning styles that offered a publicly available set of labels for various 'learning processes.' Thus, in many settings, students were formally taught how to derive learning strategies (Ellis & Sinclair, 1990) in order to use what they would do as learners in the world explicitly in instructional settings. Articulated primarily through work on learning styles (Oxford, 1990) and multiple intelligences (Gardner, 1983), this approach cast classroom learning as a potentially diagnostic activity to bring the learners' natural functions within the architecture of instruction. As Oxford (2001: 166) asserts, 'Learning strategies help learners become more autonomous. Autonomy requires conscious control over one's own learning process.'

In this move to learner autonomy, as based in learning styles and strategies, a new Discourse (in Gee's sense) was created around what learners do anyway, so that teachers and their students could talk about how they learn. This social language brought opportunities for diagnosis (e.g. 'I'm a visual learner ... I need to see things written'), as well as pedagogical imperatives (e.g. 'Good lessons will address multiple intelligences or all learning styles'). This Discourse brought with it an illusion of control. Now that learning could be disassembled, labeled, and manipulated, there was a technology for incorporating learners' needs and identities into the architecture of instruction.

On a procedural level during the same period, many institutions built 'Learning Centers' as pedagogical delivery mechanisms through which students could exercise their newfound autonomy as learners by pursuing structured learning in a quasi self-directed way. These Learning Centers initially included usually only tape recorders, but later, as technology progressed, video, CD-ROMs, and computers were added. It is interesting that embedded in many of these Learning Centers was the history of the activity of language learning. The new Learning Center often drew its actual hardware from the technology of the older audio-lingual Language Laboratory. The same physical set-up was used, but the definition of purpose and therefore of community of users changed. Thus language as content was reconceived, from patterns to be drilled and practiced in an ALM Language Lab, to a resource library of material to meet independently framed student-learner needs in a Self-access Learning Center.

This activity of managing learning created a professional community with a new social language; it is a group that has formed a new club. All of which amounts, it seems to me, to an exercise in what Stein in Chapter 2 calls 're-sourcing,' in this case, classroom learning. To further their autonomy in classrooms, students are asked to articulate their experiences as learners. Through the quasi-diagnostic use of this new Discourse, the process takes learning that has been invisible and unarticulated and re-creates 'learning' as a visible, stable, and predictable classroom phenomenon, as something that students and teacher can talk and write about, can document, and can harness. Oxford concludes:

> Learning strategies are teachable, and positive effects of strategy instruction emerged for proficiency in listening, speaking, reading and writing ... Strategy instruction led to greater strategy use and self-efficacy, anxiety reduction, and to increased motivation, strategy knowledge and positive attitudes.[3] (Oxford, 2001: 170)

In this Discourse and its associated tools, the architecture of instruction – the ways in which teaching goes on in classrooms and schools – overlays a generic veneer on the learning process, describing it in 'learning styles and strategies' to make it more amenable to regulation and control. By organizing this seemingly broad diversity of learning into a manageable form the stability of language as subject matter is extended and preserved. By creating 'autonomous' learners in classrooms through attention to 'learning styles' and 'multiple intelligences' and the like, to put it too simply, the learner becomes the 'problem' and diagnosis and labeling offer the solution. In this redesign of the architecture of instruction, the unpredictability of individual and social learning is tamed, the stability of the subject matter is maintained and even strengthened.

Linguicism

In some ways, something similar is happening with the concept of 'linguicism.' As argued by Phillipson (1992) and others, 'linguicism' is the assumption that one language, or version of it, dominates others. It is evident in such social facts as privileging 'native speakers' as better users or teachers of the language. There is little doubt in my mind that arguments about linguicism have heightened awareness of the privilege that can accompany being a mother-tongue speaker of English, for example. Like the parallel concepts of 'whiteness' and 'heterosexism', among others, linguicism illuminates the power of the 'default category', of what is perceived as usual or customary. Thus it can engage those in dominant positions, who may be social members of the labeled group, to acknowledge the power and privilege that may seem 'normal' accompaniments of their social roles and identities.

The strength of the concept of linguicism notwithstanding, there are some conceptual flaws. Canagarajah (1999) has argued that the extreme of the position that a language can dominate its users tends to overlook or downplay the realities of personal agency, namely that people use languages for their own purposes. Gee makes a similar case, but on the theoretical level, in his argument that there is no one English because all language is 'social languages.' A risk in asserting linguicism is that one is inadvertently supporting just that singular view of English that one seeks to dismantle. By arguing that one form of language can be hegemonic, one is actually according a singular social power to that form. As Canagarajah argues, personal agency can, under some circumstances, subvert the apparent and actual power of the dominant code. To put it perhaps too simply, people use language; language doesn't use people.

So in linguicism, there seems to be a perverse process by which the critique itself may well be appropriate; but those who make it risk asserting the very stability of language that needs to be questioned. In this case, given the pervasiveness of these default categories such as 'English' or 'native speaker,' like heterosexism or whiteness for example, the importance of the critique may outweigh the risk. The value of re-centering our thinking may well overwhelm the logical inconsistency that by recognizing and naming these categories we are according them the very power we may want to question.

The Big Paradox: The Social Benefits of Accountability vs. the Ethical Problems of Access

These cracks in the architecture of instruction introduce a broader paradox in the sociocultural view of language, namely that, while language is constantly evolving in and through social interaction and is therefore not fixed, there seem to be more (and less) dominant, canonical forms of language. These are what Gee refers to as 'cultural models.' Education generally, and the architecture of classroom instruction in particular, foregrounds this paradox. On the one hand, classrooms are clearly social environments: what they teach, the content, and how they function, participation and instruction, are hardly neutral. This is particularly the case when the content is language, which can pass so fluidly and contagiously from the world at large in and out of the classroom. This dynamic suggests – and even reinforces – the notion of personal agency that Canagarajah (1999) writes about: namely that learners, as students in classrooms, can and do subvert language (and other forms) of content to their own needs and identities. In a social world that values individual responsibility and accountability, this appears to be the 'good news': *Can't students manage the benefits of language learning to meet their own ends? And if they don't, can't their failure to do so be ascribed to their own shortcomings?*

On the other hand, there is widespread evidence (e.g. Heath, 1983; also Canagarajah, 1999) that, among forms of language-as-content, some are valued more – in a social and political sense – than others. Whether we refer to them as codes, genres, or Discourses, it is quite evident that language-as-content is not simply a set of neutral words to be learned and used according to individual purposes. Depending on where one locates the problem, classrooms, instruction, and even communities are all seen as creating different levels of access and expertise from these 'valued' and 'valuable' forms of language-as-content (e.g. Delpit, 1995). Such discrepancies in access and learning expertise can promote and sustain social inequalities. This is a point of criticism in Gee's disturbing example of the Korean graduate student: the university failed, in and through the practices of various individual professors, to provide the student with explicit access to the social languages of English through which she could accomplish her intent to write an acceptable dissertation and graduate with a doctorate. In an ethical world that values social justice, this is the 'bad news'. *Don't those with access to language power bear some ethical responsibility to recognize what they know how to do and to offer others access to it?*

These are the plate tectonics of social languages that pit the malleability of human nature and learning against the powerful dynamics of dominant cultural models. I question the bleak framing of this paradox, however, especially in light of this focus on social languages examined in this book. In so far as the paradox is cast (as I have done just above) as a contest between individual agency and social organization, its scale seems so large and ungainly as to be basically unmanageable. I wonder whether, in fact, we need more particular analytical tools to unpack this contradiction. It seems to me that real issues, in an analytic and indeed an operational sense, may well lie in the constructs of subject matter and content, and of instruction. I have referred to them in metaphorical terms – as the *technology* of subject matter and the *architecture* of instruction – in part to open up their potential uses as tools. As such, they are meant, hopefully to bring the stuff of social languages into focus.

To summarize my argument thus far: I have examined how what I called the architecture of instruction maintains and supports the technology of subject matter. In the CLT example, which focuses on teaching, language is cast as singular and stable, although it is amenable to multiple purposes in the CLT hub–spoke design of instruction. I have further suggested that concepts such as learner autonomy and linguicism may actually serve this same stability of language as subject matter even as they critique it. In focusing on learning as the variable, as the plastic concept, the concept of learner autonomy advances the notion of a singular language to which learners gain access through multiple learning styles that they can 'learn' to regulate and control. In focusing on language as content, linguicism argues simultaneously both for and against the notion of a hegemonic form of language that can encourage a perception that stability and singularity dominate the people who use it.

So how does all this relate to the preparation of second language teachers? The bridge, it seems to me, lies in what I have been calling 'the architecture of instruction' or, to co-opt a phrase, 'the way it's supposed to be' in the language classroom. This is what Willett and Miller call, in Chapter 3, the dominant 'D' Discourse of education: the constellation of identity, activity, meanings, cultural models and language design that are the medium of teaching and learning in schools. As is shown in various chapters in this book, in educational settings there are plural Discourses working even as there is a singular Discourse linked to power and privilege.

The post-apartheid South Africa situation provides an instructive example. Faced with massive needs and disparities in the national educational system, and the imperative to extend educational equity to all its people, the first Mandela government made many changes in education. Among these was the dismantling of racially-separate schools and education authorities, redefining the national curriculum, racially integrating the teaching force at local, provincial and national levels. All of this work represented the melding of different, formerly separate and profoundly unequal, Discourses in the realm of education. One visible aspect of education that the national government held constant, however, was the pre-1994 national school-leaving examination, known as 'the Matric.' This Discourse – knowing what 'doing matric' is – is an emblem of privilege that was shared in the old and the new South Africa. Maintaining this talisman was – and is – a controversial step. Yet, however one may argue the particulars, the Matric functions to sustain a 'standard' and a value that creates some historical and social continuity in education from pre- to post-apartheid society. To do away with the Matric might recognize its inadequacy in capturing the multiple Discourses of the new society; to maintain it acknowledged the previous (and perhaps continuing) power of the dominant Discourse. This dilemma illustrates the constant tension between shared and specific Discourses.

The architecture of instruction is based on Discourses, 'or rules of the game' as Gee has called them. One function of the dominant Discourse in most educational settings is to create the notion – or cultural model – of a subject matter. In the case of TESOL, like other language teaching, these cultural models support subject matter – English or language – as singular.

Singularity is the foundation of stability; that stability, across curricula, materials, assessment, and teacher preparation, is critical in order for teaching to 'work'. Just as the now and former 'Matric' created a somewhat stable horizon in the rapidly-changing world of post-1994 South African education, so too, in a much broader sense, does the singular notion of language in language teaching create stability in second language classrooms. But it is stability with a price. From this view flow many of the practices that are taken as normative, as 'usual and customary' in language teaching, practices that teacher educators, like those writing in this book, argue we must critique and change in order to realize broader and more equitable instruction, what they call 'a social justice agenda' in and through education.

Teacher Education as Re-sourcing: Outside in and Inside out

This leads to the third and last issue in this analysis: Teacher education as re-sourcing, to borrow Stein's phrase from Chapter 2. If this 'thing' that we call English is not actually a singular subject matter, if it is not a stable entity around which to organize materials, curricula, testing and the like, then clearly how we prepare people to teach it changes in definition. If to be taught, this content is not simply packaged in a method or activity, but exists in a dynamic of representation that includes how teachers see what they do and how their students perceive what they are learning (as with Nora and her book report), then how we prepare teachers must also change in practice. The question is, how does it need to change? How might we define these new directions?

Because the nature of the subject matter is not what educational Discourses have defined it to be, because the ways in which that subject matter – social languages – works in the world at large are different from what students and teachers are used to, the work of teacher education also needs to change. For example, in this social languages view, literacy – as we see in the accounts of Stein (Chapter 2), Miller (Chapter 5), and Beynon (Chapter 6) – is not a neutral technical undertaking of learning to decode written texts. Rather, to quote from Stein in Chapter 2, 'What literacy is, how people acquire it (or don't), what it does and its relationship to language power, and access, is critical.' Similarly, on a broader level, as Willett and Miller argue in Chapter 3, preparing to be second language teachers is not simply a matter of learning knowledge and skills, it is also about becoming 'educators who contribute deliberately and critically to the Discourses and practices that constitute schools and society.' In these views, the challenge to change the status quo is unmistakable. Interestingly, they frame the challenge to teacher education in two ways; it must change both from the inside out and from the outside in.

Changing from the outside in ...

Changing from the *outside in* responds to the imperatives of access and equity in the world that I discussed earlier. If access to social language is not only a matter of individual initiative and agency, if representational resources, in the broadest sense from Discourse to vocabulary and register, are unequally distributed in communities and societies, then what is the role of language teacher education in reorganizing equitable access? In their chapters, Stein, Hawkins, and Willett and Miller each write about changing from the outside in: how they prepare teachers because of the situation and imperatives that they understand from the wider societies and social orders in which they live. Through this sense of responsibility, they and their colleagues are re-positioning their work as teacher educators. They are shifting from what Schon (1983) referred to as the 'technical rational' view of teaching to a moral one based on social justice.

While it is admirable, there are, however, risks in moving to a values-based stance in teacher education. What if the values are not ones that we subscribe to? Personally I support this outside-in change; it is one that we have grappled with, and continue to grapple with, in my own department at the School for International Training. I believe in it, as no doubt will many readers. Stepping back, however, one can argue that there is a certain risk involved in this outside-in change that shifts teacher education from the technical-rational to a values-based stance. While we may applaud the moral stance of social justice that underlies the teacher education described in these chapters and practiced in many teacher preparation programs, we can equally envision a stance whose values we might not support. To draw a very loose parallel: while I think it is good that my children's high school biology classes examine the values and attitudes that undergird the science they are learning, I would be personally troubled if they were to adopt the values and attitudes of creationism in their biology class. So an argument can be leveled that this re-positioning of teacher education to a values-base is fine so long as we like the directions it is heading; it would not be so good if we didn't.

From the inside out ...

There is a fallacy in this argument that we need 'better values' to undergird teacher education, however, a fallacy that directs us to the need to change teacher education from the *inside out*. It begins with the realization that the technical-rational view of teaching and its notion of a singular and stable subject matter are not values-neutral. This view of teaching as packaging stable chunks of language for students to learn how to use to their own ends is neither true nor benign simply because it is – and has been – the status quo within our institutions and teacher education programs. In fact, the technical-rational view of teaching is as values-based as are these transformative proposals.

But the inside-out argument for change in teacher education does not pursue this line. Instead, it points to the central flaw in the technical-rational view (a flaw that is – not coincidentally – also its central value), namely the assumption that subject matter is neutral, constant, stable, and therefore accessible to all through good instruction. In assuming that all students and teachers have equal access to cultural models (or cultural capital), and that representational resources are broadly available and equitably distributed throughout our societies, the technical-rational view advances the position (and value) that success is based on aptitude and effort, rather than on access. If language students fail, if they do not learn to read, to use English for their own ends, the shortcoming must lie either in the students as learners or in the teachers and the way they provide instruction. By holding the subject matter constant, the equation shifts responsibility and accountability to the actors: the teacher and her students.

In their rich accounts of middle school classrooms in Australia and South Africa, Jennifer Miller and Alison Beynon reveal the real flaws in this line of reasoning. As their work demonstrates, by *not* challenging this fallacy, we are arguably complicit in it. This is the *inside-out* argument. The architecture of instruction that flows from, reproduces, and is reproduced by the technical-rational view of teaching that is widely promulgated in our teacher education programs is a major part of the problem. This architecture, and the classrooms and schools that make it up, promotes a view of language that is not accurate, that is not accessible to many students, and that does not lead many of them to the control and use of language as they need and are seeking to do. The Korean graduate student in Gee's chapter is a case in point.

This realization alone seems to me enough to argue that teacher education programs need to change from the inside out, even if we do not accept the moral social justice arguments to re-position them from the outside in. In view of the fact that languages are socially positioned and constructed, teacher education programs must work in ways that are compatible – both theoretically and practically – with that reality. As they currently function, most teacher education programs are mis-representing – or mis-teaching if you will – what language (as subject matter) is all about. Working within, and not questioning, this technical-rational view of teaching as teacher educators, we are selling teacher-learners a bill of goods. They therefore become complicit in an architecture of instruction that promotes and sustains that damaging fiction.

Closing

All of this is demanding stuff. It is also fundamentally necessary to the on-going viability of our enterprise as teachers and as teacher educators, particularly in second language teaching. It is a mistake to think that the technical-rational view of teaching, and its allied architecture of instruction and technology of subject matter, will somehow yield easily. In fact, here in the United States, with the increasing political rhetoric of accountability (for teachers through teacher testing and for students through state curricular frameworks and testing programs) the technicist view seems ascendant. The external structures of subject matter and instruction are easy to see and to assess. Which is where the inside-out argument comes in. It may be more straightforward to change the values and practices in language teacher education by recognizing and exposing the fictions of language as a stable subject matter, and language teaching as packaging content, on which most of our current work rests. This process amounts to what Stein calls 're-sourcing' the content. The material is still there; it is familiar and known, but how it is used changes.

The great French structural anthropologist, Claude Levi-Strauss (1966) wrote about theory building and myth making as forms of 'bricolage', an activity that roughly translates into 'cobbling together odds and ends' to make some needed or new object. The dynamic of bricolage lies in using what you find in your surroundings to create an explanation – be it a myth or a theory – that helps make sense out of things that need to be explained. Re-sourcing seems to me a lot like bricolage. We re-use what we have to do the new work that needs doing; and this has at least two advantages. First, it makes the task immediate and feasible. If, in teacher education, we are to continue present practices but to think about and do them differently, that strategy may be more accessible to us than inventing new ways of doing things. So, for example, student teaching will continue to exist in teacher preparation; but it may be approached differently.

Second, by re-sourcing existing practices, we are re-valuing them or giving them new and different meanings. By absorbing the former ways of doing things into the new ones, we can in some senses neutralize the old. Education, like many social practices, is full of pendulums that have swung from one old practice to a new one and back again. By re-sourcing the known and commonplace, we absorb the old so it is no longer an option as it was before, as with the illustration of the new South African Matric. In teacher preparation for example, when we shift our way of thinking and talking about the role of the classroom teacher vis-à-vis the student teacher from 'cooperating teacher' to 'mentor', we initiate a re-sourcing of the role and the know-how of that individual as a participant in the activity of student teaching. Changing words does not itself change practices, and I am not naive enough to argue that new labels alone create new ways of doing things. But, as George Orwell pointed out in Newspeak, language can and does co-opt and reform (for better and for worse); so, as we rename common practices and roles in teacher education, we re-source and thus transform them. The classroom teacher who has been a 'mentor' and who has played that role, will probably not go back to the role of cooperating teacher.

All of this is necessary simply because we cannot really go back. The influence of sociocultural theory in general, and the specifics of this book in particular, indicate a different way of understanding and doing the work of language teaching and language teacher education. The raw material is there; it's up to us to create from it, to *bricoler*.

Notes

1. It is interesting to note that this dynamic in foregrounding/backgrounding captures the instructional shifts that go on as ESL teaching in many settings moves from direct English language teaching to 'content-based' or 'sheltered instruction'. In these shifts language is adjusted to support content, or content can be tailored to language abilities (e.g. Short, 2002).
2. For a more extended discussion of the applied linguistics as discipline/ language as content debate in second language teaching, see Allwright & Tarone (in press) and, in response, Freeman & Johnson (in press); also Yates & Muchisky (2003).
3. For full references to support these statements, please see the original article (Oxford, 2001).

References

Allwright, D. and Tarone, E. (in press) Language teacher-learning and student language learning: Shaping the knowledge base. In D. Tedick (ed.) *Second Language Teacher Education: International Perspectives*. Mahwah, NJ: Lawrence Erlbaum.

Calkins, L.M. (1986) *The Art of Teaching Writing*. Portsmouth, NH: Heineman.

Canagarajah, A.S. (1999) *Resisting Linguistic Imperialism in English Teaching*. Oxford: Oxford University Press.

Cazden, C. (1998) *Classroom Discourse* (2nd edn). Portsmouth, NH: Heineman.

Delpit, L. (1995) *Other People's Children: Cultural Conflict in the Classroom*. New York: New Press.

Ellis, G. and Sinclair, B. (1990) *Learning to Learn English: A Course in Learner Training*. Cambridge: Cambridge University Press.

Freeman, D. (1996) The 'unstudied problem': Research on teacher learning in language teaching.' In D. Freeman and Jack C. Richards (eds) *Teacher Learning in Language Teaching* (pp. 351–377). New York: Cambridge University Press.

Freeman, D. and Johnson, K.E. (1998) Reconceptualizing the knowledge base of language teacher education. *TESOL Quarterly* 32 (2), 397–418.

Freeman, D. and Johnson, K.E. (in press) Response to 'Language teacher-learning and student language learning: Shaping the knowledge base.' In D.J. Tedick (ed.) *Language Teacher Education: International Perspectives on Research and Practice.* Mahwah, NJ: Lawrence Erlbaum Associates

Gardner, H. (1983) *Frames of Mind: The Theory of Multiple Intelligences.* New York: Basic Books.

Gee, J.P. (1996) *Social Linguistics and Literacies.* London: Taylor and Francis.

Gee, J.P. (1999) *An Introduction to Discourse Analysis: Theory and Method.* Routledge: New York.

Graves, K. and Rice, A. (1994) *East–West Basics.* Oxford University Press.

Grossman, P. (1990) *The Making of a Teacher.* New York: Teachers College Press.

Halliday, M.A.K. (1978) *Language as a Social Semiotic.* London: Edward Arnold.

Heath, S.B. (1983) *Ways with Words.* New York: Cambridge University Press.

Hyon, S. (1996) Genre in three traditions: Implications for ESL. *TESOL Quarterly* 30 (4), 693–722.

Kachru, B. (1990) *The Alchemy of English.* Urbana, IL: University of Illinois Press.

Lampert, M. and Ball, D. (1998) *Teaching, Multimedia, and Mathematics: Investigations of Real Practice.* New York: Teachers College Press.

Lantolf, J. (ed.) (2000) *Socio-cultural Theory and Second Language Learning.* Oxford: Oxford University Press.

Larsen-Freeman, D. (1986) *Techniques and Principles in Language Teaching* (1st edn). New York: Oxford Press.

Larsen-Freeman, D. (2003) *Teaching Language: From Grammar to Grammaring.* Boston: Heinle/ITP.

Levi-Strauss, C. (1966) *The Savage Mind.* Chicago: University of Chicago Press.

Lemke, J. (1988) Genres, semantics classroom education. *Linguistics in Education* 1, 81–99.

Mehan, H. (1979) *Learning Lessons.* Cambridge: Harvard University Press.

New London Group (1996) A pedagogy of multiliteracies: Designing social futures. *Harvard Educational Review* 66 (2), 60–92.

Oxford, R. (1990) *Language Learning Strategies: What Every Teacher Should Know.* Boston: Heinle/ITP.

Oxford, R. (2001) Language learning strategies. In R. Carter and D. Nunan (eds) *The Cambridge Guide to Teaching English to Speakers of Other Languages* (pp. 166–172). New York: Cambridge University Press.

Phillipson, R. (1992) *Linguistic Imperialism.* Oxford: Oxford University Press.

Reynolds, M. (1989) *The Knowledge Base of the Beginning Teacher.* New York: Pergamon Press.

Richards, J. and Rodgers, T. (1986) *Approaches and Methods in Language Teaching.* New York: Cambridge University Press.

Schon, D. (1983) *The Reflective Practitioner.* New York: Basic Books.

Shulman, L.S. (1987) Knowledge and teaching: Foundations of the new reform. *Harvard Educational Review* 57 (1), 1–22.

Short, D. (2002) Language learning in sheltered social studies classes. *TESOL Journal*, 11 (1), 18–24.

Sizer, T. (1992) *Horace's School: Redesigning the American High School*. Boston: Houghton-Mifflin.

Tyack, D. and Cuban, L. (1995) *Tinkering Toward Utopia: A Century of Public School Reform*. Cambridge: Harvard University Press.

Wertsch, J. (1991) *Voices of the Mind.* Cambridge: Harvard University Press.

Wertsch, J. (1998) *Mind as Action.* Oxford: Oxford University Press.

Wilkins, D.A. (1976) *Notional Syllabuses.* Oxford: Oxford University Press.

Yates, R. and Muchisky, D. (2003) On reconceptualizing teacher education. *TESOL Quarterly* 37 (1), 135–147.

Index

Authors

Subjects